# DESIGNING HEALTH MESSAGES

Approaches
From
Communication
Theory
and
Public
Health
Practice

**Edward Maibach**
**Roxanne Louiselle Parrott**
editors

 **SAGE** Publications
*International Educational and Professional Publisher*
Thousand Oaks   London   New Delhi

*For information address:*

SAGE Publications, Inc.
2455 Teller Road
Thousand Oaks, California 91320
E-mail: order@sagepub.com

SAGE Publications Ltd.
6 Bonhill Street
London EC2A 4PU
United Kingdom

SAGE Publications India Pvt. Ltd.
M-32 Market
Greater Kailash I
New Delhi 110 048 India

Printed in the United States of America

Library of Congress Cataloging-in-Publication Data

Main entry under title:

Designing health messages: Approaches from communication theory and
    public health practice / edited by Edward Maibach, Roxanne Louiselle
    Parrott.
    p.  cm.
    Includes bibliographical references and index.
    ISBN 0-8039-5397-6.  —  ISBN 0-8039-5398-4 (pbk.)
    1. Mass media in health education.  2. Health promotion.
I. Maibach, Edward.  II. Parrott, Roxanne.
RA440.5.D46  1995
362.1'014—dc20                                                    94-40646


                    99  10  9  8  7  6


Sage Production Editor: Astrid Virding

# Contents

# Preface

> *"There is nothing so practical as a good theory."*
> —Professor Kurt Lewin
> *The Practical Theorist*

Theory. There is no other term in the field of communication that inspires such passion (positive and negative) and provokes such divisiveness. Communication researchers are often passionate about, one might even say love struck by, the theories that drive their research. Communication practitioners can be equally passionate about theory. Unfortunately, their passion often concerns the irrelevance of theory to the realities of the practitioners' world. There are communication practitioners who value theory; however, they often face skepticism or opposition at the hands of their less academically oriented colleagues.[1] Theory has also been known to polarize teachers and students. Professors tend to lecture in abstract about the importance of theory, whereas students prefer concrete guidance on how to accomplish communication objectives.

As communication researchers who are deeply involved in the practice of public health communication, we are concerned about the division between theory and practice. The division is a false dichotomy that seriously inhibits advancement of the field of public health communication. We wholeheartedly embrace Professor Lewin's adage that "there is nothing so practical as a good theory" (Marrow, 1969). Moreover, we believe that communication researchers, practitioners, and students alike will be willing to embrace that adage once the field has advanced some "good" theories, and once these theories have been explained in a manner that makes clear their value in practice.

Fortunately, theorists in the field of communication and other related behavioral fields have advanced many "good" theories. The challenge now is to explain these theories in ways that prove their worth.

There are a number of obvious reasons why published discussions of theory tend to be esoteric. Theorists may consider such explanations to be a distraction from their work. After all, communication theories are conceived in abstract terms to explain communication processes and effects at an abstract level (Reynolds, 1971). It may also be that forces operative in today's academic institutions discourage academics (who do most of the writing) from writing about the practical implications of theory. For example, academic careers are generally elevated on the basis of advancing original theories or disproving other people's theories, not explaining and applying theories. Second, academic books and journals are biased against the overtly practical because their reading audience is composed primarily of other academics, not practicing professionals. Moreover, the standard format in most academic journals relegates discussions about the practical aspects of theory to the concluding section of research articles. Introductory textbooks are generally broadly inclusive, which inhibits their ability to delve deeply into theory or make an adequate case for linking theory to practice. There may be other reasons as well why so few practical explanations of "good" theories have been forthcoming.

Rising to the challenge of explaining "good" theories in a way that proves their worth is the first goal of this book. The contributing authors in Part I (Theory-Driven Approaches to Health Message Design) were carefully selected both for their exuberance about the communication theories with which they work, and for their interest in explaining those theories in a way that proves their worth. The contributing authors were directly and explicitly challenged to prove Kurt Lewin's adage by laying bare the message design implications of their theories. As editors, we feel they have met the challenge, and in doing so have honored the memory of Professor Lewin, a founding member of the academic field of communication. Moreover, these chapters speak to what psychologist Albert Bandura (1986) has called the ultimate test of a theory: when a theory indicates methods that are "capable of effecting significant changes in human affect, thought, and action" (p. 3).

"Good" theories of human behavior and communication processes provide only half the necessary information for effective health message design. The other half of the equation is a thorough knowledge of the target audience. A detailed, vivid knowledge of the intended audience enables the message designer to select appropriate communication objectives, to create messages that can accomplish those communication objectives, to contextualize the messages properly, and to deliver the messages through communication channels frequented and preferred by members of the audience. There are many ways that message designers can attempt to gain a thorough knowledge of their target audience. Some of these approaches are likely to be more effective than others. The more effective strategies are those that systematically use research both to identify the audience(s) and to assess what the audience currently wants, thinks, feels, and does regarding the health issue. Ideally, this is an ongoing process throughout the campaign, with the information fed forward for the purpose of refining campaign messages to the changing situation and needs of the audience members.

Thus, the second goal of this book is to recommend and illustrate a series of information gathering strategies from contemporary public health practice that will enable appropriate audience-centered communication planning. The contributing authors in Part II (Audience-Centered Strategies for Health Message Design) were selected for their ability to discuss and illustrate (with their own work) health communication planning activities that put a face on both the target audience and on intermediaries who stand between message planner and target audience. As editors, we are extremely pleased both with the logical and practical nature of the proposed approaches, and with the level of complementarity among ideas advanced in these chapters. These chapters will assist communication planners at all levels in refining their approaches to message design and delivery.

As previously indicated, our motivation for editing this book was to advance in clear terms, and to illustrate across a variety of public health problems, theory-grounded and audience-centered approaches to health message design. In our minds, the need for this book is so pressing not because of the lack of health information in the information environment, but because of the overabundance of ineffectual information. Beyond the myriad activities that can be construed as some form of health information campaign (see Rogers & Storey [1987] for an excellent discussion of what constitutes an information campaign), health messages are pervasive in our schools, health care organizations, workplaces, and in all aspects of our mass media. Moreover, Vice President Albert Gore is leading a nationwide charge to expand dramatically our information environment in the form of the National Information Infrastructure (i.e., the "information superhighway"), one major component of which will be devoted to health information (Gore, 1994).[2] Not all of this health information is specifically intended to improve the health of our citizens. News and entertainment programming about health, for example, may be created with little concern about people's health. Conversely, a vast amount of health information, including news, entertainment, and advertising, is developed with health improvement as a primary or secondary communication objective. Our concern is that the majority of these health messages are produced in such a haphazard fashion as to ensure that they have little or no positive impact. By creating clutter in the health information environment, they may actually have a negative impact to the extent that they interfere with the relatively fewer well-designed and well-communicated health messages.

We are encouraged by preliminary signs that academics in the field of communication are becoming more concerned with theory for the sake of practice (see Avery & Eadie, 1993; Monahan & Collins-Jarvis, 1993). Among other places, this change can be observed in the rapidly expanding health communication section rosters of the International Communication Association and the Speech Communication Association, the two largest professional associations in the academic field of communication. We are equally encouraged by signs that communication professionals at all levels are becoming increasingly interested in promoting health and other prosocial outcomes (see Montgomery [1990] and Nariman [1993] for discussions about the entertainment industry). The single most spectacular example of this trend is the efforts over the past decade of the Partnership for a Drug-Free America, a media industry consortium that produced and distributed approximately $1,000,000 worth of public service advertising *per day* for several consecutive years (the 10th largest advertising campaign in the country at that time). Our hope is that this book will encourage the continued development of these trends by focusing more health communication efforts on theory-driven, audience-centered approaches.

## Intended Users of the Book

This book was written with a number of audiences in mind. Both editors and many of the chapter contributors teach advanced undergraduate or graduate-level courses in health communication, social marketing, and information campaigns. Students in these and related courses should find the chapters in this book refreshingly direct and instructive. The second audience is the large group of public health professionals who, as part of their job requirements, develop health messages or campaigns but without the benefit of having had specific training in health communication. An equally large audience is communication professionals who, with no public health training, find themselves directing or assisting in the development of public health messages or campaigns. The final audience is composed of our academic colleagues in departments of communication, public health, and related areas. We hope that this volume's emphasis on the practical side of theory will generate new insights and inspirations.

Part I of the book (Theory-Driven Approaches to Health Message Design) opens with a chapter by Parrott that broadly overviews variables that affect audience members' attention to health messages, regardless of their level of involvement with the topic. Several language-use principles are suggested for maximizing attention to health messages, and context of the message is discussed as a potential mechanism for heightening message effectiveness. In the second chapter Holtgrave, Tinsley, and Kay introduce Prochaska and DiClemente's (1984) stages of change model, and demonstrate how principles drawn from the behavioral decision-making literature can be used to help move people through the initial stages.

In Chapter 3, Maibach and Cotton continue the discussion by presenting a complementary approach to moving people through all five stages of change using message design constructs presented in Bandura's (1986) social cognitive theory. These three chapters address the first theme within Part I of the volume: how to use behavioral theory to organize message design decisions.

The subsequent five chapters address the second theme within Part I: a presentation of specific theory-grounded considerations in message design. In Chapter 4, Hale and Dillard initiate the theme by reviewing the theory and findings on the use of fear appeals in health campaigns, providing insights on intelligent use of this strategy. In Chapter 5, Monahan elaborates the utility of using the other end of the affective scale: positive feelings. In doing so, she presents a promising perspective on an underutilized health communication strategy.

In Chapter 6, Pfau discusses and illustrates the importance of behavioral inoculation with (primarily) young audiences who demonstrate a predisposition to adopt unhealthful practices. In Chapter 7, Austin completes our consideration of young audiences by meticulously reviewing the developmental literature and making some bold message-related recommendations.

In Chapter 8, Witte rounds out the section by presenting her original template for campaign message design and dissemination. Witte's approach, called the Persuasive Health Message Framework Approach, utilizes persuasion theory and research to provide a decision tree of choice points and paths for health message designers to consider in specifying plans and objectives.

In Part II of the book (Audience-Centered Strategies for Health Message Design), we present four chapters that focus on the data gathering and related activities needed to develop effective health messages. In Chapter 9, Nowak and Siska beautifully illustrate how audience and evaluation research can be used throughout the life span of a campaign. In Chapter 10, Slater provides a deeply insightful look at audience segmentation, and recommends approaches to segmentation in both high- and low-resource situations.

In Chapter 11, McGrath reminds us that a whole cast of characters—gatekeepers—typically stand between the message designer and the target audience. Based on his extensive experience, he presents a series of important recommendations to enlist the help of gatekeepers. In the final chapter of Part II, Lefebvre and colleagues illustrate that the brave new world of database marketing can be harnessed in service of greater goals than selling dish soap.

Part III (Combining Theory and Practice: Additional Considerations) consists of two chapters that address several additional issues that health message designers ought to consider before and during their design activities. First, in Chapter 13, Hammond reviews steps that have been taken to increase patients' understanding of medication regimens. These initiatives exemplify the importance of considering how media and interpersonal communication interface in the design of health messages. These efforts also illustrate how multiple media messages in the information environment supplement campaign efforts, at times reinforcing but at other times contradicting campaign messages. In the final chapter, Parrott, Kahl, and Maibach acknowledge the critical constraints imposed on message designers by health and other administrative policies, expanding on the ideas about gate keeping advanced by McGrath in Chapter 11. Such policies may facilitate or inhibit the design and delivery of health campaigns. Message designers should consider the relevance and implications of these policies before proceeding with their message design activities.

Finally, these 14 chapters challenge everyone involved in the construction of the health information environment to practice the principles provided by "good theory." Doing so will have two important consequences: It will help enable our citizens to live healthier and more productive lives; and it will ultimately, through its impact on subsequent research and evaluation efforts, advance our understanding of the mechanisms and dynamics of effective public health communication.

## Notes

1. This point is nicely emphasized by the third definition of the term *academic* in Webster's (New Riverside) Dictionary: "not practical: theoretical."

2. Universal service—that is, assuring all segments of society full access to the information superhighway through the use of subsidies—is a major tenet of the federal government's proposed plan. This provision is specifically intended to level the playing field between the information haves and have nots.

# References

Avery, R. K., & Eadie, W. F. (1993). Making a difference in the real world. *Journal of Communication, 43,* 174-179.

Bandura, A. (1986). *Social foundations of thought and action: A social cognitive theory.* Englewood Cliffs, NJ: Prentice Hall.

Gore, A. (1994, February 28). We're all going to be connected. *The Wall Street Journal,* p. A15.

Marrow, A. J. (1969). *The practical theorist. The life and work of Kurt Lewin.* New York: Basic Books.

Monahan, J. L., & Collins-Jarvis, L. (1993). The hierarchy of institutional values in the communication discipline. *Journal of Communication, 43,* 150-157.

Montgomery, K. (1990). Promoting health through entertainment television. In C. Atkins & L. Wallack (Eds.), *Mass communication and public health* (pp. 114-128). Newbury Park, CA: Sage.

Nariman, H. (1993). *Soap operas for change.* New York: Praeger.

Prochaska, J. O., & DiClemente, C. C. (1984). *The transtheoretical approach: Crossing traditional boundaries of therapy.* Homewood, IL: Dow-Jones-Irwin.

Reynolds, P. D. (1971). *A primer in theory construction.* New York: Macmillan.

Rogers, E., & Storey, J. D. (1987). Communication campaigns. In C. Berger & S. Chaffee (Eds.), *Handbook of communication science* (pp. 814-846). Newbury Park, CA: Sage.

# PART I

# Theory-Driven Approaches to Health Message Design

The opening and in many ways the main section of this book addresses theory-driven approaches to health message design. Theory plays many roles in helping us understand communication processes. The most basic role of theory in behavioral science involves description. Our theories describe aspects of the complex world in which we live, and in doing so, render them more comprehensible. Philosopher John Dewey commented on this role of theory by proposing the following question as a test of the adequacy of a theory: "Does it end in conclusions which, when they are referred back to ordinary life experiences, render them more significant, more luminous to us, and make our dealings with them more fruitful? Or does it terminate in rendering the things of ordinary experience more opaque than they were before?"[1]

A second role of behavioral theory involves prediction of outcomes. Predictive theories extend descriptive theories to the next logical level by stating: "if X occurs, then Y is more (or less) likely to occur." This is said to be a higher role of theory because the process of postulating and proving relationships among antecedents and outcomes confers an even greater degree of comprehensibility to the world around us.

Yet another goal of theory, in addition to description and prediction, is explanation. Although theories that predict relationships among variables are often highly heuristic, generating volumes of testable hypotheses and research, these theories do not necessarily explain why "If X occurs then Y is more (or less) likely." Theories that are able to answer the question "why" create greater understanding. They are often necessary to attain yet another goal of theory—the ability to prescribe effective interventions.

The final role of theory we will discuss involves prescription. Prescriptive theories build on the other two roles of theory by extending them to the final logical level: "X can be made more likely to occur by doing A, B, and C, which, in turn, will make Y more (or less) likely to occur." Such understanding confers the greatest degree of comprehensibility. It is the difference between understanding that apples are good food, understanding that apple trees grow from apple seeds, and understanding that an apple tree will bear the most fruit when properly watered, fertilized, and pruned. The latter degree of comprehension is clearly more useful to those people concerned with regularly putting food on the table. The prescriptive function of theory, needless to say, is the central concern of this section.

The main challenge issued to contributing authors in this section was to explore the prescriptive value of behavioral theories. All authors responded to our challenge. Many of them even took the assignment one step farther. They integrated their description of the theories we asked them to address with descriptions of other theories, and in doing so, they extended the prescriptive value of the original theories in important ways.

In Chapter 1, Parrott explores linguistic theories advanced in the fields of communication and psychology that contend that word choice matters. She builds the case that particular word choices lead members of the target audience to recognize some concepts as more central or important to focus on than others. The prescriptive value of these theories is seen in Parrott's recommendations for guiding the selection of the exact words to maximize audience attention to the critical message content. Parrott extends the prescriptive value of linguistic theories by integrating them with theories that specify which forms of media presentations evoke the most active thought processes. The integration provides significant insight into why people attend to and become more involved with some health messages than others, even when the messages do not initially appear to be personally relevant.

In Chapter 2, Holtgrave, Tinsley, and Kay examine certain key behavioral decision-making constructs. Moreover, they extend the prescriptive value of these constructs by examining them within the context of Prochaska and DiClemente's stage of behavior change framework. Their discussion centers on decision-making processes at the early (decision-oriented) phases of the behavior change process. The result is an illuminating set of recommendations on how to move target audience members through early behavior change stages (Precontemplation and Contemplation).

In Chapter 3, Maibach and Cotton explain the prescriptive value of key constructs from Bandura's social cognitive theory. Moreover, following the approach presented in Chapter 2, they examine these constructs in a stages of behavior change context. The discussion grants the reader a significant opportunity to understand an audience member's experience at each stage of the behavior change process. Explicit guidance is given, by stage of behavior change, regarding which social cognitive constructs are likely to be most influential, and recommendations are made regarding how to most reliably influence those constructs. The discussion is a direct complement to that presented in Chapter 2.

In Chapter 4, Hale and Dillard provide a comprehensive review and integration of the theoretical perspectives advanced to explain the role of using negative affect in health message design. Fear appeals have historically been aligned with health campaigns, perhaps because some of the classic examples are so indelibly imprinted in the minds of persons exposed to them. In addition, individuals have often been presumed to perform behaviors represented as being in their own best health interests if they understand the dire consequences associated with failure to do so. As Hale and Dillard illustrate, such assumptions may be misleading, whereas other principles more appropriately and frequently lead to intended outcomes. In comparing and contrasting these issues, Hale and Dillard provide an excellent synthesis of understanding to guide the pragmatic considerations of health message designers.

In Chapter 5, Monahan takes up where Hale and Dillard leave off, discussing the obverse—that is, the role of using positive affect in health message design. As she duly notes, this approach is far too often neglected when health campaigners are considering how to present the content of health information to an audience. Her review of theory and research relating to the impact of promoting benefits associated with behavior leads to Monahan's identification of ways to encompass this knowledge in the construction of health messages. Moreover, Monahan compares and contrasts varied approaches to utilizing positive affect, each with its own strengths and weaknesses.

In Chapter 6, Pfau examines the issue of adolescent smoking prevention and argues that, when targeting children and early adolescents, appropriate messages are those that positively reinforce existing behavior, not those that attempt to persuade children to oppose a health risk behavior. He specifically examines the theoretical rationale for one approach to primary prevention through positive reinforcement: behavioral inoculation. Pfau presents an explicit set of theory-driven recommendations for the creation of inoculation and booster messages. This chapter is an important complement to Maibach and Cotton's chapter on social cognitive approaches because it focuses on the development of abilities and confidence to resist experimenting with and adopting risk behaviors.

In Chapter 7, taking up where Pfau left off, Austin integrates a vast and divergent set of literatures on developmental theory and youth audiences. Her developmental stage-specific review gives readers the means to understand the cognitions, motivations, sources of influence, media use habits, and a variety of other important message design considerations for children in six age groups (0-5, 5-7, 7-10, 10-13, 13-16, and over 16). Austin's thorough review presents and defends four important message design recommendations for youth audiences: start early; segment and target by age group and environmental differences; strive for consistent messages from a variety of sources over a long period of time; and emphasize giving children control and ownership of their own destinies.

In Chapter 8, Witte proposes a transtheoretical model to guide health message designers' actions. In addition to integrating diverse behavior change theories, Witte's model provides a step-by-step guide to the process of designing health messages. As such, it is an important bridge to the second section of this book. The model emphasizes the interrelationships among decisions made about selecting the content of a message based on the particular audience for whom the message is designed, in conjunction with the source and channel selection.

The specific examples used for illustration in these chapters are largely drawn from the personal experiences of the authors. The examples address a wide variety of health promotion issues including the prevention of cancer, substance use, AIDS, and accidents. The reader can thus benefit both from the authors' efforts to integrate and extend theory into prescriptions for health message design, and by seeing these prescriptions illustrated in application to "real-world" examples along the way.

## Note

1. Dewey, J. (1929). *Experience and nature.* New York: Norton.

# 1 Motivation to Attend to Health Messages

PRESENTATION OF CONTENT
AND LINGUISTIC CONSIDERATIONS

ROXANNE LOUISELLE PARROTT

*Mass media can be extremely powerful in involving audiences with the
abstract matters of health in exciting personalized ways and in so involving
people they can become quite capable of affording insights that might produce
ameliorative actions ultimately.*

—Mendelsohn (1968, p. 136)

Despite Mendelsohn's (1968) promise regarding media's potential to positively affect people's behaviors in relation to health, evidence suggests that many mediated health messages fall short of attaining this goal. The failure occurs, in part, because of the ways that people process information once they have been exposed to it (Levy & Windahl, 1985). This chapter discusses audience information processing, and proposes specific presentation of content and linguistic approaches to increase individuals' mental effort to process health messages.

## Audience Attention Levels

Campaign theorists and researchers generally agree that after exposure to a message, audience attention comprises the next stage in response (McGuire, 1989). The attention an audience gives to a message may be conceptualized along a continuum (Langer, 1978). At one end of the continuum, the audience pays very little attention, a passive or mindless response. At the other end of the continuum, listeners attend a great deal, an active or mindful response:

Audience Attention

<------------------------------------------------->

Mindless/Passive                          Mindful/Active

An important predictor of the amount of cognitive effort an audience exerts to attend messages is the audience's level of involvement with the topic of the message (Petty & Cacioppo, 1986). Involvement has been conceptualized in a number of ways (see Pfau & Parrott, 1993), with each promoting active information processing via a central route (Borgida & Howard-Pitney, 1983; Petty, Cacioppo, & Goldman, 1981). An audience who is involved with the topic of cancer prevention, for example, will actively seek, attend, and process messages about cancer prevention (Johnson, Meischke, Grau, & Johnson, 1992). This has also been referred to as top-down information processing, which occurs when an individual's goal or conscious awareness leads to active processing (Green, Lightfoot, Bandy, & Buchanan, 1985; Park & Smith, 1989). Uninvolved audiences, on the other hand, process information in a passive fashion, which has been conceptualized to occur via a peripheral route:

Information Processing

<------------------------------------------------->

Passive/Peripheral                        Active/Central
                                          Top-down

Peripheral information processing lacks the active awareness, comprehension, and evaluation of arguments to support positions (Petty, Cacioppo, & Schumann, 1983). Although relatively enduring attitude and behavior formation, change, and reinforcement occur via both active and passive modes of information processing (Pechmann & Stewart, 1989), the health message designer's goal often is to prompt active thought in a passive audience. Message designers thus should reckon with how, when, and why people exposed to health messages might be motivated to switch to more active rather than automatic message processing, as well as when and how to motivate more active versus passive thought.

## "Switching Cognitive Gears": Invoking Active Thought

For the most part, individuals rely on automatic processing of health information, depending on past knowledge or experience with similar messages to assign meaning and interpretation to a present message (Chanowitz & Langer, 1981). One does not have to exert much effort to be exposed to health messages, as popular television programs, both entertainment and educational, deal with health topics (Larson, 1991), and commercial campaigners make health claims in relation to their products to promote sales (Maibach, 1991). This information dissemination occurs simultaneously with more traditional media and interpersonal forms, such as public service announcements (PSAs) presented via posters, pamphlets, radio, and television (e.g., Freimuth, Hammond, Edgar, & Monahan, 1990); and physician recommendations delivered face to face and over the telephone (Parrott, Greene, & Parker, 1992). The mode of message presentation may affect information processing, as evidence suggests that people expend more cognitive effort to process print messages than television messages (Chaiken & Eagly, 1976). This assumes, however, that an audience has already decided to attend the print message; one cannot actively exert effort to process a message that one simply chooses to ignore.

A number of theories address the differences between active and passive cognitive functioning and why individuals actively or passively process information (e.g., Behrman, Moscovitch, & Mozer, 1991; Petty & Cacioppo, 1986). Less research has addressed how to motivate individuals to move from the passive to the active mode (Park & Smith, 1989; Reeves & Thorson, 1986). Louis and Sutton (1991) have begun a systematic program of research to identify conditions that encourage people to enter an active processing mode, prompting bottom-up attentional processing in contrast to top-down processing:

Information Processing

◄─────────────────────────────────►

Passive/Peripheral          Active/Central
Bottom-up  Top-down

Louis and Sutton's model of "switching cognitive gears" posits that individuals are motivated to become actively cognitively engaged:

1. when presentation of content is unusual, unfamiliar, or novel;

2. when presentation of content represents a discrepancy between expectations and reality; and

3. when an external or internal request causes an individual to deliberately initiate an increased level of conscious attention (Louis & Sutton, 1991).

Each condition will be examined within a framework of health message design and of motivating people to attend health messages actively, via bottom-up information processing.

## UNUSUAL, UNFAMILIAR, AND NOVEL PRESENTATION OF CONTENT

Consider the following message, which appears on the back page of a pamphlet titled, "It's Never Too Early to Stop Skin Cancer . . . or Too Late" (The Skin Cancer Foundation, 1985):

Know the signs of skin cancer
• A skin growth that increases in size and appears pearly, translucent, tan, brown, black or multicolored.
• A mole, birthmark or beauty mark that
    changes color
    increases in size or thickness
    changes in texture
    is irregular in outline
• A spot or growth that continues to itch, hurt, crust, scab, erode or bleed.
• An open sore or wound on the skin that does not heal or persists for more than four weeks, or heals and then reopens.
If you have any of these symptoms, see your doctor. Now.

Clearly, the goal of this message is to educate readers about the physical symptoms of skin cancer, which, if observed, should lead a person to seek a physician for consult. For this education to occur, however, an individual must obtain the brochure, read it, and pay enough attention to comprehend and retain information that may or may not be personally relevant at the time.

The material contained in the skin cancer message may be unfamiliar to the reader, but the method of presentation is a highly familiar one: a lengthy and dry clinical exposition containing words that are not commonly used by most people. Everyone has seen numerous health brochures that look just like this message. Louis and Sutton's (1991) first condition to promote active information processing—present the content in an unusual way—is lacking in this message. Because printed health messages are often factual, straightforward, clinical directives, positive affect appeals (see Chapter 5 in this volume) may garner more attention. No one feels positively about cancer in general, but a print message could be designed to promote positive feelings in relation to the behavior being promoted, by an opening statement constructed in the following fashion: "Knowing these signs of skin cancer gives people one more way to safeguard their health." Audience members feel positively about having the ways and means to control their own well-being, but health messages too seldom explicitly emphasize this as a reason to process information actively. Messages can also be designed to invoke a sense of personal responsibility, which has been shown to motivate people to process issue-relevant arguments (Petty & Cacioppo, 1986) but is not frequently found in presentations of health content: "Knowing these signs of skin cancer helps friends and families to detect the disease early for themselves and their loved ones."

Another way to present the content in an unusual way is to explicitly state a basic motive to attend rather than stating a clinical directive: "Knowing these signs of skin cancer can help you detect any unusual skin conditions before they become a serious health problem." Each of these openings would be novel in comparison to how the message presently opens, and so they should invoke more active processing. To keep the audience's attention, the rest of the content should be revised to present the information in an unusual fashion relevant to audience needs.

Unusual modes of printed health messages should also be considered by message designers who seek to trigger more active thought about specific health matters through the unusual presentation of content. Among the more novel print media currently being used to disseminate health messages is the comic book (Parrott, in press-a). *The Amazing Spiderman* comics, for example, have devoted a number of issues to the development of stories in which the main character promotes awareness about health matters. In one issue (McDuffie, 1993a), Spiderman discusses drug use and abuse with several teenage boys. In another (McDuffie, 1993b), the main character promotes wearing helmets when cycling. Through the medium of comic books, the health message may take on a conversational rather than didactic tone. More personal matters, such as strategies to deal with peer pressure to use drugs, may be addressed. Although an audience member does not actually have an interpersonal relationship with a fictional character, audience members often feel as though they have formed such social relationships (Pfau, 1990). By invoking these already formed parasocial relationships with comic book characters, opportunities occur to reinforce healthy behaviors while attempting to change unhealthy behaviors. The finding that unusual, unfamiliar, and novel presentations of content promote more active message processing may also explain why audiences attend and remember health information presented in television soap operas and situation comedies (Larson, 1991). Yet another way to present skin cancer information in a novel fashion is to have a character on a prime-time situation comedy or a daytime soap opera suddenly notice a mole that has changed in color and texture and is increasing in size. The character's visit to a physician provides an opportunity to model the appropriate behavioral response and for conversations to occur in which family and friends, in addition to medical professionals, discuss the character's skin cancer. These novel methods of presenting health information also provide opportunities explicitly to address potentially private topics. The very nature of the soap opera provides an excellent setting for the character to reveal personal doubts and concerns, the same ones an audience member might hesitate to reveal to a physician because of their sensitive nature (Parrott, in press-b). In relation to skin cancer, individuals may be concerned about the scarring that could result from having a skin cancer removed but hesitate to express such a concern in the fear that it seems vain or inappropriate. The soap opera character, however, could express this same concern and provide the opportunity for his or her physician to explain how seldom surgery is necessary to treat a skin cancer and how minimal scarring is likely to be if surgery is needed. In sum, novel content, situations in which to present content, or modes to deliver content provide means to prompt people to engage in more active thought about health messages. Health message designers should consider novel ways to introduce health information, particularly when the information to be presented deals with matters that might be considered sensitive or potentially private:

Information Processing

Passive/Peripheral                     Active/Central
                                       Bottom-up      Top-down
                                    • Novel/unusual:
                                       = Information
                                       = Mode of delivery
                                       = Situation

## DISCREPANT OR UNEXPECTED
## PRESENTATION OF CONTENT

A second condition that Louis and Sutton (1991) identify as a means to motivate an audience's active thought is the presentation of content that is discrepant or unexpected. Based on previous experience or observation, individuals form expectations about what health messages will say and where particular health messages will appear. These expectations provide people with the opportunity to think and behave in response to the content or the setting in an automatic fashion (Langer, 1985; Langer, Blank, & Chanowitz, 1978). When an actual message is inconsistent with what is expected, active thought is triggered.

Consider messages about exposure to the sun as one example of how discrepant presentation of content invokes thought. For years, exposure to sunlight was promoted as a means to enhance health, specifically in relation to obtaining adequate amounts of vitamin D. In recent years, exposure to the sun is more likely to be criticized in terms of the damage that such exposure causes to the skin. For audiences who have been exposed to both messages, the discrepancy is likely to produce more thought about the latter message than would occur in the absence of exposure to the former message. The thoughts generated may, however, lead to the development of counterarguments to the discrepant message (see Chapter 6 in this volume), so message designers must consider all possible outcomes associated with active thought about a discrepant message to predict the audience's most likely response.

Messages about condoms are also likely to have associations in the minds of many audience members who have been exposed to previous messages that promote condom use to prevent venereal disease. As a method to reduce the spread of HIV, messages that promote condom use may invoke more active thought for audiences who have already been exposed to messages about condoms and sexually transmitted diseases than in audience members who have not had such exposure. In this instance, audience members may well be able to assimilate rather than contrast the information, for although the information is unexpected in view of earlier learning, the information does not disagree with what has already been learned. For audience members who use condoms as a method to prevent venereal disease, awareness that condoms reduce the spread of HIV may reinforce behavior.

In relation to expectations for health messages about skin cancer and AIDS, message designers should consider, too, how and where audience members expect to be exposed to such messages (or to purchase the products promoted in the messages—sunscreen and condoms). These health messages are most likely expected to be part of public service announcements (PSAs) and commercial campaigners' displays in drug stores. What if, however, farmers—who are accustomed to encountering health messages about farm injuries at feedstores—suddenly also find messages about skin cancer in feedstores. These unexpected messages, although similar to skin cancer prevention messages, which they have been exposed to in their physicians' offices, are more likely to generate active thought.

Some fast food restaurants have introduced salads and skin-free broiled chicken sandwiches into their menus, partially in response to the public's request for such food fare. This, however, provides all consumers with unexpected messages about nutritional options that promote more active thought about eating choices and health. Consumers expect to encounter messages about the restaurant's "healthy," "beefy," "juicy" burgers—they do not expect messages about fat and cholesterol in relation to fast food. If consumers come to expect such messages in restaurants as part of the information provided about the menu, however, this will reduce the effectiveness of their presence to motivate active thought.

The "Meat-out" campaign takes advantage of this method of invoking more conscious thought in relation to the campaign's goal of getting individuals to eat less meat (Pfau & Parrott, 1993). The annual date for "The Great American Meat-out" falls on the first day of spring, with campaigners' messages intentionally invoking thoughts about new life. Such thoughts are discrepant with messages that also discuss the destruction of life that eating meat requires. Moreover, the campaigners solicit participation from restaurants who agree to post messages about "Meat-out" and provide meatless menus on the first day of spring. Because such messages are inconsistent with people's expectations for restaurants' menus, they should produce more active thought about the issues surrounding the campaign.

In sum, when a health message designer's goal is to invoke active thought, in addition to considering novel presentations of content, discrepant or unexpected messages should be considered. Consideration should also be given to the settings in which health messages and products are usually delivered and whether or not to expand these. Designers may want to include settings where one kind of health message and/or product is expected, and still other messages are salient, and products should be used, but neither are available:

Information Processing

←——————————————————————→

Passive/Peripheral                    Active/Central
                          Bottom-up          Top-down
                    • Unexpected/discrepant:
                      = Information
                      = Mode of delivery
                      = Situation

## EXTERNAL OR INTERNAL
## REQUESTS TO ATTEND

Louis and Sutton's (1991) third condition to promote active message processing—use of an external or internal request to attend—is extremely relevant for health message design. External requests are overt statements by a message source that explicitly or implicitly tell an audience to increase their attention to the message (e.g., "Looking for the answer to fast weight loss? Pay attention to this."). Internal requests are a message receiver's psychological or physiological response to message stimuli, which produces a self-command to attend. Although novel or unexpected messages may produce a command to attend, some linguistic forms and word choices facilitate the reaction in audiences regardless of whether or not the core message content is novel or unexpected. By stipulating what language features prompt external or internal requests to attend, message designers may intentionally construct content to take advantage of these relationships. Novel or unexpected messages might be combined with these suggestions to further facilitate conscious consideration of message content.

External requests to increase conscious attention occur most directly in the form of a command to the audience:

Now hear this.

Pay attention to what's coming next.

Don't let anything interrupt this message.

Stop whatever else is going on, and get on over here.

These examples of explicit external requests to increase conscious attention were all taken directly from a single radio show aired in Atlanta, Georgia, one morning. There is nothing unusual about the approach. In fact, if asked, people seem more likely to report that these messages annoy them than to report that they increase attention. Yet, Louis and Sutton's review (1991) posits that such messages orient the listener to attend to the content that follows. External requests may also be constructed in the form of a question with varying levels of directness:

> Is everyone listening for information about the upcoming flu season? (Implicit: If not, please do.)

> How many listeners know what to do when faced with someone who has an alcohol or drug problem? (Implicit: Pay attention to find out.)

Many campaign messages are formed around such questions, which facilitate increased audience attention.

Whereas designing messages that direct audiences to "Pay attention to the upcoming announcement" exemplifies the use of external cues to attend, internal requests to attend may also be triggered by intentional message design. Internal requests to attend are audience members' prompts to themselves to "pay more attention" to the content of a message in reaction to what they have heard. In one sense, all of the methods described to increase active thought produce such a response. However, an analysis of the former methods that produce active responses in listeners leads to the identification of macro themes or reasons for the audience members' cognitive effort, such as the use of novel, discrepant, or unexpected information, and overt commands to attend. Message designers should also examine the many micro-level decisions that must be made, as these avenues provide other means to motivate audiences to process information actively. Perhaps most critically, message designers must decide what words to use in constructing content.

Internal requests to attend may occur in response to the precise words selected to design health messages. Numerous message design researchers recommend avoiding ambiguous language in the design of health messages (Siegel, 1988). One reason for this recommendation is that these messages are likely to be misunderstood by audiences. Phrases such as *multiple partners* and *sexual activity* carry more than one meaning. Moreover, to personalize health messages, the selection of some words versus others creates psychological distance between the message and the audience. The language construct of verbal immediacy provides insights about how to avoid distancing the message from the audience. *Verbal immediacy* is defined as the degree of directness between a communicator and the objects or events about which he or she is communicating, as determined by pronoun choice, verb tense, object referents, and the context of language use (Wiener & Mehrabian, 1968).

Immediacy increases sensory stimulation (Anderson, 1985), with verbal immediacy facilitating a message receiver's awareness of information contained in utterances but not necessarily asserted in the discourse (Wiener & Mehrabian, 1968). Nonimmediate language communicates avoidance, whereas immediate language communicates approachability, enhancing the attention given to issues (Hess & Gossett, 1974) or persons (Kuiken, 1981). Wiener and Mehrabian (1968) have identified several categories of speech that communicate avoidance versus approachability. Four forms that should be considered when evaluating the immediacy of language use will be discussed in relation to designing health messages.

*Denotative Specificity.* Denotatively specific speech explicitly states the agent, object, and/or action in a message (Wiener & Mehrabian, 1968). Message designers must decide between the use of immediate words that make explicit references to specific agents, objects, or actions—or nonimmediate words that refer to general categorical agents, objects, and actions. In the statements, "You should wear sunscreen to protect your skin from the sun" versus "People should wear sunscreen to protect their skin from the sun," the first person pronoun specifically designates an explicit agent in reference to the action, whereas the second sentence contains a categorical class for the agent in reference to the action.

The use of denotatively specific language enhances the attention given to the message by personalizing and simplifying the message: The listener does not have to consider whether or not the message is relevant because the message contains trigger words that state its relevance. Simpler messages have been found to be processed with more cognitive effort than are complex messages, as evidenced by the longer reaction times that result from exposure to simple versus complex messages (Reeves & Thorson, 1986). This may be due to such messages triggering perceptions of personal responsibility, for example, which have been found to facilitate active thought (Langer & Rodin, 1976), or the use of self-references, which increase persuasive effectiveness of appeals (Burnkrant & Unnava, 1989). Consider the following message, which appears in a skin cancer brochure published by the American Cancer Society (1985):


How is skin cancer treated?
    Physicians have several different methods to choose from depending on the size of the skin cancer, position on the body and risks to the patient. Mainly they are surgery, electrical current, radiation therapy, and freezing. Sometimes a combination of therapies are used. Afterward, if the extent of the defect warrants it, some form of plastic surgery may be used to improve appearance.

*Physicians, methods,* and *risks* are all examples of use of categorical terms. The first two statements can be stated more specifically in the following way: "Your dermatologist may choose surgery, electrical current, radiation therapy, or freezing, or some combination of these to treat your skin cancer." This denotatively specific wording more explicitly and simply informs the reader of the type of physician to see for treatment of skin cancer. In addition, the self-reference ("your") triggers active information processing by clarifying the audience's relationship to the message; the revised message also concisely identifies the "methods" of treatment. More explicit information about the "risks" that physicians consider in order to make a treatment decision would reduce the likelihood that a patient will reach unwarranted conclusions in this regard. "Risks," in other words, may appear ominous and act as a barrier to thought about the message.[1] In sum, to invoke more conscious thought about a verbal message, message designers should select more denotatively specific language.

*Spatial Immediacy.* A second form of speech that may be used to enhance verbal immediacy is the use of demonstratives, such as *this, these,* and *here* in contrast to use of *that, those,* and *there* (Wiener & Mehrabian, 1968). Moreover, the introduction of adverbial clauses with *where* or other words and phrases denoting physical or spatial separation detracts from immediacy of expression. Examine these messages:

Message A:
"This is your brain . . . This is your brain on drugs . . . Any questions?"

Message B:
"That was a person's brain . . . That was a person's brain after using drugs . . . Any questions?"

The widely disseminated version contained in Message A is both spatially immediate and denotatively specific. In contrast, Message B seems less personal, involving, or explicit. The use of spatially immediate demonstratives enhances the attention given to a verbal message.

*Temporal Immediacy.* A third form of language use that enhances verbal immediacy is the selection of present tense verbs in reference to present events (Wiener & Mehrabian, 1968). A number of researchers studying the effects of language use during therapeutic encounters have found that verb tense affects perceptions of context: "The verb tenses, as context markers, will function at an out-of-awareness level and be vitally important to the therapist who wishes to deal with the overall context of the interaction" (Phoenix & Lindeman, 1982, p. 8).

Research on learning has demonstrated that learning is impaired if instructional material misdirects attention, with one method of misdirecting attention being to use inappropriate verb tense (Sweller, Chandler, Tierney, & Cooper, 1990). Message B above is also temporally nonimmediate, further inhibiting the likelihood that an audience will understand and remember the vivid verbal metaphor, even when the visual image of an egg frying remains constant, and only the words selected to convey the message change. Use of temporally immediate language generates an internal request to attend.

*Qualifiers.* One final type of language that designers should consider when evaluating the immediacy of a message is use of qualifiers, the words or phrases that express uncertainty (Wiener & Mehrabian, 1968). Such words as *perhaps, may, maybe,* and *possibly* all introduce room for doubt. Similarly, phrases such as *it could be* and *it might be* suggest uncertainty. The following message from the Georgia Department of Human Resources' WIC Program and the Office of Nutrition in the brochure, *Good Beginnings for Having a Healthy Baby,* exemplifies such use: "Avoid eating laundry starch, cornstarch, dirt, clay, flour, chalk, and ashes because they may be harmful." Among many rural women in some Southeastern states, the practice of eating white dirt or clay is common, with the consumption being related to anemia (Beasley, 1993). Yet, the message that appears in the WIC brochure is qualified through the use of *may* and appears unlikely to motivate many pregnant women to give the message or their behavior, if they are eating dirt, a second thought. Avoid use of qualifiers to facilitate attention to a health message.

In sum, to motivate audiences to attend health messages consciously and actively, consideration should be given to the selection of specific speech indices to trigger internal requests to attend:

Information Processing

◄—————————————————————————————►

Passive/Peripheral                          Active/Central
                                 Bottom-up          Top-down
                        • Immediate language
                          = Denotatively specific
                          = Spatially immediate
                          = Temporally immediate
                          = Without qualifiers

These forms of language use provide the means not only to increase aware-ness but to prompt behavioral change as well. One study that examined adults' understanding of skin cancer's causes found that an immediate message increased awareness more than a nonimmediate message (Parrott, 1993). Another study demonstrated that college students increased condom use after receiving an immediate message promoting AIDS prevention, but students who received the nonimmediate message demonstrated no differences in use (Saisslin & Parrott, 1993).

## Conclusion

The desire to discover what motivates people to behave or not to behave in their own best health interests has puzzled and inspired researchers from many disciplines for many years (e.g., Glanz, Kirscht, & Rosenstock, 1981; Talkington, 1978; Webb, 1980; Zifferblatt, 1975). At times, people inten-tionally seek information about health matters, a goal-oriented activity that is likely to be associated with conscious attention and the exertion of mental effort toward the end of satisfying a particular need. Unfortunately, the goal-oriented need for health information most often occurs because in-dividuals or someone they know acquire an illness or disease that might have been prevented had they actively processed information earlier. In order to facilitate active thought about health messages in the absence of a perceived need, several guidelines should be considered, as developed in this chapter, in relation to presentation of content and linguistic variables that motivate cognitive effort:

1. Use novel messages, settings, and media to present health messages.
2. Consider discrepant and unexpected messages, settings, and media to present traditional health messages.
3. Instruct the audience to pay attention to the message.
4. Construct health messages in a denotatively specific manner.
5. Choose spatially immediate demonstratives.
6. Use temporally immediate speech.
7. Avoid the use of qualifiers in relation to establishing a need to change behaviors; instead, identify the probabilities associated with specific outcomes of certain behaviors.

As a result of considering these matters, Mendelsohn's (1968) promise regarding media's potential to affect people's behaviors positively in relation to health will more often be attained.

## Note

1. Moreover, as the message appears, the use of the personal pronoun *they* in reference to surgery, electrical current, radiation therapy, and freezing may be misinterpreted in reference to "risks to the patient," due to the location of the pronoun in relation to *methods* versus *risks*. *They*, as the message reads, modifies the risks to the patient—undoubtedly not the intended meaning of the writer.

## References

American Cancer Society. (1985). *Fry now: Pay later* (No. 2611-LE). New York: Author.

Anderson, P. A. (1985). Nonverbal immediacy in interpersonal communication. In A. W. Siegman & S. Feldstein (Eds.), *Multichannel integrations of nonverbal behavior* (pp. 105-128). Hillsdale, NJ: Lawrence Erlbaum.

Beasley, D. (1993, January 9). Trying to stop a dirty habit: Macon doctor behind drive against unhealthy, age-old craving for kaolin. *Atlanta Journal & Constitution*, p. B2.

Behrman, M., Moscovitch, M., & Mozer, M. C. (1991). Directing attention to words and nonwords in normal subjects and in a computational model: Implications for neglect dyslexia. *Cognitive Neuropsychology, 3,* 213-248.

Borgida, E., & Howard-Pitney, B. (1983). Personal involvement and the robustness of perceptual salience effects. *Journal of Personality and Social Psychology, 45,* 560-570.

Burnkrant, R. E., & Unnava, H. R. (1989). Self-referencing: A strategy for increasing processing of message content. *Personality and Social Psychology Bulletin, 15,* 628-638.

Chaiken, S., & Eagly, A. H. (1976). Communication modality as a determinant of message persuasiveness and message comprehensibility. *Journal of Personality and Social Psychology, 34,* 605-614.

Chanowitz, B., & Langer, E. J. (1981). Premature cognitive commitment. *Journal of Personality and Social Psychology, 41,* 1051-1063.

Freimuth, V. S., Hammond, S. L., Edgar, T., & Monahan, J. L. (1990). Reaching those at risk: A content-analytic study of AIDS PSAs. *Communication Research, 17,* 775-991.

Glanz, K., Kirscht, J. P., & Rosenstock, I. M. (1981). Linking research and practice in patient education for hypertension. *Medical Care, 19,* 141-152.

Green, S. K., Lightfoot, M. A., Bandy, C., & Buchanan, D. R. (1985). A general model of the attribution process. *Basic and Applied Social Psychology, 6,* 159-179.

Hess, A. K., & Gossett, D. (1974). Nixon and the media: A study of non-immediacy in newspaper editorials as reflective of geographical attitude differences. *Psychological Reports, 34,* 1055-1058.

Johnson, J. D., Meischke, H., Grau, J., & Johnson, S. (1992). Cancer-related channel selection. *Health Communication, 4,* 183-196.

Kuiken, D. (1981). Nonimmediate language style and inconsistency between private and expressed evaluations. *Journal of Experimental Social Psychology, 17,* 183-196.

Langer, E. J. (1978). Rethinking the role of thought in social interaction. In J. H. Harvey, W. J. Ickes, & R. F. Kidd (Eds.), *New directions in attribution research* (Vol. 2, pp. 35-58). Hillsdale, NJ: Lawrence Erlbaum.

Langer, E. J. (1985). Playing the middle against both ends: The usefulness of adult cognitive activity as a model for cognitive activity in childhood and old age. In S. R. Yussen (Ed.), *The growth of reflection in children* (pp. 267-285). New York: Academic Press.

Langer, E., Blank, A., & Chanowitz, B. (1978). The mindlessness of ostensibly thoughtful action: The role of "placebic" information in interpersonal interaction. *Journal of Personality and Social Psychology, 36,* 635-642.

Langer, E. J., & Rodin, J. (1976). The effects of choice and enhanced personal responsibility for the aged: A field experiment in an institutional setting. *Journal of Personality and Social Psychology, 34,* 191-198.

Larson, M. S. (1991). Health-related messages embedded in prime-time television entertainment. *Health Communication, 3,* 175-184.

Levy, M. R., & Windahl, S. (1985). The concept of audience activity. In K. E. Rosengren, L. A. Wenner, & P. Palmgreen (Eds.), *Media gratifications research: Current perspectives* (pp. 109-122). Beverly Hills, CA: Sage.

Louis, M. R., & Sutton, R. I. (1991). Switching cognitive gears: From habits of mind to active thinking. *Human Relations, 44,* 55-76.

Maibach, E. (1991). Selling prevention: A public health communication perspective. *Cosmetics & Toiletries, 106,* 39-40.

McDuffie, D. (1993a, February). Hit and run. In T. DeFalco (Ed.), *The amazing Spiderman, 1-3,* pp. 1-30.

McDuffie, D. (1993b, February). Skating on thin ice. In T. DeFalco (Ed.), *The amazing Spiderman, 1-1,* pp. 1-30.

McGuire, W. J. (1986). The myth of massive media impact: Savagings and salvagings. In G. Comstock (Ed.), *Public communication and behavior* (Vol. 1, pp. 173-257). Newbury Park, CA: Sage.

McGuire, W. J. (1989). Theoretical foundations of campaigns. In R. E. Rice & C. K. Atkin (Eds.), *Public communication campaigns* (2nd ed.) (pp. 43-66). Newbury Park, CA: Sage.

Mendelsohn, H. (1968). Which shall it be: Mass education or mass persuasion for health? *American Journal of Public Health, 58,* 131-137.

Park, C. W., & Smith, D. C. (1989). Product-level choice: A top-down or bottom-up process? *Journal of Consumer Research, 16,* 289-299.

Parrott, R. (1993). *Adults' knowledge, perceptions of vulnerability, and outcome expectations: A formative evaluation.* Manuscript submitted for publication.

Parrott, R. (in press-a). Comic book heroes battle a tough enemy in AIDS. In L. K. Fuller (Ed.), *Media-mediated AIDS: Messages about transmission and risk.* Amherst, MA: Human Resource Development Press.

Parrott, R. (in press-b). Topic and person-centered "sensitive subjects": Managing barriers to disclosure about health. In L. K. Fuller & L. M. Shilling (Eds.), *Communicating about communicable diseases.* Amherst, MA: Human Resource Development Press.

Parrott, R., Greene, K., & Parker, R. (1992). Negotiating child health care routines through paediatrician-parent conversations. *Journal of Language and Social Psychology, 11,* 35-45.

Pechmann, C., & Stewart, D. W. (1989). The multidimensionality of persuasive communications: Theoretical and empirical foundations. In P. Cafferata & A. M. Tybout (Eds.),

*Cognitive and affective responses to advertising* (pp. 31-56). Lexington, MA: Lexington Books.

Petty, R. E., & Cacioppo, J. T. (1986). The elaboration likelihood model of persuasion. *Advances in Experimental Social Psychology, 19,* 123-205.

Petty, R. E., Cacioppo, J. T., & Goldman, R. (1981). Personal involvement as a determinant of argument-based persuasion. *Journal of Personality and Social Psychology, 37,* 1915-1926.

Petty, R. E., Cacioppo, J. T., & Schumann, D. (1983). Central and peripheral routes to advertising effectiveness: The moderating role of involvement. *Journal of Consumer Research, 10,* 135-146.

Pfau, M. (1990). A channel approach to television influence. *Journal of Broadcasting and Electronic Media, 34,* 195-214.

Pfau, M., & Parrott, R. (1993). *Persuasive communication campaigns.* Needham Heights, MA: Allyn & Bacon.

Phoenix, V. G., & Lindeman, M. L. (1982). Language patterns and therapeutic change. In R. D. Pietro (Ed.), *Linguistics and the professions: Proceedings of the second annual Delaware Symposium on Language Studies* (pp. 3-11). Norwood, NJ: Ablex.

Reeves, B., & Thorson, E. (1986). Watching television: Experiments on the viewing process. *Communication Research, 13,* 343-361.

Saisslin, R., & Parrott, R. (1993). *Use of verbal immediacy to personalize an AIDS message: Effects on college students' condom use.* Manuscript under review.

Siegel, K. (1988). Public education to prevent the spread of HIV infection. *New York State Journal of Medicine, 88,* 642-646.

Skin Cancer Foundation. (1985). *It's never too early to stop skin cancer . . . or too late.* New York: Skin Cancer Foundation.

Sweller, J., Chandler, P., Tierney, P., & Cooper, M. (1990). Cognitive load as a factor in the structuring of technical material. *Journal of Experimental Psychology, 119,* 176-192.

Talkington, D. R. (1978). Maximizing patient compliance by shaping attitudes of self-directed health care. *The Journal of Family Practice, 6,* 591-595.

Webb, P. A. (1980). Effectiveness of patient education and psychosocial counseling in promoting compliance and control among hypertensive patients. *The Journal of Family Practice, 10,* 1047-1055.

Wiener, M., & Mehrabian, A. (1968). *Language within language: Immediacy, a channel in verbal communication.* New York: Appleton-Century-Crofts.

Zifferblatt, S. M. (1975). Increasing patient compliance through the applied analysis of behavior. *Preventive Medicine, 4,* 173-182.

# 2 Encouraging Risk Reduction

## A DECISION-MAKING APPROACH
## TO MESSAGE DESIGN

DAVID R. HOLTGRAVE

BARBARA J. TINSLEY

LINDA S. KAY

D ecisions are made in the hope that they will result in good outcomes (Yates, 1990). However, short-term benefits (e.g., the perceived pleasure of having sex without a condom) sometimes are chosen over long-term benefits (e.g., a reduced probability of developing AIDS with consistent condom use). Other times, the effort required to make a decision may be overwhelming, and people may elect simply not to decide (e.g., someone may choose to do whatever their sexual partner wants to do regarding condom use). On other occasions, people might arrive at very different decisions just because they hear identical information worded in slightly different ways (e.g., a couple might disagree on the usefulness of condoms because one person has heard a report that condoms are 98% effective against HIV transmission, whereas the other has heard that condoms have a 2% failure rate). The study of these and related phenomena is the domain of the field of behavioral decision making (BDM) (Arkes & Hammond, 1986; Dawes, 1988; Hogarth, 1987; Hogarth & Reder, 1986; von Winterfeldt & Edwards, 1986; Yates, 1990).

AUTHORS' NOTE: The authors thank J. Carlos Rivero, Rob Hamm, Ann Bostrom, Caryn Christensen, and the editors for insightful theoretical discussions and commentary. Although the original empirical research on environmental decision making described herein was funded wholly or in part by the United States Environmental Protection Agency under assistance agreement #CR817465 to the University of Oklahoma while David R. Holtgrave was a faculty member there in the Clinical Decision Making Program, Department of Family Medicine, it may not necessarily reflect the views of the Agency and no official endorsement should be inferred.

BDM is largely concerned with the cognitive processes by which humans perceive, structure, and evaluate alternative courses of action. It goes far beyond the relatively simplistic cost-benefit components included in the health belief model, the theory of reasoned action and protection motivation theory (for a comparison of those theories, see Weinstein, 1993). BDM research includes the study of risk perception, problem structuring, consequence (outcome) valuation, probability judgment, and heuristics and biases. The last area considers how people use cognitive shortcuts in their decision making and how their judgment displays consistent biases (Kahneman, Slovic, & Tversky, 1982). Although much effort in the BDM field has been expended in developing *descriptive* theories of how people actually *do* make decisions (Camerer, 1992; Lopes, 1990; Yates, 1990, 1992), none has gained universal acceptance. For that reason, this chapter does not put forth one particular descriptive BDM theory, but rather draws broadly on the BDM literature.

## CHAPTER OVERVIEW

In this chapter, we take from the BDM literature theoretical constructs and empirical lessons that can be used to guide and improve the development of health communication messages. Here we modify and update Fischhoff's (1989b; Fischhoff, Bostrom, & Quadrel, 1993) survey of BDM research for use in risk communication campaigns, emphasize developmental considerations, and combine the BDM lessons with a stage of behavior change framework. A stage of behavior change framework is important to use because, at best, communication campaigns will cause people to make incremental movements toward behavior change, and various BDM constructs are more appropriate for use at particular stages of these incremental steps (Prochaska, DiClemente, & Norcross, 1992). It is also important to consider developmental issues because it has been shown that child and adolescent decision making differ from adult decision making (Baron & Brown, 1991; Fischhoff, 1992; Holtgrave, Tinsley, & Kay, in press); however, developmental BDM data is less available than data on adults.

This material is covered in three major sections below. First, stage of change models are briefly reviewed. Second, specific BDM constructs are described that can be used by communication campaigns to help move audience members from one stage of behavior change to the next. These are accompanied by examples, most of which are related to HIV prevention messages. Developmental issues are also covered throughout this section whenever relevant data is available. The final section gives conclusions and describes a proposed research agenda.

## Stage Models of Behavior Change

Nonstage theories and models of preventive behavior (e.g., the health belief model, theory of reasoned action, and protection motivation theory) view behavior change or adoption as movement along a single continuum of action. They assume that the relative probability of a person taking action is a mathematical function of that individual's attitudes and beliefs. Which factors are included in this function, how they are weighted, and their interactions are assumed to be constant from the time one learns of a threat to the time action is taken (Weinstein, 1988).

In contrast, stage models view behavior change as a series of actions or events. These models allow researchers to detect movement toward a behavior change among people who have not yet attained the behavior change. In addition, investigators can see the influence of factors at the beginning and through-out the change process, rather than expecting all factors to impact the end product of actual behavior change or adoption (Prochaska et al., 1992; Weinstein & Sandman, 1992).

According to Weinstein (1988), a stage theory suggests that (a) people at different stages in the change process behave in qualitatively distinct ways, and (b) the interventions needed to move people toward the desired behavior vary by stage. Thus, an effective program in one situation may be inappropriate in another (Catania, Kegeles, & Coates, 1990; Prochaska et al., 1992; Weinstein & Sandman, 1992). Three of the stage models currently in use are the AIDS risk reduction model (ARRM) (Catania, Kegeles, & Coates, 1992), the precaution adoption process (PAP) (Weinstein, 1988; Weinstein & Sandman, 1992), and the stages of change model (DiClemente & Prochaska, 1985; Prochaska et al., 1992; Baranowski, 1992-1993). We have chosen to elaborate here on the *stages of change (SOC)* model and to use it as the framework for the selected BDM constructs because of the extensive testing of the model and the wealth of empirical data that support it.

The SOC model, derived from diverse theories of psychotherapy, proposes five stages: *Precontemplative (PC)*—not recognizing the problem or the need to change; *Contemplative (C)*—seriously thinking about the problem and the possibility of change; *Preparation (P)*—making a commitment to change and taking steps to prepare for that change; *Action (A)*—successful modification of behavior for a period of from 1 day to 6 months; and *Mainte-*

*nance (M)*—continuation of change from 6 months to an indefinite period. Research has shown that relapse and recycling through the stages of behavior change happens often as individuals try to stop or change particular behaviors. Therefore, the original model of linear progression through the stages was modified to a spiral model. The factors and processes that help individuals progress through the stages of behavior change vary from stage to stage. For example, consciousness raising, emotional arousal, and environmental reevaluation are influential processes for moving people from PC to C, and decisional balance and self-reevaluation are important for movement from C to P (DiClemente & Prochaska, 1985; DiClemente, 1993; Prochaska et al., 1992).

Weinstein and Sandman (1992) conclude that, "knowing which factor one would like to change is not the same as knowing how to change it" (p. 180). In this chapter we propose using BDM lessons not only to indicate which factors to change, but also to provide important instruction on "how to" change these factors.

## The Influence of Behavioral Decision-Making
## Constructs on Progression Through Stages of Change

### MOVING FROM THE PRECONTEMPLATIVE
### TO CONTEMPLATIVE STAGE: LESSONS FROM BDM

Consciousness raising, one of the change processes found to underlie movement from PC to C, is defined as increasing information about oneself and a particular problem being faced (Prochaska et al., 1992). An increased perception of personal risk by people engaged in potentially risky behaviors (which may include the absence of a preventive behavior) easily fits within this definition, and points to four constructs from the BDM literature that are especially relevant and compelling: (a) Dimensional Models of Risk Perception and Risk Comparisons, (b) Cumulative and "One-Shot" Probability Judgments, (c) Qualitative and Quantitative Probability Terms, and (d) the Framing Effect. These concepts, all of which relate to level of perceived risk, can be employed by designers of health messages to foster movement from the PC to C stage of behavior change.

*Dimensional Models and Risk Comparisons.* Scientists, policy makers, and risk analysts often think of risk as the objective probability that some harm will come to a person exposed to a particular hazard (Cohrssen & Covello,

1989; Fischhoff, Watson, & Hope, 1990). Empirical BDM research, however, has shown that lay people have a much richer way of conceptualizing risk. In well-replicated research, Slovic and colleagues have shown that people categorize diverse risks into a taxonomy defined by several dimensions (Kraus & Slovic, 1988; Slovic, Fischhoff, & Lichtenstein, 1990; Yates & Stone, 1992). Although there is some controversy over the exact set of dimensions used by lay persons in categorizing risks (Holtgrave & Weber, 1993; National Research Council, 1989), there is general agreement that at least the following major dimensions are involved: voluntariness, dread, control, knowledge, catastrophic potential, novelty, and equity (Kraus & Slovic, 1988). Certain characteristics lead to higher perceived risk: involuntariness, high level of dread, lack of control, low level of knowledge, high catastrophic potential, high level of novelty, and low level of equity (National Research Council, 1989).

It is often argued that people reject comparisons of risks that possess very different dimensions of risk (National Research Council, 1989). For instance, people may become angry when their involuntary exposure to man-made outdoor air pollutants is compared to voluntary exposure from cigarette smoke. Such a comparison is seen as comparing apples with oranges, and may also be seen as an attempt at manipulation. When a target audience perceives manipulation, the communicator may be perceived as untrustworthy and the messages dismissed (National Research Council, 1989).

Hence, the most important lesson for health message designers to draw from the risk perception literature is that *only risks with similar dimensional profiles should be compared in communication campaigns.* Health communicators may encourage people to move from the PC to C stage of behavior change by increasing the risk perceived to be associated with a particular behavior and by making comparisons with activities widely regarded by society as risky. Inappropriate comparisons, however, may be rejected by the audience or have other undesirable or unintended consequences.

Message designers must take care to elicit or locate the risk dimension profiles of activities that they would like to compare in their communications. For instance, a message designer constructing an HIV prevention campaign might be tempted to compare HIV risks and epidemiological statistics to other STD risks and statistics. We must ask, however, whether the risk dimension profiles of HIV and other STDs are adequately similar. It would seem that these two types of risk differ mainly on four dimensions: *dread, control, catastrophic potential,* and *novelty.*

HIV infection, at present, leads to a fatal consequence. This is largely not the case for other STDs. HIV is therefore likely to be seen as a more *dreaded* risk. HIV and other STDs can both be avoided via careful avoidance of high-risk behaviors. However, other STDs can be much more readily treated than can HIV infections. Hence, there is less *control* associated with HIV infection. Although basic epidemiology tells us that HIV and other STDs can be transmitted widely, an HIV epidemic would result in death for a greater proportion of the population than would, say, a syphilis epidemic. Therefore, HIV infection has greater *catastrophic potential.* HIV infection has arrived on the public health horizon within the past several years; other STDs have been known for centuries. So, HIV infection is a more *novel* risk than other STDs.

Overall, HIV infection is a more *dreaded,* less *controllable,* more *catastrophic,* and more *novel* health risk than other STDs. The risk perception model would predict, therefore, that people are more likely to rate HIV infections as a greater risk than other STDs. A better comparison to HIV risks might be driving under the influence of drugs or alcohol. Inebriate driving has more in common with HIV infection risk in terms of dread and control than do other STDs. Hence, although an imperfect comparison, it may be viewed (perhaps surprisingly) as a more acceptable risk comparison than a comparison of HIV and other STDs. The National Research Council (1989) provides other examples of poor and "better" risk comparisons.

There are other considerations when devising risk comparisons (National Research Council, 1989; Roth, Morgan, Fischhoff, Lave, & Bostrom, 1990; Slovic, Kraus, & Covello, 1990). One important consideration is that there are individual differences in the way people use dimensions in their risk perceptions (Holtgrave & Weber, 1993). An important individual difference is the age and developmental status of the audience members. Risk perception of adolescents, for example, is highly influenced by dimensions related to perceived social norms (Benthin, Slovic, & Severson, 1992). This is an important difference from adult dimensional models.

*Cumulative and One-Shot Probability Judgments.* The BDM literature contains empirical evidence that people have difficulty processing probabilistic information. They often overweight small probabilities and underweight large ones (Slovic, Fischhoff, & Lichtenstein, 1990), have trouble revising probability judgments in light of new information (Hogarth, 1987; Tversky & Kahneman, 1982b), and overestimate the probability of easy-to-imagine events (Hogarth, 1987; Sox, Blatt, Higgins, & Marton, 1988; Tversky & Kahneman, 1982a).

Even when provided with a true probability of an event occurring once from one opportunity, people have trouble estimating the cumulative probability that the event will occur once over many opportunities. This was strikingly demonstrated when Linville, Fischhoff, and Fischer (Fischhoff, 1989a) asked college students for the probability that HIV would be transmitted between a heterosexual couple, one of whom is HIV positive, in 1 instance of unprotected sexual intercourse. They asked similar questions specifying sex with and without condom use, and specifying male-to-female or female-to-male transmission. They then asked these questions again but for 10 sexual encounters (not 1), and again for 100 sexual encounters. Assuming as correct the subjects' estimates for transmission on 1 sexual encounter, the subjects made gross underestimates of the cumulative probability of transmission after 10 and 100 encounters. Similar findings have been obtained in studies related to seat belt use and contraceptive failure (Fischhoff, 1989a).

For health message designers, the important lesson is that *people tend to underestimate cumulative risks.* If the communication designer wishes to move someone from the PC to C stage of behavior change, emphasizing cumulative probabilities would be more useful than emphasizing single incident probabilities. For instance, a message related to HIV prevention might avoid mentioning that the probability of transmission of HIV in a *single* incident of unprotected sexual intercourse is quite low. Rather the message should emphasize that over time, after a number of unprotected sexual encounters, the probability of contracting HIV infection rises to nearly 1. For example, a message to a group of persons engaged in high-risk behavior might state, "Think of the times that you are likely to have sex in the next 2 years. Every one of those times that you don't use a condom, you increase your chances of getting HIV, the AIDS virus. Before you know it, unsafe sex will catch up with you, and you will become HIV infected. So why not protect yourself and start using condoms now. Make condoms a habit." Although we know of no supporting empirical data on the effectiveness of such a message in the HIV arena, similar messages have been found effective in the seatbelt usage literature (Fischhoff, 1989a; Slovic, Fischhoff, & Lichtenstein, 1978).

*Qualitative and Quantitative Probabilities.* Aside from the nightly weather forecast, people tend to communicate about probabilistic concepts using words instead of numbers. Rather than saying, "There is a 10% chance that I will get this job," people tend to say something like, "It is unlikely that I will get this job." The use of such qualitative terms to refer to quantitative concepts involves much imprecision. Imprecision in communications about probabilistic terms can lead to confusion and even conflict.

Several researchers have attempted to understand exactly what people mean when they use qualitative probability expressions (Bryant & Norman, 1980; Mostellor & Youtz, 1990; Spedden & Ryan, 1992). These studies generally find that there is great disagreement about what numerical values should be linked with particular verbal expressions. Indeed, the error bars around the mean quantitative values given for a majority of verbal expressions span the value 50%. This is important because it means that someone hearing a term such as *possibly* would not know whether to bet that the event in question will or will not occur.

Therefore, before using a qualitative expression of uncertainty (see Chapter 1 in this volume), communication designers should *consult the qualitative probability literature to find the (range of) quantitative equivalents* that have been expressed by research subjects. Further, given the broad range of disagreement typically expressed by subjects over the quantitative meaning of some qualitative phrases, message designers should *consider providing both qualitative and quantitative expressions* so as to make their meaning clear.

As an example of message design intended to move people from PC to C, consider a hypothetical HIV prevention street outreach worker who wishes to convey to an injection drug-using population that—when used correctly—bleach kills HIV with a probability of more than .99. The outreach worker also needs to convey that highly improper usage of bleach can drop the probability of bleach killing HIV to less than .20 (these are *illustrative* numbers only). The research literature indicates that *virtually always* and *high probability* have average quantitative probability meanings relatively near .99 (Bryant & Norman, 1980) and that the phrases *unlikely, doubtful,* and *low probability* are consistent with a probability value of .20 with some audiences (Bryant & Norman, 1980). If intravenous drug users understand these terms in the same way as other audiences, the street outreach worker can use the qualitative terms to supplement and emphasize the numerical probabilistic information.

*Framing Effects.* The framing effect refers to the phenomenon in which subjects respond differently to equivalent verbal stimuli when the stimuli are worded differently (Elstein, 1987). In a classic study, McNeil, Pauker, Sox, and Tversky (1982) asked both patients and physicians whether they would prefer surgical or radiation treatment for lung cancer. All subjects received information about the potential consequences of the two therapies. The subjects, however, were randomly assigned to receive either (a) information presented as survival statistics, or (b) information presented as mortality statistics. Of course, a 5-year survival rate of, say, 30% is equivalent to a 5-year mortality rate of 70%. Both patient and physician subjects receiving survival-framed information had different expressed preferences among therapy modalities than did those receiving the mortality frame. This difference in preferences between frames is startling because the only thing that changed between the two scenarios was the wording—the underlying information conveyed was the same. Even using somewhat different stimuli, researchers have found this "framing effect" to be quite robust (Elstein, 1987; Fischhoff, 1989a; Tversky & Kahneman, 1974, 1986).

The implications for communication designers are clear. What may appear to be *arbitrary choices of wording—even alternative wording with the same underlying meaning—can have profound impacts in terms of the decisions and behaviors they elicit* from the target audience. The message designer may opt to use the frame that seems most likely to elicit the desired behavior. For instance, supporters of condom use in HIV prevention might craft messages touting condom success rates, whereas critics of condom usage might tout failure rates. A 95% success rate is equal to a 5% failure rate, but messages that use only one or the other of these statistics are likely to lead to different behavioral responses. Fischhoff (1989a) demonstrated that people receiving condom information framed as success rates were more likely to report that they would use condoms than subjects receiving equivalent failure rate information. Clients' responses to various frames should be tested in formative evaluation. Further, if message receivers perceive that they have been given only one frame as a means of manipulation, the maneuver may backfire and the receivers may come to distrust the message sources.

## MOVING FROM THE CONTEMPLATIVE
## TO PREPARATION STAGE: LESSONS FROM BDM

Movement from C to P involves a person developing and committing to a course of action, a process that necessarily includes selection among options (i.e., a tipping of the decisional balance toward one option). Three BDM concepts that deal with option selection are particularly compelling: (a) Decision-Making Perspective, (b) Time Horizon, and (c) Importance Assessment of Decision-Making Factors. These three aspects of health decision making can in some way be influenced by communication campaign messages.

*Decision-Making Perspective.* For public health workers, the decision of whether or not to smoke may seem to have one and only one obviously right answer. The "right" choice may not seem quite so transparent to a smoker, however. Perhaps someone hears an antismoking message but does not respond because cigarettes are a source of perceived comfort in a life with few other sources of positive influence.

In another health area, Pinkerton and Abramson (1992) have discussed under what conditions unsafe sexual behavior may actually seem perfectly rational to the participants. In the case of radon testing, Svenson and Fischhoff (1985) have drawn a decision tree from the perspective of social policy makers and another from the perspective of an individual homeowner. The two decision trees are quite different, and inspection of them makes it clear that conflicts between policy makers and homeowners could easily arise over this issue, because quite different issues and structures are incorporated in the trees.

When decision analysis is used in the normative sense, one of the very first steps in the analysis is to outline the decision-making perspective. In communication campaigns, *message designers need to elicit and address the decision-making perspective of the message recipients,* bearing in mind that the designer's perspective is not necessarily the same as the message recipient's perspective. This elicitation takes place during periods of formative research; then messages are designed to help the client choose an option that will move him or her from the C to P stage of behavior change.

As a concrete example of encouraging people to change their decision-making perspective, consider a counselor providing ongoing, one-on-one behavior change counseling to a male client, recently tested HIV seropositive, who is considering consistent condom use but has yet to commit to this course of action. This continued failure to use condoms consistently with persons of unknown HIV serostatus is clearly of concern. In order to help the client move from the C to P stage of condom use, the counselor should attempt to assess the client's decision-making perspective. If the client is using himself as the referent point in his decision-making perspective, he may think that because he is already infected, there is little benefit in using condoms, but there is mainly the financial cost and perceived potential physical and social discomfort of condom usage.

In such a case, the counselor has at least two options. One is to try to shift the client's perspective to that of the sexual partners of unknown serostatus. As a second option, if the client refuses to acknowledge another decision-making perspective, the counselor can work within the client's own perspective to tip the balance of perceived costs, benefits, and probabilities related to condom use and nonuse.

*Time Horizon.* Whether consciously or subconsciously constructed, all decisions are made, in part, by taking into account the time horizon over which consequences are to be considered. For instance, people in a very stable environment may consider the long-term health effects of possible HIV infection when making a decision about whether or not to use a condom with a new sexual partner of unknown HIV serostatus. If, however, a person lives in an area where homicide and other death rates are so high that life expectancy is numbered in years rather than decades, or has to procure food and shelter on a day-to-day basis, then condom use may seem superfluous. BDM research has shown that people in actuality do have quite different planning horizons (Kirsch, Nijkamp, & Zimmermann, 1988; McGrath, 1988; Svenson, 1991; Vlek & Keren, 1992). Health message designers *need to incorporate message recipients' time horizon(s) into health communication.*

By helping the client to take on a different time horizon or by working within the client's current time horizon, message designers can assist movement from the C to P stage. For example, an HIV prevention counselor can assess an adolescent client's time horizon by inquiring about whether the client typically makes plans for the next day, week, month, year, several years or decades (or a combination of such plans). It may be discovered that the client usually considers activities for the next month or two but seldom considers events taking place in the next school year. With this short time horizon it seems unlikely that HIV infection would be a major concern of the client. The counselor might therefore probe to see whether the client has any dreams for certain occupations. Perhaps the client has thought about being a physician, but feels that is so far out in the future it will probably never be achieved. In this case the counselor might try to focus the client on considering this occupational dream, thereby lengthening the client's time horizon. Only after the time horizon has been stretched will it make sense to consider the issue of condom use for HIV infection prevention, which is an issue requiring long-term thought.

Of course, the client's time horizon might not be easily changed. If the client continues to focus on short-term issues, the counselor will need to make condom use a short-term issue. For instance, it may make sense to talk about condoms as a guard against other STDs and unintended pregnancy in the near term.

*Assessment of Importance of Decision-Making Factors.* People may differ in the choices they make about health behaviors because they value or weight the importance of various decision-making factors differently. Methods have been developed for studying how people access and use information across multiple factors when making decisions (Carroll & Johnson, 1990; Ford, Schmitt, Schechtman, Hults, & Doherty, 1989; Montgomery & Svenson, 1989). The BDM literature also contains well-developed normative and descriptive theories of how people take into account multiple outcome factors in their decision making, the most famous theory being multi-attribute utility theory (MAUT) (von Winterfeldt & Edwards, 1986). In a simplified example, assume that there are four factors relevant to the decision about whether or not to use condoms with a casual sex partner: (a) disease protection, (b) physical comfort, (c) cost, and (d) partner's reaction. One person might use condoms because he put the most weight on the disease protection factor. If someone else put most of the importance weighting on physical comfort, he might choose not to use condoms.

For purposes of communication campaigns, it is useful to determine what importance weights people place on the factors in a given decision-making problem and *incorporate the factors with the highest importance weights into the message*. We will describe very briefly our success in using this strategy in the design and evaluation of a recycling education curriculum (for more details, consult Holtgrave & Tinsley, 1993; Holtgrave, Tinsley, & Kay, in press).

Before assembling the curriculum, extensive formative research was conducted to understand how children and adolescents make decisions about recycling. We surveyed 1,278 students, 731 from Oklahoma City, Oklahoma, area schools and the rest from Riverside, California, area schools. In one portion of the survey, students rated the importance of 41 different factors on their decision making about putting trash in a recycling container rather than a garbage can. The students rated each factor from 0 if it was not at all important in their decision making up to a 10 if the factor is the most important in their decision making. The 41 factors covered such domains as the feelings of various people (e.g., family, friends, and teachers) and other features of recycling, such as (a) habit, (b) difficulty, (c) benefits to human health, wildlife, and the environment, (d) problems that arise from failure to recycle, and (e) financial benefits.

The results obtained were remarkably stable with only slight differences seen across cities and grades. The most important factors in recycling decision making included concerns about wildlife, health, the environment, natural resources, reducing the amount of garbage in dumps, and the opinion of environmental groups (not necessarily in that order). These 6 factors, rather than all 41 relevant factors, were stressed prominently in the recycling educational curriculum that was implemented in some schools in the Riverside,

California, area. The curriculum met with a favorable evaluation in terms of short-term attitude and self-reported recycling behavior change (Holtgrave & Tinsley, 1993).

## Conclusions and Research Agenda

The BDM literature also contains constructs and findings relevant to progression through the later stages of the behavior change process (P to A and A to M), as well as to preventing possible relapse from any stage to a previous one. However, space constraints do not permit a detailed coverage here. Rather, we simply note that BDM researchers have concerned themselves with how people make sequential choices (e.g., Coombs, Dawes, & Tversky, 1981; Ford et al., 1989; Hutchison, 1986), make decisions in real time (e.g., Holtgrave, 1990), and use feedback in their decision making (e.g., Hammond, Stewart, Brehmer, & Steinmann, 1986). These constructs are relevant to message designers attempting to help clients "spiral" through the remaining stages of behavior change.

Although important BDM discoveries have been made that are of considerable utility for the design of health communication campaigns, *more research* is clearly needed in at least the following areas. First, there is a need for further *empirical* testing of the utility of BDM for message design. Although it would be difficult to demonstrate directly that BDM is more useful than an atheoretical approach to message design (Hochbaum, Sorenson, & Lorig, 1992; van Ryn & Heaney, 1992), it would be possible to test further the effectiveness of BDM-based messages for changing audience members' behaviors.

Second, it was stated above that developmental considerations are important in BDM, but this is a relatively new area of BDM study and further work is needed (Baron & Brown, 1991). For instance, the effectiveness of teaching general decision-making skills as part of health communication campaigns targeted toward adolescents should be evaluated. Third, there is a need to evaluate the relative effectiveness of persuasive campaigns to those designed to engage the client in a decision-making partnership (Ballard-Reisch, 1990). Another fruitful area of research would be comparing the effectiveness of decision aiding devices for client decision making (de Dombal, 1988; Shortliffe, 1990; Watson & Buede, 1987) to the effectiveness of persuasive campaigns.

In conclusion, we have demonstrated the potential and utility of BDM constructs for designing more effective health messages and hope such considerations will be encompassed in campaign planners' repertoire.

# References

Arkes, H. R., & Hammond, K. R. (1986). *Judgment and decision making: An interdisciplinary reader.* Cambridge: Cambridge University Press.

Ballard-Reisch, D. S. (1990). A model of participative decision making for physician-patient interaction. *Health Communication, 2,* 91-104.

Baranowski, T. (1992-1993). Beliefs as motivation influences at stages in behavior change. *International Quarterly of Community Health Education, 13,* 3-29.

Baron, J., & Brown, R. V. (1991). *Teaching decision making to adolescents.* Hillsdale, NJ: Lawrence Erlbaum.

Benthin, A. C., Slovic, P., & Severson, H. (1992). *A psychometric study of adolescent risk perception.* Unpublished manuscript, Decision Research, Eugene, OR.

Bryant, G. D., & Norman, G. R. (1980). Expressions of probability: Words and numbers. *The New England Journal of Medicine, 302,* 411.

Camerer, C. F. (1992). Recent tests of generalizations of expected utility theory. In W. Edwards (Ed.), *Utility theories: Measurements and applications* (pp. 207-251). Boston: Kluwer Academic.

Carroll, J. S., & Johnson, E. J. (1990). *Decision research: A field guide.* Newbury Park, CA: Sage.

Catania, J. A., Kegeles, S. M., & Coates, T. J. (1990). Towards an understanding of risk behavior: An AIDS risk reduction model (ARRM). *Health Education Quarterly, 17,* 53-72.

Cohrssen, J. J., & Covello, V. T. (1989). *Risk analysis: A guide to analyzing health and environmental risk* (NTIS No. PB89-137772). Washington, DC: Executive Office of the President's Council on Environmental Quality.

Coombs, C. H., Dawes, R. M., & Tversky, A. (1981). *Mathematical psychology: An elementary introduction.* Ann Arbor, MI: Mathesis Press.

Dawes, R. M. (1988). *Rational choice in an uncertain world.* San Diego, CA: Harcourt Brace Jovanovich.

de Dombal, F. T. (1988). Computer-aided diagnosis of acute abdominal pain: The British experience. In J. Dowie & A. Elstein (Eds.), *Professional judgment: A reader in clinical decision making* (pp. 196-199). Cambridge: Cambridge University Press.

DiClemente, C. C. (1993). Changing addictive behaviors: A process perspective. *Current Directions in Psychological Science, 2,* 101-106.

DiClemente, C. C., & Prochaska, J. O. (1985). Processes and stages of self-change: Coping and competence in smoking behavior change. In S. Shiffman & T. A. Willis (Eds.), *Coping and substance abuse* (pp. 319-343). San Diego, CA: Academic Press.

Elstein, A. S. (1987). Cognitive processes in clinical inference and decision making. In D. C. Turk & P. Salovey (Eds.), *Reasoning, inference and judgment in clinical psychology* (pp. 17-50). New York: Free Press/Macmillan.

Fischhoff, B. (1989a). Making decisions about AIDS. In V. M. Mays, G. W. Albee, & S. F. Schneider (Eds.), *Primary prevention of AIDS* (pp. 168-205). Newbury Park, CA: Sage.

Fischhoff, B. (1989b). Risk: A guide to controversy. In National Research Council, *Improving risk communication* (pp. 211-319). Washington, DC: National Academy Press.

Fischhoff, B. (1992). Risk taking: A developmental perspective. In J. F. Yates (Ed.), *Risk taking behavior* (pp. 133-162). Chichester, England: John Wiley.

Fischhoff, B., Bostrom, A., & Quadrel, M. J. (1993). Risk perception and communication. *Annual Review of Public Health, 14,* 183-203.

Fischhoff, B., Watson, S. R., & Hope, C. (1990). Defining risk. In T. S. Glickman & M. Gough (Eds.), *Readings in risk* (pp. 30-41). Washington, DC: Resources for the Future.

Ford, J. K., Schmitt, N., Schechtman, S. L., Hults, B. M., & Doherty, M. L. (1989). Process tracking methods: Contributions, problems & neglected research questions. *Organizational Behavior and Human Decision Processes, 43,* 75-117.

Hammond, K. R., Stewart, T. R., Brehmer, B., & Steinmann, D. O. (1986). Social judgment theory. In H. R. Arkes & K. R. Hammond (Eds.), *Judgment and decisionmaking: An interdisciplinary reader* (pp. 56-76). Cambridge: Cambridge University Press.

Hochbaum, G. M., Sorenson, J. R., & Lorig, K. (1992). Theory and health education in practice. *Health Education Quarterly, 19,* 295-314.

Hogarth, R. M. (1987). *Judgement and choice* (2nd ed.). Chichester, England: John Wiley.

Hogarth, R. M., & Reder, M. W. (1986). *Rational choice: The contrast between economics and psychology.* Chicago: University of Chicago Press.

Holtgrave, D. R. (1990). Constructing models of dynamic choice behavior. In K. Borcherding, O. I. Larichev, & D. M. Messick (Eds.), *Contemporary issues in decision-making* (pp. 409-428). Amsterdam: Elsevier Science (North-Holland).

Holtgrave, D. R., & Tinsley, B. J. (1993). *Risk communication, recycling and young people* (Cooperative Agreement No. 817465). Washington, DC: Environmental Protection Agency.

Holtgrave, D. R., Tinsley, B. J., & Kay, L. S. (in press). Heuristics, biases and environmental health risk analysis. In L. Heath, F. Bryant, J. Edwards, E. Henderson, J. Myers, E. Posavac, Y. Suarez-Balcazar, & R. S. Tindale (Eds.), *Applications of heuristics and biases in social issues.* New York: Plenum.

Holtgrave, D. R., & Weber, E. U. (1993). Dimensions of risk perception for financial and non-financial stimuli. *Risk Analysis, 13,* 553-558.

Hutchison, J. W. (1986). Discrete attribute models of brand switching. *Marketing Science, 5,* 350-371.

Kahneman, D., Slovic, P., & Tversky, A. (1982). *Judgment under uncertainty: Heuristics and biases.* Cambridge: Cambridge University Press.

Kirsch, G., Nijkamp, P., & Zimmermann, K. (1988). *The formulation time preferences in a multidisciplinary perspective.* Berlin: WZB-Publications.

Kraus, N., & Slovic, P. (1988). Taxonomic analysis of perceived risk: Modeling individual and group perceptions within homogeneous hazard domains. *Risk Analysis, 8,* 435-455.

Lopes, L. L. (1990). Re-modeling risk aversion: A comparison of Bernoullian and rank dependent value approaches. In G. M. von Furstenberg (Ed.), *Acting under uncertainty: Multidisciplinary conceptions* (pp. 267-299). Boston: Kluwer.

McGrath, J. E. (1988). Introduction: The place of time in social psychology. In J. E. McGrath (Ed.), *The social psychology of time: New perspectives* (pp. 7-20). Newbury Park, CA: Sage.

McNeil, B. J., Pauker, S. G., Sox, H. C., & Tversky, A. (1982). On the elicitation for preferences for alternative therapies. *The New England Journal of Medicine, 306,* 1259-1262.

Montgomery, H., & Svenson, O. (Eds.). (1989). *Process and structure in human decision making.* Chichester, England: John Wiley.

Mostellor, F., & Youtz, C. (1990). Quantifying probabilistic expressions. *Statistical Science, 5,* 2-34.

National Research Council. (1989). *Improving risk communication.* Washington, DC: National Academy Press.

Pinkerton, S. D., & Abramson, P. R. (1982). Is risky sex rational? *The Journal of Sex Research, 29,* 561-568.

Prochaska, J. O., DiClemente, C. C., & Norcross, J. C. (1992). In search of how people change: Applications to addictive behaviors. *American Psychologist, 47,* 1102-1114.

Roth, E., Morgan, M. G., Fischhoff, B., Lave, L., & Bostrom A. (1990). What do we know about making risk comparisons? *Risk Analysis, 10,* 375-388.

Shortliffe, E. H. (1990). Clinical decision-support systems. In E. H. Shortliffe & L. E. Perrealt (Eds.), *Medical informatics: Computer applications in health care* (pp. 466-502). Reading, MA: Addison-Wesley.

Slovic, P., Fischhoff, B., & Lichtenstein, S. (1978). Accident probabilities and seatbelt usage: A psychological perspective. *Accident Analysis and Prevention, 10,* 281-285.

Slovic, P., Fischhoff, B., & Lichtenstein, S. (1990). Rating the risk. In T. S. Glickman & M. Gough (Eds.), *Readings in risk* (pp. 61-75). Washington, DC: Resources for the Future.

Slovic, P., Kraus, N., & Covello, V. T. (1990). Comment: What *should* we know about making risk comparisons? *Risk Analysis, 10,* 389-392.

Sox, H. C., Blatt, M. A., Higgins, M. C., & Marton, K. I. (1988). *Medical decision making.* Boston: Butterworths.

Spedden, S. E., & Ryan, P. B. (1992). Probabilistic connotations of carcinogen hazard classifications: Analysis of survey data for anchoring effects. *Risk Analysis, 12,* 535-541.

Svenson, O. (1991). The time dimension in perception and communication of risk. In R. E. Kasperson & P.J.M. Stallen (Eds.), *Communicating risks to the public* (pp. 263-285). Dordrecht, the Netherlands: Kluwer.

Svenson, O., & Fischhoff, B. (1985). Levels of environmental decisions: A case study of radiation in Swedish homes. *Journal of Environmental Psychology, 5,* 55-68.

Tversky, A., & Kahneman, D. (1974). Judgment under uncertainty: Heuristics and biases. *Science, 185,* 1124-1131.

Tversky, A., & Kahneman, D. (1982a). Availability: A heuristic for judging frequency and probability. In D. Kahneman, P. Slovic, & A. Tversky (Eds.), *Judgment under uncertainty: Heuristics and biases* (pp. 163-178). Cambridge: Cambridge University Press.

Tversky, A., & Kahneman, D. (1982b). Evidential impact of base rates. In D. Kahneman, P. Slovic, & Tversky, A. (Eds.), *Judgment under uncertainty: Heuristics and biases* (pp. 153-160). Cambridge: Cambridge University Press.

Tversky, A., & Kahneman, D. (1986). Rational choice and the framing of decisions. *Journal of Business, 59,* 5251-5278.

van Ryn, M., & Heaney, C. A. (1992). What's the use of theory? *Health Education Quarterly, 19,* 315-330.

Vlek, C., & Keren, G. (1987). Behavioral decision theory and environmental risk management: Assessment and resolution of four "survival" dilemmas. *Acta Psychologica, 80,* 249-278.

von Winterfeldt, D., & Edwards, W. (1986). *Decision analysis and behavioral research.* New York: Cambridge University Press.

Watson, S. R., & Buede, D. M. (1987). *Decision synthesis: The principles and practice of decision analysis.* Cambridge: Cambridge University Press.

Weinstein, N. D. (1988). The precaution adoption process. *Health Psychology, 7,* 355-386.

Weinstein, N. D. (1993). Testing four competing theories of health-protective behavior. *Health Psychology, 12,* 324-333.

Weinstein, N. D., & Sandman, P. M. (1992). A model of the precaution adoption process: Evidence from home radon testing. *Health Psychology, 11,* 170-180.

Yates, J. F. (1990). *Judgment and decision making.* Englewood Cliffs, NJ: Prentice Hall.

Yates, J. F. (1992). *Risk-taking behavior.* Chichester, England: John Wiley.

Yates, J. F., & Stone, E. R. (1992). Risk appraisal. In J. F. Yates (Ed.), *Risk-taking behavior* (pp. 1-26). Chichester, England: John Wiley.

# 3 Moving People to Behavior Change

## A STAGED SOCIAL COGNITIVE
## APPROACH TO MESSAGE DESIGN

EDWARD W. MAIBACH

DAVID COTTON

In Chapter 2, Holtgrave, Tinsley, and Kay described stages of change theory and illustrated how behavioral decision-making principles inform messages designed to encourage people through the initial steps of behavior change. We, too, will base our message design recommendations on a stages of change approach, but rather than draw on the decision-making literature, we will examine Bandura's social cognitive theory and its implications for moving people to behavior change in a staged fashion. To this end, we briefly review both the transtheoretical model and social cognitive theory, and then describe and illustrate social cognitive message design strategies to move target audience members through the stages of change. The messages we use to illustrate the recommended strategies are drawn from two multisite, community-level, HIV prevention projects funded by the Centers for Disease Control and Prevention (CDC): the AIDS Community Demonstration Projects and the Prevention of HIV in Women and Infants Demonstration Project.

## The Transtheoretical Model

The transtheoretical model (Prochaska & DiClemente, 1983, 1985; Prochaska, DiClemente, & Norcross, 1992), also called stages of change

AUTHORS' NOTE: Portions of this chapter have been borrowed from E. Maibach & D. Murphy, Conceptualization and Measurement of Self-Efficacy in Health Promotion Research (in press), *Health Education Research*. This chapter was supported in part by a Cooperative Agreement between the Association of Schools of Public Health/CDC and Emory School of Public Health (Edward Maibach, P.I.).

theory, describes behavior change as a process in which individuals progress through a series of discrete phases or stages of change. These stages of change have been documented with individuals undergoing behavior change in the areas of smoking cessation (Prochaska & DiClemente, 1983; Prochaska, DiClemente, Velicer, Ginpil, & Norcross, 1985), substance use (DiClemente & Hughes, 1990), weight control (O'Connell & Velicer, 1988; Prochaska, Norcross, Fowler, Follick, & Abrams, 1992), sun screen use (Rossi, 1989), and most recently in the area of condom use (Galavotti, Cabral, Grimley, Riley, & Prochaska, 1993; O'Reilly & Higgins, 1991; Prochaska, Redding, Harlow, Rossi, & Velicer, in press).

The five stages have been labeled Precontemplation, Contemplation, Preparation, Action, and Maintenance. *Precontemplation* is the stage at which an individual has no intention to change the relevant behavior in the foreseeable future. People at this stage are either unaware that their behavior places them at risk, refuse to acknowledge their risk, or have decided for some other reason not to adopt the healthier behavior. *Contemplation* is the stage at which an individual begins to consider the need to change the behavior in question at some point in the future. People often remain at this stage for a long period of time because of the difficulty in evaluating the costs and benefits of changing their behavior (Prochaska, DiClemente, & Norcross, 1992). *Preparation* is the stage at which an individual makes a decision to change the behavior. Although some particularly resolute individuals are able to adopt new behaviors immediately and consistently upon making a decision to change, this is not the case for most people. The Preparation stage is more commonly characterized as a time of planning a behavior change strategy. Engaging in the new behavior on a trial basis can be an important part of the Preparation stage. *Action* is the stage at which individuals implement their behavior change plan and begin performing the behavior consistently. The final stage, *Maintenance,* entails solidifying and routinizing the behavioral practice and is characterized by efforts to prevent relapse into the old form of behavior. Relapse may occur at any part of this sequence and may or may not be followed by a resumption of progress through the stages of change.

The stages of change provide a description of when particular shifts in attitudes, intentions, and behaviors occur. A second component of the transtheoretical model, the processes of change, describes how these shifts in stage occur. Change processes are covert and overt coping activities and experiences that individuals engage in when they attempt to modify problem behaviors. Each process is a broad category encompassing multiple techniques, methods, and interventions traditionally associated with disparate theoretical orientations (Prochaska & DiClemente, 1984, 1992). Detailed information about the processes of change is beyond the scope of this chapter; interested readers are therefore encouraged to refer to Prochaska and DiClemente (1986). The important point about processes of change for the purpose of this chapter is that each process is more influential at certain stages than at other stages (Prochaska & DiClemente, 1984; DiClemente & Prochaska, 1982). People move more efficiently through the stages when stage-appropriate processes are used; similarly, if some processes are used excessively at inappropriate stages, they can actually obstruct change or precipitate a relapse to an earlier stage.

The transtheoretical model (TM) has a number of important implications for health message design. First and most obviously, it can serve as the basis for an effective audience segmentation analysis. An analysis of this type is conducted by assessing a representative sample of the target audience to establish their current stage of change and other relevant psychosocial and behavioral variables (see Chapter 10 in this volume for a full discussion of audience segmentation strategies). When members of the sample are subdivided into five audience segments based on their current stage of change, program designers will know both the size and the psychosocial composition of each potential audience segment. Primary data collection and analysis of this type can greatly enhance message design by informing decisions about which audience segment(s) to target (and in what order), with what objectives, and in what manner. Second, the TM literature on processes of change provides a rich source of message design information on strategies to move people through the stages of change. Message design decisions will benefit greatly by taking advantage of information on the staging distribution of a target audience, as well as how to move people through the various stages.

Chapter 2 in this volume examines the behavioral decision-making literature for additional insights on how to move people through the early stages of change. An article by Baranowski (1989-1990) drew on the transtheoretical model to recommend both individual- and environmental-level strategies with the potential to move target audiences through each of the stages of change. As a complement to these two works, the remainder of this chapter presents a message design view of how to move people through the stages of change using a social cognitive approach.

## Social Cognitive Theory

Social cognitive theory (SCT) describes human behavior as being reciprocally determined by internal personal factors and the environment in which a person lives (Bandura, 1986). Figure 3.1 portrays a representation of this reciprocal determination among behavior, person, and environment. SCT presents a balanced and optimistic view of the human condition: People and their behaviors are shaped by their environments, yet people also shape their environments through their behavior and expectations. The social cognitive perspective on health behavior change is that individual behavior change can be facilitated by modifying people's personal factors and by altering environmental factors to encourage healthful behavior. Although both options are viable, health communication campaigns generally attempt to influence personal factors rather than environmental factors (see Maibach [1993] and Wallack [1990] for discussions about the role of communication campaigns in promoting macro-social change).

SCT is an important theory for health message design for a number of reasons. There is a large and rapidly growing literature that substantiates the predictive and explanatory value of social cognitive factors across a diverse group of health behaviors. These behaviors include diet and nutrition; weight loss; exercise; control of addictive substance use such as tobacco, alcohol, and opioid drugs; contraception and STD/HIV prevention; pain and disability reduction; stress reduction; and adherence to prescriptive and rehabilitative regimens (see Bandura [1991, in press] and Strecher, DeVellis, Becker, & Rosenstock [1988] for reviews). Interventions that enhance relevant social cognitive factors significantly improve the rate at which their associated health behaviors are enacted (see Bandura [1992, in press] for comprehensive reviews of this literature). Moreover, SCT elucidates mechanisms for enhancing social cognitive factors to promote appropriate health behavior changes. Strategies for enhancing the personal factors specified in SCT are examined in the next section. The subsequent section proposes a method to optimize social cognitive behavior change strategies by tailoring messages according to the relevant stage of change.

## The Role of Personal Factors in Health Behavior Change

### KNOWLEDGE

It takes little more than common sense to appreciate the fact that knowledge is a necessary precondition for behavior change. Before behavior change is likely to occur, people must have knowledge both about their risk factors (the behaviors or conditions that place one at risk) and the ways in which their risk factors can be reduced (the alternative behaviors). Without

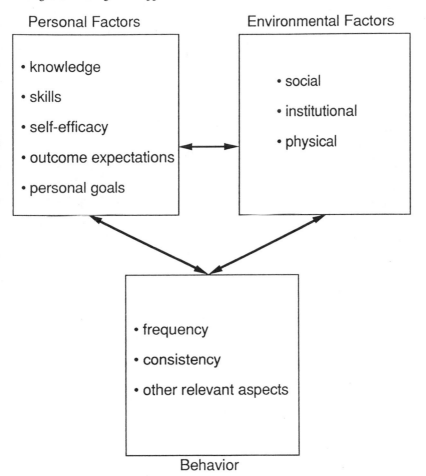

**Figure 3.1.** The Reciprocal Determination of Behavior, Person and Environment

such knowledge, people are unlikely to engage in the process that can ultimately lead to behavior change. Conversely, although knowledge is necessary, it is not sufficient to motivate or activate behavior change.

The transfer of knowledge is an inherent strength of the communication process. Health communication campaigns can be highly effective at generating appropriate levels of knowledge among members of the target audience (e.g., Maccoby & Alexander, 1980). Health message designers should, however, pay close attention to the principles of effective message design to ensure the effectiveness of their communication efforts in enhancing knowledge (see Chapters 1, 2, 9, and 10 in this volume).

## SKILLS

One reason why knowledge gains do not lead inevitably to behavior change is the lack of skills necessary to perform the behavior. Adoption of a new health-promoting behavior often requires the enactment of a constellation of complex cognitive, social, behavioral, and self-regulatory skills (Bandura, 1986, 1991, in press). Examples of these respective skills as they relate to the promotion of safer sex include the ability to recognize situations that may lead to sexual coercion (a cognitive skill), the ability to negotiate safe behavior with a sexual partner (a social skill), the ability to use a condom properly (a behavioral skill), and the ability to adhere to a previously made decision to engage only in safe sex (a self-regulatory skill). Without the necessary skills to support a new health behavior, people are unlikely to initiate and less likely to sustain behavior change efforts.

Skill development can be another strength of the communication process when properly conducted. The steps to structuring messages for skill development follow directly from the observational learning process as described by Bandura (1986). Generally speaking, skill-building messages systematically deconstruct the behavior of interest into its component parts and demonstrate how to reconstruct the behavior from those parts. Skill-building messages typically begin by conveying, through demonstration and explanation (i.e., modeling), a sense of what successful behavioral performances look like, preferably using a variety of different models. If the behavior is complex or composed of numerous steps, the behavioral components of the larger behavior should each be explicitly demonstrated.

The cognitive, social, and behavioral (and in some instances, the self-regulatory) skills required to perform the behavior must be systematically identified and modeled. In the case of complex behaviors, this modeling should be conducted for each of the behavioral components. Verbal and behavioral modeling should also be used to explain and demonstrate how the component skills and behaviors should be integrated into a successful performance of the larger behavior. Ideally, message recipients should be provided with the opportunity to practice the modeled behaviors (either behaviorally or mentally) to maximize their skill acquisition (Bandura, 1986) and confidence to apply those skills (Maibach & Flora, 1993).

SELF-EFFICACY

Self-efficacy is a pivotal factor in SCT in that it mediates the application of knowledge and skills in the pursuit of behavioral attainments. Self-efficacy refers to people's belief in their capability to organize and execute the course of action required to perform a given behavior successfully (Bandura, 1986, in press). This includes people's confidence in their capability to regulate their motivation, thought processes, emotional states, and their physical and social environment to attain their behavioral goals. When people judge themselves to be efficacious, they are confident in their capability to overcome the difficulties inherent in changing and maintaining a *specific* behavior.[1]

Efficacy judgments affect the adoption and maintenance of health behaviors through four important mechanisms: choice of behaviors, effort expenditure and persistence, thought patterns, and emotional reactions.

*Choice of Behavior.* Self-efficacy influences health behavior choices in that people tend to avoid tasks they feel exceed their capabilities, while pursuing those they feel competent to perform (Bandura, 1986). For example, smokers with low efficacy to control their smoking behavior attempt to quit less often than those who judge themselves more efficacious (DiClemente, Prochaska, & Gilbertini, 1985).

*Effort Expenditure and Persistence.* Mastering new behaviors requires both effort and persistence. A strong sense of efficacy motivates people to engage themselves fully in the tasks they undertake. For example, highly efficacious cardiac patients can get themselves to exercise harder on a treadmill than patients with weaker efficacy (Ewart, Taylor, Reese, & DeBusk, 1983). Self-efficacious individuals are also more persistent in the face of difficulties than those persons with lower efficacy. For example, efficacy to regulate eating behavior predicts decreased attrition from weight loss programs (Bernier & Avard, 1986). When obstacles to behavior change attempts arise, people of low efficacy tend to give up or reduce their effort, whereas those of high efficacy generally intensify their efforts until they succeed (Bandura & Cervone, 1983; Brown & Inouye, 1978).

*Thought Patterns and Emotional Reactions.* Efficacy beliefs affect thought patterns that can enhance or undermine behavior change. These patterns include goals and aspirations, visualization of successful versus failed efforts, and the use of analytical thought processes to cope with setbacks and difficulties (Wood & Bandura, 1989). Perceived self-efficacy also influences the regulation of affective states in that people who have a low sense of efficacy are more vulnerable to stress and depression when coping with taxing situations (Bandura, 1986).

Like knowledge and skills, self-efficacy to engage in various health behaviors is open to influence through the communication process. Perceptions of self-efficacy can be altered by four major modes of influence: performance mastery experiences, vicarious experiences (i.e., observational learning), verbal persuasion regarding one's capabilities, and inferences from physiological and affective states (Bandura, 1986).

*Performance Mastery Experiences.* The most direct way to enhance self-efficacy is to have members of the target audience attempt and succeed in performing the behavior in question. Even success with an approximation of the behavior, under practice conditions rather than real-life circumstances, will help to bolster perceptions of efficacy. Repeated successes in a safe setting will further enhance perceptions of efficacy and increase the likelihood of trying (and succeeding) in more difficult situations. Health messages should therefore encourage people to try out the new behavior in some manageable fashion and in an environment in which they are most likely to succeed.

*Vicarious Efficacy Information.* Other people's behavioral performances, whether live or depicted in print or electronic media, provide an abundant source of efficacy information. This vicarious efficacy information can have a powerful impact on an observer's efficacy beliefs, especially in the absence of much direct personal experience with the behavior. Health messages can enhance perceptions of efficacy by modeling successful demonstrations of the behavior. The impact of modeled behavior, however, is mediated by characteristics of the models and the manner in which the demonstration is performed. For example, the most effective models are those who are similar (demographically and behaviorally) to members of the target audience but somewhat more competent at the behavior being modeled. The most effective modeling demonstrations (of complex behaviors) are those that conform to the style described in the preceding section on skill development. Other important characteristics of effective modeling demonstrations include contrasting effective and ineffective performances of the behavior, making crucial but unobservable aspects of the performance (such as thought processes) observable to the audience, and providing the audience with instructive feedback about the strong (and weak) elements of the modeled performance (see Bandura [1986], Hosford & Mills [1983], Maibach [1992], and Perry & Furukawa [1986] for more detailed discussions of effective modeling performances).

*Persuasory Efficacy Information.* People often accept the appraisals of credible others as valid assessments of their own ability. Such feedback can influence perceptions of efficacy (Chambliss & Murray, 1979a, 1979b), especially for behaviors where it is difficult to judge one's own capabilities objectively. Health messages can be used to enhance audience members' self-efficacy by highlighting their existing skills and relevant experiences. This type of information can help recipients focus on and utilize their existing strengths. Similarly, health messages can be used to bolster efficacy by directing attention to successful aspects of failed behavioral attempts, rather than focusing exclusively on the outcome. And finally, health messages can enhance efficacy by providing positive feedback regarding progress toward behavior change (Schunk, 1982).

*Physiological and Affective Efficacy Information.* People make inferences about their capabilities from emotional arousal and other physiological cues they experience while enacting or anticipating a difficult behavior. Arousal that is interpreted negatively (e.g., fear or anxiety) diminishes perceptions of efficacy, whereas arousal that is interpreted positively (e.g., excitement) can raise efficacy beliefs. With instruction on anticipation and reinterpreting physiological cues, people are able to reduce or eliminate this negative anticipatory arousal and thereby increase their perceptions of efficacy (Bandura & Adams, 1977). Health message designers can encourage reinterpretation by alerting the audience that the arousal experience is normal and common, even among the most proficient models, and by naming the experience in a way that emphasizes its performance enhancing qualities.

## OUTCOME EXPECTANCIES

SCT makes a clear distinction between beliefs about ability to enact a behavior (i.e., self-efficacy) and beliefs about the outcomes that will result from the behavior. Bandura (1986) has termed the latter concept outcome expectations. These anticipated outcomes can take the form of physical effects (e.g., increasing or decreasing health or the pleasures of living), social effects (incurring the approval or disapproval of other people), or self-evaluative effects (incurring self-approval or self-disapproval). People are motivated to perform behaviors that they believe will produce outcomes they desire.

Self-efficacy mediates this motivation in two important ways, however. First, the stronger a person's judgments of efficacy for a particular behavior, the more likely he or she is to have positive outcome expectations associated with performance of that behavior. Second, people can believe a behavior will lead to desirable outcomes, but if they have no confidence that they can perform the required behavior they are not likely to be motivated to attempt it (Bandura, 1986).

Outcome expectations are open to influence through the communication process. Similar to self-efficacy, people develop their outcome expectations through some combination of direct experience, observational learning, and persuasive communication. Health messages that manage to establish new positive outcome expectations or to reinforce existing positive expectations, through demonstration or persuasion, are likely to increase people's motivation for engaging in the relevant health behavior. Health messages that reduce or eliminate negative outcome expectations associated with the new behavior are also likely to increase people's motivation to enact the behavior. Although the ideal balance between these two strategies (promoting positive expectations vs. minimizing negative expectations) is unknown, Baranowski's (1992, p. 304) analysis of diverse research literatures suggests emphasizing the benefits and establishing appropriate expectations of the costs. Regardless of the mix, health messages attempting to influence outcome expectations portray the outcomes resulting from the recommended behaviors, in contrast to self-efficacy messages, which focus on skills necessary to perform the behavior.

## PERSONAL GOALS

SCT describes personal goals as one of the major sources of motivation for behavior change and maintenance (Bandura, 1986, in press). The process of setting challenging personal goals has consistently been shown to enhance motivation across a variety of behavioral domains, populations, and time spans (Bandura, in press; Locke & Latham, 1990). Goals provide both a direction and a reference point against which people can compare their progress. When progress is made (or when behavior is maintained at a level that meets the goal), people tend to be satisfied and have positive self-appraisals. Conversely, when people fail to progress toward their goals, they tend to be dissatisfied and have negative self-appraisals. In either event, the consequence of having a closely held personal goal is enhanced motivation and effort. When goals are attained, people often adjust their goal upward and increase their level of effort; when people fail to progress, they will generally renew their effort toward attainment of the original goal.

The health message design implications of this self-regulatory process are clear. Messages that encourage people to set personal goals can have a strong motivational effect. People must be able to monitor their progress toward their goal, however, in order to sustain their motivation. Therefore, short-term goals are more effective than long-term goals, because it is difficult to monitor progress toward long-term goals. The attainment of a short-term goal is likely to motivate people to set a more challenging, longer term goal. The American Cancer Society's Great American Smokeout is a good example of a set of health messages whose objective is to encourage short-term goal setting. Smokers are encouraged to quit for one day, the day of the Great American Smokeout. They are also encouraged to feel proud of their success with the short-term effort and to use this as a springboard for future quit attempts.

## Influencing Social Cognitive Factors the Transtheoretical Way

In this chapter, we are recommending the integration of social cognitive theory with the transtheoretical model for the purpose of health message design. SCT offers a parsimonious set of internal personal factors that influence the production of behavior (i.e., a compelling explanation of why people do what they do). TM offers an equally parsimonious temporal framework and model of behavior change dynamics (i.e., a compelling explanation of how people change what they do). As such, TM offers a clear framework for addressing the internal personal factors suggested by SCT as causal determinants of behavior.

The transtheoretical model suggests several important message design considerations. First, messages must be tailored to the specific cognitive and behavioral conditions of people at each given stage. For example, a message designed for people in Precontemplation (to help them move to Contemplation) will be different than a message designed for people in the Action stage (to help them move to Maintenance). This strategy is a distinct advancement over the all-too-common approach in health campaigns where it is assumed that all message recipients are ready and willing to change their behavior immediately upon being persuaded.

| Precontemplation to Contemplation | Contemplation to Preparation | Preparation to Action | Action to Maintenance |
|---|---|---|---|
| Knowledge About Risk | | | |
| Outcome Expectations: • risk behaviors – physical (–) • alternative behaviors – physical (+) – social (+) | Outcome Expectations: • alternative behaviors – physical (+) – social (+) – self-evaluation (+) | Outcome Expectations: • social reinforce- ment of the new behavior | Outcome Expectations: • self-evaluative rein- forcement of the new behavior |
| | Self-Efficacy: • reduce risk behavior or • attempt an alterna- tive behavior | Self-Efficacy: • adopt the alterna- tive behaviors | Self-Efficacy: • overcome setbacks |
| | | Skills: • environmental restructuring • planning and problem solving | Skills: • relapse prevention |
| | | Personal Goals: • set proximal goals to adopt the alter- native behaviors | Personal Goals: • monitor progress • extend goals |

**Figure 3.2.** Internal Social Cognitive Factors That Encourage Change From One Stage to the Next

The second important consideration suggested by TM is that the order in which internal personal factors are addressed has important implications for the likelihood of promoting sustained behavior change. Figure 3.2 illustrates which internal personal factors are important at the various stages of change (based on previous work by Hemophilia Behavioral Intervention Evaluation Projects, 1993; Prochaska & DiClemente, 1984). This information can be used to guide message design and intervention tailoring.

As noted in the chapter's introduction, the investigators in the AIDS Community Demonstration Projects (ACDP) used a stages of change ap- proach to develop prevention messages for audiences at high risk of HIV infection (O'Reilly & Higgins, 1992; Pulley, McAlister, Kay, & O'Reilly, in press). These messages featured the stories and pictures of "role models" from the communities being targeted. The role models are members of the local community whose true stories of behavior change best represented the various stages of change from Contemplation to Maintenance.[2] Their stories were printed in a variety of formats (e.g., flyers, newsletters, "baseball" type cards) and distributed by peer volunteers in that community. Role model stories (the name given to these printed materials) for any given stage of change were intended to influence target audience members at the previous stage of change. The communication objectives of these role model stories correspond to the factors depicted in Figure 3.2.

The ADCP approach to intervention is currently being refined by a second set of investigators in the Prevention of HIV in Women and Infants Demonstration Projects (WIDP) (Centers for Disease Control [CDC], 1994; Cotton et al., 1994; Liebman et al., 1994). WIDP employs both paid outreach staff and volunteer community members to distribute role model stories, reinforce progress toward behavior change, and encourage further risk reduction efforts. As with the ACDP, the role model stories are staged; that is, they contain information from the woman that clearly describes her current readiness to change and the processes of change she has used to make the transition from the prior stage to her current one. The paid outreach workers attempt to "stage" (i.e., determine the stage of change of) each person they interact with so that they can deliver a stage-appropriate outreach encounter.

The mix of these role model stories is intended to reflect the current needs of women (i.e., their readiness to change) and provide messages to help them move toward consistent safer sex. For instance, if most women in the desired audience are in Contemplation for condom use, then a majority of the stories will be about women in Ready-for-Action, telling how they were able to move from Contemplation. The distribution of women in the target community across the stages was determined through pilot work and baseline surveys (and modified as successive waves of follow-up data are collected).

The distribution of role model stories through peer networkers is one example of how to influence personal factors using a stage-based approach. The next section will present general recommendations on moving people to behavior change. Examples of role model stories from ACDP and WIDP are used to illustrate our recommendations.

## Influencing Personal Factors to
## Move People Through the Stages of Change

### MOVEMENT FROM PRECONTEMPLATION
### TO CONTEMPLATION

The common characteristic shared by individuals in Precontemplation is their lack of intention to modify their risk behavior. The primary goals for facilitating change among Precontemplators are to encourage reevaluation of current behavior, and to engage them in preliminary consideration of the alternative behavior. Active consideration of, and deliberation about, both current and alternative behaviors will encourage movement to the Contemplation stage.

Because Precontemplators have such low motivation, they will generally ignore or reject action-oriented suggestions. They are more likely to respond positively to messages that encourage self-examination rather than behavior change. Messages of this type might include information about the risk behavior itself; the likelihood of experiencing consequences as a result of the risk behavior (personal risk); personalization of the risk message by reminding the person of recent episodes of the risk behavior; potential consequences of the person's risk behavior on family, friends, or valued others; and the likelihood of those consequences to others (e.g., risk to passengers of drunk driving or risk of infecting a sex partner with a sexually transmitted disease). *Thus, enhancing Precontemplators' knowledge of—and outcome expectancies about—the risk behavior, and personalizing the risk, are key strategies for encouraging movement to subsequent stages.*

A second key strategy for moving Precontemplators is related to positive and negative outcome expectancies for the alternative (i.e., risk-reducing) behavior. Precontemplators generally believe that the disadvantages of and barriers to practicing the alternative behavior far outweigh the advantages. They may even have difficulty listing positive aspects associated with the alternative behavior, although they often welcome new information about positive aspects. Therefore, *messages targeting Precontemplators should emphasize the positive attributes of the alternative behavior and encourage a reevaluation of outcome expectancies that includes the new positive information* (see Chapter 5 in this volume, for additional rationale regarding the use of positive messages). Such reevaluation of outcome expectancies is a critical element in helping to tip the balance in favor of the alternative behavior.

The radio commercial *Basketball Court #1* (see Figure 3.3), drawn from WIDP, is an adaptation of the role model story approach. In this commer-

**Setting:** Two young women (18-20) meet at a basketball court.

| | |
|---|---|
| Woman 1: | Hey girl. What's up? |
| Woman 2: | Hey, what's up? |
| Woman 1: | Did you check out that jump shot? |
| Woman 2: | Yeah, it was slammin'. |
| Woman 1: | Your man here too? |
| Woman 2: | Oh, I'm supposed to meet him here later. The reason I'm here is standing right . . . over . . . there. |
| Woman 1: | You thinking about giving him some? |
| Woman 2: | Check him out girlfriend. His body is cut. I'm dying to get with him. |
| Woman 1: | Careful. You might get your wish. |
| Woman 2: | Where you comin' from with that? You checkin' him out too? |
| Woman 1: | Don't even try it. It's just that things are getting scary out here. That's why me and my man started using condoms. You know what I'm sayin'? |
| Woman 2: | I don't know what you're talking about, but he's got it goin' on. Tell me you don't see it? |
| Woman 1: | Oh yeah, he's all that. I'll give him his props, but one at a time for me. |
| Woman 2: | What? Since when? |
| Woman 1: | Like I said, you gots to be careful out here now. |
| Woman 2: | Girl, you trippin . . . you talkin' about. |

TAG: RAP . . . Real AIDS Prevention. Ladies, for more information about how you can protect yourself, call the Family Health Council at 361-RAPP. Find out how you can prevent the spread of AIDS. Call now . . . 361-RAPP.

**Figure 3.3.** Script of a Radio Commercial Targeting Women in Precontemplation for Condom Use

cial, one young woman (who is in the Action stage for condom use) provides positive modeling for a second young woman (who is clearly in the Precontemplation stage). In her modeling she includes an explicit acknowledgment of the risks associated with multiple partners and unprotected sex, and she endorses several positive outcomes of monogamy and condom use.

## MOVEMENT FROM CONTEMPLATION TO PREPARATION

People in Contemplation are aware of the need to practice a healthier behavior but are not ready yet to take action. Contemplators often like to talk about their problem and seek information from a variety of sources.

Contemplators may be in a state of distress as a result of acknowledging their problem when having inadequate emotional, cognitive, or behavioral ability to mount an effective behavior change effort. This distress may be compounded by concern about valued behaviors that must be given up to adopt the alternative behavior. In the absence of a specific stimulus to change, the Contemplation stage can become a chronic condition for many people. *In order to help people move beyond this stage, Contemplators must be encouraged specifically to consider changing something about themselves. Moreover, they should be encouraged to gain behavioral experience with the change.* This can be accomplished by trying the new behavior (at least once), trying an approximation of the behavior, refraining from the risk behavior on a specific occasion, or partially substituting the new behavior for the risk behavior.

Outcome expectations remain a key issue in the Contemplation stage. It is useful for Contemplators to examine their risk behavior and weigh its costs versus its benefits. These costs and benefits may include physical (e.g., health risks vs. enjoyment), social (e.g., the praise of friends vs. family) and self-evaluative (e.g., self-esteem and self-concept) consequences. Although all behavior changes entail costs or negative consequences, people are more likely to move beyond the Contemplation stage when the positive outcomes are seen to be more salient than the costs (at least in the long term). Moreover, people are less likely to experience subsequent relapse if they have thoroughly examined these expected costs and benefits and reconciled their values before taking action.

Positive social and self-evaluative consequences may be particularly important in moving people beyond this stage. For example, data from the ACDP indicates that promoting trust in intimate relationships and feeling pride as a result of doing the "right thing" were important expectations for people who had moved beyond Contemplation. *Intervention messages at the Contemplation stage should continue to promote new positive outcome expectations and reinforce existing positive expectations. Disputing commonly believed but untrue negative consequences and suggesting ways to minimize bona fide negative consequences may also be useful at this stage,* although it is generally easier to promote advantages than to challenge perceived disadvantages.

Contemplators must begin to see themselves as capable of behavior change. Such perceptions of capability will, in turn, enhance positive outcome expectations and motivation for change. Therefore, *self-efficacy enhancement is another key strategy for moving people out of Contemplation and toward the Preparation stage.* People may begin to consider barriers to behavior change at this stage, which can have detrimental effect on perceptions of self-efficacy.

# My Girlfriend Insists On It

My name is Harold. I'm 28 years old. I started smoking marijuana when I was 14. I experimented with cocaine back then, but I didn't like it. Lately I started shooting it up.

I have heard about AIDS. My brother is infected. I have done a lot of reading and I've seen it on television. I've heard that AIDS is increasing at a rapid rate.

My girlfriend is an IV drug user. She uses bleach to sterilize her equipment. Now she is insisting that I use it too. We already use condoms. We could really feel safe if I use the bleach too. I am planning to use bleach the next time I share needles. I enjoy life, I don't want to die.

**Figure 3.4.** Harold's Story—A Role Model Story Targeting Bleach Use Contemplators

*Messages should therefore identify how to effectively overcome perceived barriers to change.*

Harold's story (see Figure 3.4), a role model story developed for the ACDP, is a good example of a message designed to move injecting drug users currently in the Contemplation stage for proper needle hygiene to the preparation stage (McAlister, Pulley, Kay, & O'Reilly, in press). The message is clear, simple, and compelling. Harold is aware of his HIV risk; he tells the reader of his personal experience with his brother and about what he has seen and heard on television and through print media. He also tells the reader about the social pressure he feels from his girlfriend. He provides important vicarious efficacy information by stating: "We already use condoms. We could feel really safe if I use the bleach too." Finally, he makes a clear statement about his short-term behavioral goal: "I am planning to use bleach the next time I share needles."

MOVEMENT FROM
PREPARATION TO ACTION

People who are preparing for Action often have some experience with the new behavior and are now attempting to modify their behavior, experiences, and environment in order to practice the new behavior consistently. Their behavior at this stage is at best inconsistent, but they are forming goals regarding complete adoption of the new behavior. To move beyond this stage, people must maintain their motivation to eliminate the risk behavior while simultaneously building their repertoire of safer alternative behaviors. This may require the acquisition of skills and the confidence to use those skills in a variety of situations. It may also require that people restructure their environments to remove cues and social support for practicing the old behavior and to install cues and social influences that support the new behavior. This may include enlisting the assistance of friends, parents, partners, and other important social network members.

Skills for behavior change are crucial at this stage. One important set of skills for people attempting to move beyond this stage is knowing how to restructure their personal and social environment to ensure the presence of cues and social relationships that support the new behavior. The lack of such environmental cues and reinforcers can lead to returned involvement in the unhealthy behavior. *Messages at the Action stage should instruct and encourage people to restructure their environments so that important cues for practicing the new behavior are obvious and supported socially.*

Another important set of skills for moving beyond this stage is the ability to consider the obstacles to behavior change and to plan ways to circumvent those obstacles. Successful movement from Preparation to Action requires that people plan ahead for situations that will jeopardize their change efforts and work out specific strategies for dealing with these circumstances. This type of planning will also help individuals identify people in their social environments who can provide social and other forms of support. Therefore, *messages at the Action stage should encourage people to identify and plan solutions to the behavior change obstacles they are most likely to face.*

A third important set of skills for moving people to the Action stage is the ability to set appropriate behavioral goals. People who set personal goals will be better able to maintain their motivation for the behavior change. The manner in which they set these goals, however, has an important mediating influence. Establishing and accomplishing a series of clear short-term goals (to work toward a long-term goal) is highly motivating, whereas establishing only the long-term goal is fraught with problems and is likely to undermine motivation. *Messages at the Action stage should encourage people to set specific behavior change goals, and instruct them on appropriate ways to set incremental goals.*

A strong sense of self-efficacy is also crucial for movement beyond this stage. People who are feeling highly efficacious are more likely to set behavior change goals and to apply their knowledge and skills effectively in pursuit of these goals. A drop in self-efficacy at this stage will discourage goal setting and may cause people to reevaluate their motivations. Reevaluation at this stage is dysfunctional, because excessive reevaluation now (as opposed to task-oriented coping or problem solving) is associated with relapse. *Messages at the Action stage should promote enhancement of self-efficacy. Wherever possible, these messages should bolster self-efficacy to cope with specific situations and other obstacles that people are likely to encounter in their change efforts.*

Reinforcement for change is also an important consideration at this stage. Sources of such reinforcement can be internal or external to the person. External reinforcers, such as social approval, are particularly influential in moving people into the Action stage, and care must be taken to shape these influences in ways that support healthy choices. *Messages at the Action stage should model social reinforcement of appropriate behaviors.*

Shavonne's story, drawn from WIDP, is a good example of a message targeting women in the Preparation stage of condom use (see Figure 3.5). In the first paragraph, she describes her reevaluation of her motivations to have sex, and the unique situations that led her to practice risky behaviors. She acknowledges that she has put herself at risk, and that she has already suffered some consequences. She reveals to the reader some of her outcome expectations by stating, "I found out that [condoms] weren't as bad as those myths said." Further, she lets the reader know that she has not been perfect in her efforts, but that she is trying her best to be more consistent. Women in circumstances similar to Shavonne's, but at the Preparation stage for condom use, are likely to find her story interesting and useful as a role model for behavior change.

## MOVEMENT FROM ACTION TO MAINTENANCE

During the movement from Action to Maintenance, people have been practicing the new behavior regularly for a period of several months. Maintaining motivation and building habit strength for the new behavior are important to ensure that it will remain a regular part of the behavioral repertoire. Relapse is a very real threat for people in the Action stage. Self-management

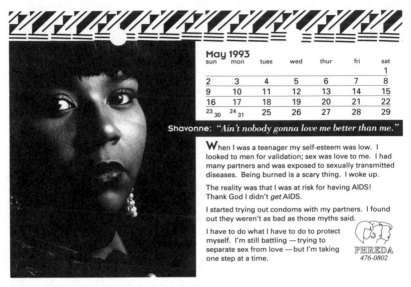

| May 1993 | | | | | | |
| sun | mon | tues | wed | thur | fri | sat |
| | | | | | | 1 |
| 2 | 3 | 4 | 5 | 6 | 7 | 8 |
| 9 | 10 | 11 | 12 | 13 | 14 | 15 |
| 16 | 17 | 18 | 19 | 20 | 21 | 22 |
| 23 30 | 24 31 | 25 | 26 | 27 | 28 | 29 |

Shavonne: *"Ain't nobody gonna love me better than me."*

When I was a teenager my self-esteem was low. I looked to men for validation; sex was love to me. I had many partners and was exposed to sexually transmitted diseases. Being burned is a scary thing. I woke up.

The reality was that I was at risk for having AIDS! Thank God I didn't *get* AIDS.

I started trying out condoms with my partners. I found out they weren't as bad as those myths said.

I have to do what I have to do to protect myself. I'm still battling — trying to separate sex from love — but I'm taking one step at a time.

PHREDA
476-0802

**Figure 3.5.** Shavonne's Story—A Role Model Story Targeting Women in the Preparation Stage for Condom Use

skills including the ability to restructure cues and social support for the behavior, to anticipate and circumvent obstacles and situations that may lead to relapse, and to modify behavioral goals in the face of set-backs or slip-ups, are crucial for the prevention of relapse. *Messages at the Maintenance stage should encourage refinement of skills, especially those skills that will help people avoid relapse and those that allow productive coping with set-backs to prevent full relapse.*

A related set of issues at this stage concerns maintaining people's sense of self-efficacy to cope with new obstacles, set-backs, and slip-ups. When people understand that new obstacles and set-backs are common during the behavior change process, and when they feel confident in their ability to correct their course in the face of such difficulty, they are more likely to cope productively with these situations and avoid relapse. *Therefore, messages at the Maintenance stage should bolster self-efficacy for dealing with new obstacles and set-backs in the behavior change process.*

Reinforcement for change remains important at this stage. Although external reinforcers are particularly influential in moving people to the Action stage, internal reinforcers become increasingly important in moving people into the Maintenance stage. Internal reinforcers take the form of positive self-evaluations, as well as the tangible rewards that people bestow upon themselves for their goal accomplishments. As a result, *messages at the Maintenance stage should encourage people to feel good about themselves when they progress toward their goals, especially in the face of temptation.* Feelings of loss concerning valued aspects of the risk behavior may be strong at this stage. Therefore, *messages should also make explicit or reiterate the concrete and the self-evaluative long-term positive consequences of the behavior change.* Furthermore, helping people to identify peers and others who have successfully engaged in the behavior and are satisfied with their changes will help the individual maintain a strong sense of self-efficacy.

## Conclusion

As the previous descriptions and role model stories illustrate, social cognitive theory and the transtheoretical model can be effectively combined to produce tailored messages designed to facilitate behavior change. SCT delineates the triadic nature of behavioral expression, that is, the reciprocal interaction among person, environment, and behavior. Furthermore, SCT identifies the internal personal factors, such as self-efficacy and outcome expectations, that influence the development and maintenance of health behaviors. The transtheoretical model provides a framework for conceptualizing the temporal sequence in which people modify their intentions and health behaviors. Efficient movement through the stages can be promoted by addressing specific internal personal factors when they are most likely to facilitate change in the behavior change progression. Health message designers can utilize this combined perspective to develop focused messages for a variety of health-related behavior change programs.

## Notes

1. Self-efficacy judgments are tied to specific behaviors and the situations in which they occur. All people have varying levels of personal efficacy depending on the behavior and the situation. An individual cannot be thought of as having high or low self-efficacy in general, but rather as having high or low self-efficacy to engage in a specific behavior.
2. Their identities are typically altered to protect their privacy.

# References

Bandura, A. (1986). *Social foundations of thought and action: A social cognitive approach.* Englewood Cliffs, NJ: Prentice Hall.

Bandura, A. (1991). Self-efficacy mechanism in physiological activation and health-promoting behavior. In J. Madden (Ed.), *Neurobiology of learning, emotion and affect* (pp. 229-269). New York: Raven.

Bandura, A. (1992). A social cognitive approach to the exercise of control over AIDS infection. In R. DiClemente (Ed.), *Adolescents and AIDS: A generation in jeopardy* (pp. 89-116). Newbury Park, CA: Sage

Bandura, A. (in press). *Self-efficacy: The exercise of control.* New York: Freeman.

Bandura, A., & Adams, N. (1977). Analysis of self-efficacy theory to behavioral change. *Cognitive Therapy and Research, 1,* 287-310.

Bandura, A., & Cervone, D. (1983). Self-evaluative and self-efficacy mechanisms governing motivational effects of goal systems. *Journal of Personality and Social Psychology, 45,* 1017-1028.

Baranowski, T. (1989-1990). Reciprocal determinism at the stages of behavior change: An integration of community, personal, and behavioral perspectives. *International Quarterly of Health Education, 10,* 297-327.

Baranowski, T. (1992). Beliefs as motivational influences at stages in behavior change. *International Journal of Community Health Education, 13,* 3-29.

Bernier, M., & Avard, J. (1986). Self-efficacy, outcome, and attrition in a weight-reduction program. *Cognitive Therapy and Research, 10,* 319-338.

Brown, I., & Inouye, D. K. (1978). Learned helplessness through modeling: The role of perceived similarity in competence. *Journal of Personality and Social Psychology, 36,* 900-908.

Centers for Disease Control and Prevention. (1994). *Prevention of HIV in Women and Infants Demonstration Project Protocol* (Unpublished document). Atlanta: Centers for Disease Control and Prevention.

Chambliss, C. A., & Murray, E. J. (1979a). Cognitive procedures for smoking reduction: Symptom attribution versus efficacy attribution. *Cognitive Therapy and Research, 3,* 91-96.

Chambliss, C. A., & Murray, E. J. (1979b). Efficacy attribution, locus of control, and weight loss. *Cognitive Therapy and Research, 3,* 349-354.

Cotton, D. C., Cabral, R., Gielen, A., Semaan, S., Tunstall, C., Oliva, G., & Hembry, K. (1994). *The transtheoretical foundation of the Prevention of HIV in Women and Infants Demonstration Projects.* Unpublished manuscript. (Available from National Center for Prevention Services, Centers for Disease Control & Prevention, Atlanta, GA)

DiClemente, C. C., & Hughes, S. O. (1990). Stages of change profiles in treatment. *Journal of Substance Abuse, 2,* 217-235.

DiClemente, C. C., & Prochaska, J. O. (1982). Self-change and therapy change of smoking behavior: A comparison of processes of change in cessation and maintenance. *Addictive Behaviors, 7,* 133-142.

DiClemente, C. C., Prochaska, J. O., & Gilbertini, M. (1985). Self-efficacy and the stages of self-change of smoking. *Cognitive Therapy and Research, 9,* 181-200.

Ewart, C. K., Taylor, C. B., Reese, L. B., & DeBusk, R. F. (1983). Effects of early post myocardial infarction exercise testing on self-perception and subsequent physical activity. *The American Journal of Cardiology, 51,* 1076-1080.

Galavotti, C., Cabral, R., Grimley, D., Riley, G. E., & Prochaska, J. O. (1993, June). *Measurement of condom and other contraceptive behavior change among women at high risk of HIV infection and transmission* (Abstract #PO-D38-4416). Paper presented at the Ninth International Conference on AIDS, Berlin.

Hemophilia Behavioral Intervention Evaluation Projects. (1993). *Hemophilia Behavioral Intervention Evaluation Projects adolescent and adult manuals.* Atlanta: Centers for Disease Control and Prevention.

Hosford, R., & Mills, M. (1983). Video in social skills training. In P. Dowrick & S. Biggs (Eds.), *Using video: Psychological and social applications* (pp. 125-150). New York: John Wiley.

Liebman, J., Bond, L., Person, B., Terry, M., Stribling, M., & Dillard-Smith, C. (1994). *Intervention design of the Prevention of HIV in Women and Infants Demonstration Project.* Unpublished manuscript. (Available from National Center for Prevention Services, Centers for Disease Control & Prevention, Atlanta, GA)

Locke, E. A., & Latham, G. P. (1990). *A theory of goal setting and task performance.* Englewood Cliffs, NJ: Prentice Hall.

Maccoby, N., & Alexander, J. (1980). Use of media in lifestyle programs. In P. Davidson & S. Davidson (Eds.), *Behavioral medicine: Changing health lifestyles* (pp. 351-370). New York: Brunner/Mazel.

Maibach, E. (1992). The use of behavioral theory in the development of AIDS information campaigns. In B. Thornton & G. Kreps (Eds.), *Perspectives on health communication* (pp. 207-217). Prospect Heights, IL: Waveland.

Maibach, E. (1993). Social marketing for the environment: Using information campaigns to promote environmental awareness and behavior change. *Health Promotion International, 8,* 209-224.

Maibach, E., & Flora, J. (1993). Symbolic modeling and cognitive rehearsal: Using video to promote AIDS prevention self-efficacy. *Communication Research, 20,* 517-545.

Maibach, E., & Murphy, D. (in press). Conceptualization and measurement of self-efficacy in health promotion research. *Health Education Research.*

McAlister, A., Pulley, L., Kay, L., & O'Reilly, K. R. (in press). Community based prevention campaigns for hard to reach populations at high risk for HIV infection: Theory and implementation. *American Journal of Health Promotion.*

O'Connell, D. O., & Velicer, W. F. (1988). A decisional balance measure of the stages of change model for weight loss. *International Journal of the Addictions, 23,* 729-740.

O'Reilly, K. R., & Higgins, D. L. (1991). AIDS Community Demonstration Projects for HIV prevention among hard-to-reach groups. *Public Health Reports, 106,* 714-720.

Perry, M., & Furukawa, M. J. (1986). Modeling methods. In F. Kanfer & A. Goldstein (Eds.), *Helping people change* (3rd ed.) (pp. 66-110). Elmsford, NY: Pergamon.

Prochaska, J. O., & DiClemente, C. C. (1983). Stages and processes of self-change of smoking: Toward an integrative model of change. *Journal of Consulting and Clinical Psychology, 51,* 390-395.

Prochaska, J. O., & DiClemente, C. C. (1984). *The transtheoretical approach: Crossing traditional boundaries of therapy.* Homewood, IL: Dow Jones/Irwin.

Prochaska, J. O., & DiClemente, C. C. (1985). Common processes of change in smoking, weight control and psychological distress. In S. Shiffman & T. A. Willis (Eds.), *Coping and substance abuse* (pp. 345-363). New York: Academic Press.

Prochaska. J. O., & DiClemente, C. C. (1986). *The transtheoretical approach: Crossing the traditional boundaries of therapy* (2nd ed.). Homewood, IL: Dow Jones/Irwin.

Prochaska, J., DiClemente, C., & Norcross, J. (1992). In search of how people change: Application to addictive behaviors. *American Psychologist, 47,* 1102-1114.

Prochaska, J. O., DiClemente, C. C., Velicer, W. F., Ginpil, S., & Norcross, J. C. (1985). Predicting change in smoking status for self-changers. *Addictive Behaviors, 10,* 395-406.

Prochaska, J. O., Norcross, J. C., Fowler, J. L., Follick, M. J., & Abrams, D. B. (1992). Attendance and outcome in a work site weight control program: Processes and stages of change as process and predictor variables. *Addictive Behaviors, 17,* 35-45.

Prochaska, J. O., Redding, C. A., Harlow, L. L., Rossi, J. S., & Velicer, W. F. (in press). The stages of change model and HIV prevention. *Health Education Quarterly.*

Pulley, L., McAlister, A., Kay, L., & O'Reilly, K. (in press). Prevention campaigns for hard-to-reach populations at risk for HIV infection: Theory and implications. *Health Education Quarterly.*

Rossi, J. S. (1989). Exploring behavioral approaches to UV risk reduction. In A. Moshell & L. W. Blankenbaker (Eds.), *Sunlight, ultraviolet radiation, and the skin* (pp. 91-93). Bethesda, MD: National Institutes of Health.

Schunk, D. H. (1982). Effects of effort attributional feedback on children's perceived self-efficacy and achievement. *Journal of Educational Psychology, 74,* 548-556.

Strecher, V., DeVellis, B., Becker, M., & Rosenstock, I. M. (1986). The role of self-efficacy in achieving health behavior change. *Health Education Quarterly, 13,* 73-91.

Wallack, L. (1990). Mass media and health promotion: Promise, problem and challenge. In C. Atkin & L. Wallack (Eds.), *Mass communication and public health* (pp. 41-51). Newbury Park, CA: Sage.

Wood, R., & Bandura, A. (1989). Social cognitive theory of organizational management. *Academy of Management Review, 14,* 361-384.

# 4 Fear Appeals in Health Promotion Campaigns

## TOO MUCH, TOO LITTLE, OR JUST RIGHT?

JEROLD L. HALE

JAMES PRICE DILLARD

When designing health promotion campaigns, there are any number of persuasive message strategies that can be used. One of these strategies involves the use of fear appeals to promote better health. Fear appeals are persuasive messages that emphasize the harmful physical or social consequences of failing to comply with message recommendations.

The use of fear appeals in the media to promote health is widespread. One well-known fear appeal depicts a harmful physical consequence of drug use. The commercial shows an egg, a frying pan, and then the egg frying. The voice-over says: "This is your brain. This is your brain on drugs. Any questions?" The intent of the message is to demonstrate that drug use kills brain cells. Health promotion messages also use fear appeals that stress harmful social consequences for failing to comply with message recommendations. A recent message for an alcohol treatment center serves as a good example. The commercial shows a husband being arrested for driving under the influence of alcohol. At the same time, a worried wife is on the telephone pleading with the man's employer not to fire him.

More systematic evidence of the use of fear appeals to promote better health comes from a study by Freimuth, Hammond, Edgar, and Monahan (1990). They examined the content of public service announcements (PSAs) related to AIDS. Fear appeals were used in roughly 26% of the PSAs. This combination of anecdotal and content-analytic evidence appears to indicate that producers of health promotion messages believe that fear appeals are an effective health promotion strategy. Interviews with health communication producers, however, show that health campaign professionals are split in their opinions on the usefulness of fear appeals. Backer, Rogers, and Sopory (1992) interviewed 30 individuals who constructed health communication campaigns and asked them whether fear appeals were effective strategies to promote health. The interview results showed that 6 of the campaign producers believed that fear appeals were effective strategies for promoting better health, another 13 believed fear appeals were ineffective, 10 were unsure, and 1 failed to respond.

Among social scientists there is no more agreement than among health promotion practitioners. There are nearly as many explanations for the effects of fear appeals as there are folk remedies for the common cold. A brief review and critique of those explanations will follow.

## Fear Appeal Explanations

Although there are several explanations for the effects of fear appeals, Dillard (in press) and Witte (1992a) posited that the explanations fall within three categories: drive explanations, parallel response explanations, and subjective expected utilities explanations.

### DRIVE EXPLANATIONS

Drive explanations for the effects of fear appeals all assume that fear-arousing content produces a drive. Drives are bodily states, in this case activation, arousal, or anxiety, that result in some general response (Newcombe, Turner, & Converse, 1965). Although the several drive explanations agree that fear-arousing content produces drive, they disagree on the general response that drive produces. For example, the original drive explanation suggested that fear-arousing content produced fear or anxiety about the negative consequences depicted in the message (Hovland, Janis, & Kelley, 1953). That anxiety prompted compliance with the message recommendations. Put another way, the more fear-arousing content contained in the message, the more effective the appeal was predicted to be. A persuasive message designed to reduce high-risk behaviors related to AIDS should, according to this explanation, rely on heavy doses of fear-arousing content.

Research by Janis and Feshbach (1953) produced a "resistance" explanation within the category of drive explanations. Janis and Feshbach gave high school students one of three messages designed to promote better dental hygiene: a low, moderate, or high fear appeal. They found that the low fear message led to better dental hygiene and argued that the drive or anxiety produced by the moderate and high fear messages triggered *defensive avoidance*. Defensive avoidance was the tendency to ignore or deny the negative consequences depicted in the message. They suggested that some students reasoned something like: "my teeth don't look like those, so my hygiene must be fine." Contrary to the previous approach, the resistance version of the drive explanation posits that as fear-arousing message content increases, compliance with the message recommendations will decrease. According to this drive explanation a message designed to reduce risk behaviors related to AIDS should minimize the use of fear appeals.

A final drive explanation posits a curvilinear relationship between fear and persuasive outcomes (e.g., Miller, 1963). As with the other drive explanations, the curvilinear hypothesis suggested that low fear messages would be ineffective because the messages did not produce enough drive to motivate compliance, and that high fear messages would be ineffective because they produced defensive avoidance. According to this drive explanation, the most effective fear appeal would be a moderate fear message. An AIDS-related message should seek middle ground in terms of fear-arousing content, according to this explanation.

Quantitative reviews by Boster and Mongeau (1984) and Mongeau (in press) of the fear appeal literature discount the validity of the various drive approaches. Both of those reviews found that the relationship between fear-arousing content and perceived fear (drive) was positive, as predicted. The relationship between fear-arousing content and persuasiveness was also positive, however. That outcome is inconsistent with the resistance version of drive, which hypothesizes a negative relationship. It is also at odds with the curvilinear variation, which predicts an inverted U-shaped relationship between fear-arousing content and persuasiveness. The original drive formulation—that is, more fear produces more persuasiveness—was found wanting because each of the meta-analyses identified several moderator variables that were not specified by the explanation and that discount the notion of a general response to the tension produced by the fear appeal.

## PARALLEL RESPONSE MODELS

Leventhal (1971) believed that fear appeals triggered two processes in the targets of the appeals. He argued that fear-arousing content produced the emotion of fear and the need to manage the fear. At the same time, fear appeals triggered a desire to eliminate the danger posed by the message. Leventhal argued that targets of fear appeals had to engage in both fear control and/or danger control. *Fear control* referred to a need to reduce the emotion of fear. Dillard (in press) pointed out that fear control could be accomplished by several means, such as denial, avoidance, distraction, or dulling the impact of the emotion via the consumption of drugs and/or alcohol. *Danger control,* on the other hand, referred to a need to reduce the negative consequence depicted in the message. Danger control would result in compliance with the message recommendations. The target of an AIDS-related fear appeal would experience the emotion of fear, which would trigger a desire to reduce the fear, a desire to reduce the danger, or both.

Leventhal's approach, although thought provoking, was not a very useful explanation for the effects of fear appeals. Dillard (in press) noted that threat control and danger control could serve contradictory purposes. It is possible for the target to manage the threat in ways that inhibit danger control, that is, consumption of alcohol to reduce fear might prevent the target from performing the behaviors needed for effective danger control. Several scientists have also noted that Leventhal's model does not spell out the conditions under which a target might opt for threat control, danger control, or some combination of the two (e.g., Boster & Mongeau, 1984).

Witte (1992a) constructed an extended parallel process model in which she did predict when threat control and/or danger control would be triggered. She argued that neither process would be activated with a low fear message, because the message would not produce the emotion of fear (a necessary condition for both threat control and danger control). With a high fear message, however, the emotion of fear would be produced. According to Witte, the extent to which danger control would operate depended on the efficacy of the message recommendations. If the recommendations offered an effective method to eliminate the negative outcome, then the target would comply with those recommendations. If the recommendations were an ineffective means to eliminate the negative outcome, then threat control in any of its manifestations would occur. Witte's approach appears to be a promising one. She has tested the effects of efficacy on the effectiveness of AIDS-related fear appeals, and found that efficacy does influence the persuasiveness of the message (Witte, 1992b). Nevertheless, the jury is still out on this explanation until more data are available and until tests of the entire explanation are reported.

## SUBJECTIVE EXPECTED
## UTILITY MODELS

Subjective expected utility models generally predict that outcomes are some function of several variables. One popular explanation for the effect of fear appeals will illustrate this point. Rogers (1975) proposed a protection motivation explanation. The protection motivation explanation hypothesized that persuasive outcomes would be a multiplicative function of (a) the severity of the threat, (b) the target's vulnerability to the threat, and (c) response efficacy. Because the variables combined multiplicatively, if any of the variables took on a zero value, then the fear appeal would be ineffective. For example, if an AIDS-related message failed to depict a negative outcome, it would not be persuasive. If the message predicted a negative outcome from AIDS (certain death) but the target did not feel vulnerable or at risk for the negative outcome, then the fear appeal would not be persuasive. If a message depicted a negative outcome and the target felt vulnerable to the outcome, but the recommended means to avoid the outcome was ineffective, the fear appeals would not produce compliance with the recommendation. Importantly, Rogers (1975) largely ignored the emotion of fear and focused instead on the notion of threats. That is, he argued that a sufficient threat (noxiousness) combined with combinations of vulnerability and response efficacy would be persuasive whether or not fear was produced.

Beck and Frankel (1981) argued that a subjective expected utility model should differentiate between *personal efficacy* on the one hand and *response efficacy* on the other. Personal efficacy refers to the ability of the target to perform the recommended response—for example, to wear a condom, remain monogamous, or avoid sharing needles. Response efficacy is related to the impact of recommended behavior(s) on the negative outcome.

Subsequent subjective expected utility models have tended to differentiate personal efficacy and response efficacy. There has been considerable disagreement about how the four variables relevant to these models would combine together to influence persuasive outcomes (e.g., Sutton & Eiser, 1984; Sutton & Hallett, 1989). Even Rogers (1983), in the face of evidence invalidating his original model (e.g., Boster & Mongeau, 1984), proposed an alternative model. In it he hypothesized that noxiousness, vulnerability, personal efficacy, and response efficacy would exert largely additive influences on compliance with message recommendations. That is, the more each quality was present, the more persuasive the message would be. He also hypothesized some interaction effects. Mongeau's (in press) meta-analysis reports some support for the additive effects of the proposed components but fails to find consistent support for the nonadditive combinations of variables.

## SUMMARIZING
## FEAR APPEAL RESEARCH

From the available evidence on the effects of fear appeals, three conclusions seem appropriate. First, the available data are inconsistent with explanations for the effects of fear appeals. This might lead some health promotion practitioners to abandon the use of fear-arousing content. Such a drastic step would certainly be premature. Second, despite disappointing results related to the various fear appeal explanations, a compelling case can be made for the persuasive impact of fear. Three quantitative reviews (Boster & Mongeau, 1984; Mongeau, in press; Sutton, 1982) all show reliable and compelling evidence that fear is persuasive. The most recent of the meta-analyses, and by virtue of including several newer studies perhaps the best of the lot, concluded that perceived fear and the attitude of the target were positively correlated, as were perceived fear and behavior. It is clear from these findings that fear-arousing message content is persuasive and that abandoning the use of fear would be to abandon an effective persuasive strategy. Third, the quantitative reviews also demonstrate that the relationship between fear and persuasion is a complex one. Several variables that influence fear-persuasiveness correlations have been identified and will be discussed later.

Although we have identified conclusions warranted by available data, there are also some limitations to what we know about fear appeals. For example, we know very little about the effects of messages containing extremely high amounts of fear-arousing content. Boster and Mongeau (1984) argued that the strength of the fear manipulations in fear appeal studies influenced the amount of fear perceived by the targets of the appeals. They also suggested that very few of the studies included stimuli that produced extreme amounts of fear. Largely for ethical reasons, we know very little about the effects of fear appeals on very young children. Even before the onset of institutional review boards, the youngest participants in fear appeal studies were typically high school students. So even though there are reliable effects for fear-arousing content, there are also important limits to the knowledge accumulated to date about fear appeals. For now, the most appropriate question is: "If fear appeals are effective, how should they be designed?"

## Designing Fear Appeals

In this portion of the chapter we will consider the basic structure of effective fear appeals, how those appeals should be organized, and relevant moderator variables that influence their effectiveness. Let us first consider the basic structure of effective fear appeals.

### THE STRUCTURE OF FEAR APPEALS

Based on the preceding discussion, it is clear that effective fear appeals include two general categories of components: threat components and action components. We will consider each category in turn.

*Threat Components.* Effective fear appeals arouse the emotion of fear. To accomplish this affective arousal, the fear appeals must include two basic threat components. First, an effective fear appeal must include a threat of severe physical or social harm if the target does not comply with the appeal's recommendations. As Boster and Mongeau (1984; Mongeau, in press) convincingly remind us, more fear-arousing message content (i.e., a severe threat) produces more perceived fear. The threat contained in the message must entail a truly negative consequence. Most AIDS-related fear appeals include the threat of death. One AIDS public service announcement content analyzed by Freimuth et al. (1990) showed a picture of a morgue. The message said, "If you have sex without a condom or share a needle with a drug addict you could end up here." The negative consequence is clear. In another AIDS appeal, Greene, Rubin, and Hale (1993) told adolescents, "AIDS is fatal—it kills people. There is no cure for AIDS."

In another recent study Hale, Mongeau, and Lemieux (1993) used fear appeals in an attempt to limit exposure to the sun and other sources of ultraviolet radiation. The high fear message emphasized that exposure to ultraviolet radiation increased the target's chances of developing non-melanoma cancers and/or malignant melanoma, disfigurement from removing cancerous growths from the face and neck, and the likelihood of permanently damaging one's skin. In short, the creator of the message must explicitly indicate the negative effects of failing to comply with the message recommendations.

Second, an effective fear appeal must personalize the risk to the target of the message. The target must be made to feel vulnerable or susceptible to the negative consequence depicted in the message. Several studies have found that although they are concerned about AIDS generally, members of high-risk groups deny personal risk of contracting the HIV virus (e.g., Gray & Saracino, 1989; Quinley, 1988). Edgar, Freimuth, and Hammond (1988) found that AIDS prevention messages that personalized the danger could lead to the performance of fewer risk behaviors. Greene and colleagues (1993) attempted to personalize the AIDS risk by including the following passage in one of the messages used in the study:

> Young people between the ages of 12 and 22 have been identified as a group at risk for contracting AIDS. You are a member of this group. The number of AIDS cases among young people is doubling each year, and young people may be more likely to get AIDS than other groups.

In their study of exposure to ultraviolet radiation, Hale and colleagues (1993) attempted to personalize the risk of skin cancer by demonstrating that college-aged students were among the most rapidly growing group of skin cancer victims. The targets of the appeal were also told that, according to one recent study, "If you are sunburned to the point of blistering, one time during the first 25 years of your life, your chances of contracting non-melanoma and melanoma skin cancers will double."

ACTION COMPONENTS

The action components of an effective fear appeal are related to the behavioral recommendations made in the appeal. There are two action components: personal efficacy and response efficacy.

*Personal Efficacy.* Personal efficacy concerns the target's perception that he or she has the ability to follow the message recommendations. Witte (1992b), for example, emphasized the ease of putting on a condom. A recent PSA, albeit not a fear appeal, did likewise by comparing putting on a condom with putting on your socks. Related to different issues, Hale et al. (1993) emphasized the simplicity of such actions as applying a sun block or avoiding sun exposure during peak hours to decrease exposure to ultraviolet radiation. Meyerowitz and Chaiken (1987) emphasized the simplicity of breast self-examinations for early breast cancer detection by women. Before the target of a persuasive appeal will comply with the message recommendations, he or she must possess the skills needed to do so. In constructing fear appeals, the producer of the appeal would be wise to consider the skills needed to avert the threat and the skills likely to be possessed by members of the target audience.

*Response Efficacy.* Response efficacy is the ability of the message recommendation to eliminate or reduce the threat depicted in the message. A recent study by Brouwers and Sorrentino (1993) examined the impact of response efficacy on individuals' willingness to undergo a diagnostic health exam. When response efficacy was high, in other words, when the test was depicted as an effective diagnostic tool, willingness to have the test performed increased. In her study of AIDS-related risks, Witte (1992b) emphasized the reliability of condoms in preventing the spread of AIDS. Rogers and Mewborn (1976) showed that increased response efficacy heightened the persuasive impact of a fear designed to promote cessation of smoking. Fruin, Pratt, and Owen (1992) reported that the response efficacy of a recommended program of exercise to reduce risks of cardiovascular disease influenced the willingness of individuals to begin the program. In his review of the fear appeal literature, Sutton (1982) concluded: "We can therefore state with some confidence that increased (response) efficacy produces stronger intentions to adopt the recommended responses" (p. 816). The creator of a fear-arousing message would do well to insure that the effectiveness of recommended responses is clearly demonstrated within the message.

## ORGANIZING THE MESSAGE

An effective fear appeal must include a severe threat, vulnerability of the target to the threat, personal efficacy, and response efficacy. There are any number of ways those components can be organized within a persuasive message. Indeed, even a casual glance through the spate of available public speaking texts will identify a quantity of organizational strategies (e.g., topical organization, cause-effect, problem-solution). Unfortunately there is very little empirical evidence regarding the effectiveness of the various organizational patterns. What we will offer as a guide is a personal preference, although sound arguments can be advanced in favor of that preference.

We recommend organizing the fear appeal using a problem-solution pattern. The problem-solution pattern is easy for audience members to follow. It is also well suited to the fear appeal components discussed above. The problem portion of the message should include both the threat and arguments designed to heighten perceptions of vulnerability to the threat. The severity of the threat could be documented with statistics regarding the number of AIDS-related fatalities and statements indicating that there is no cure for AIDS.

The solution portion of the message should recommend solutions to avoid the threat depicted earlier in the message. In an AIDS-related message one might recommend use of condoms during sex or avoiding sharing needles during intravenous drug use. In addition to making the recommendations, the solution portion of the speech must also demonstrate both response efficacy personal efficacy.

## VIVIDNESS OF THE APPEAL

Vivid information is emotionally interesting. It provokes clear images and makes content seem physically, psychologically, and temporally close to the person who experiences the information. Several researchers have contended that vivid information is more likely to keep a person's attention, to be recalled at a later time, and to be persuasive. Taylor and Thompson (1982) reviewed more than 50 studies of the effects of vividness, however, and concluded that support for vividness effects was equivocal at best.

Eagly and Chaiken (1993) suggest, despite research findings that are generally disappointing, that there are several contexts in which vividness does appear to improve persuasiveness. Those contexts include the persuasiveness of pictorial information, health appeals, and fear appeals. Because fear appeals frequently address health issues and rely on pictorial information, vividness might be especially important for such messages. And indeed, vividness has been a staple of strong fear appeals for quite some time. An early example of vivid information would be pictures of diseased teeth and gums in Janis and Feshbach's (1953) study of dental hygiene. A recent example of a vivid high fear message comes from Witte's study of AIDS prevention behaviors, where the high fear message included color photos of an emaciated victim, tumors on a penis, and lesions on a foot. Vivid visual images on any number of health related topics should be available to producers of health promotion messages, for example, mastectomy patients, skin cancer victims, or lungs of smokers.

Care should be taken in the use of vivid information. Eagly and Chaiken (1993) point out that vividness does not simply enhance message content. It may enhance source characteristics. They use videotaped versus written messages as an example, and point out that videotape makes characteristics of the message source (e.g., appearance, vocal qualities) more salient. The persuasiveness of enhanced source characteristics depends on whether those characteristics are perceived positively or negatively. Our point is that vivid information should draw attention primarily to the message content and, if attention is drawn to the source of the message, care must be taken in selecting a source that will be positively perceived.

FRAMING THE APPEAL

The threat in a fear appeal can be phrased in either a "loss frame" or a "gain frame" (see Chapter 2 in this volume). The loss frame presents the failure to perform the recommended response in terms of lost opportunities or increased negative consequences. A gain frame would present performing the recommended response in terms of gained opportunities or decreased negative consequences. The difference between the two frames of reference is the persuasive equivalent to asking whether the cup is half empty or half full. Some examples will help clarify the difference between loss and gain frames.

Two good examples of loss versus gain frames come from Meyerowitz and Chaiken's (1987) research on breast cancer detection. The recommended response in their messages was that women engage in breast self-examination. Each of the following examples, from the messages used in their study, is phrased in a gain frame. The language used in the loss framed messages is included in parentheses next to the word or phrase for which it was substituted. "By (not) doing Breast Self Examination now you (will not) can learn what your normal, healthy breast feels like so that you will be (ill) better prepared to notice any small abnormal changes that might occur as you get older" (p. 504). Another example was: "Research shows that women who (do not do) do Breast Self Examination have (a decreased) an increased chance of finding a tumor" (p. 504).

The results of the inquiry by Meyerowitz and Chaiken (1987) show that loss frames are more effective than gain frames. This was true both for participants' immediate responses to the messages and for their responses measured 4 months later. From this research, it appears that fear appeals should emphasize negative consequences for not following message recommendations as opposed to emphasizing positive consequences for complying with the recommended response, for example, "if you do not stop smoking you will significantly increase your risk of heart disease" instead of "if you stop smoking you will significantly decrease your risk of heart disease."

## Ineffective Use of Fear Appeals

In the previous section of this chapter we outlined the conditions necessary for a fear appeal to be persuasive. Even when a fear appeal contains a severe threat that is personalized by the target of the message and message recommendations that are effective and can be easily performed, the message may be ineffective. This is because fear appeals are simply ineffective for some audiences (Boster & Mongeau, 1984; Mongeau, in press). What follows is a discussion of issues extraneous to the content or form of the message that can inhibit the effectiveness of fear appeals.

### VOLUNTEERS OR NONVOLUNTEERS?

The target of a persuasive message may attend to a persuasive message either voluntarily or nonvoluntarily. There is convincing evidence to indicate volunteers and nonvolunteers respond differently to fear appeals. Horowitz (1969, 1972) examined the effects of voluntarism on the persuasiveness of fear appeals designed to prevent drug abuse. He found that high fear messages were more persuasive for volunteers than were low fear messages. For nonvolunteers, people who have no choice about being exposed to the message, high fear messages were ineffective. He reasoned that nonvolunteers engaged in *reactance*. Reactance is a psychological process that occurs when a person feels that his or her freedom to act is being restricted. The result of the reactance is that the individual refuses to follow the message recommendations, in an effort to recoup the lost freedom.

These results clearly show that fear appeals are a poorly conceived strategy for an audience of nonvolunteers. For example, high school students who attend a drug abuse prevention program because their presence is compelled by a principal or teacher would not respond favorably to a fear appeal. A patient whose doctor uses a strong fear appeal may not respond positively to it depending on who initiated the conversation and the patient's perceived degree of voluntarism. Fear appeals would be best for public presentations where attendance was not compelled or for conversations explicitly initiated by the target of the appeal.

Some health communication campaigns that involve fear appeals and use television do not succeed (Kohn, Goodstadt, Cook, Sheppard, & Chan, 1982). One reason may be that television viewers, although voluntarily choosing to watch entertainment programming, involuntarily watch commercials. If viewers believe they are compelled to watch commercials or that the response costs (see below) for avoiding the commercials are too high, they will engage in reactance and the fear appeal will fail. Producers of health promotion campaigns must consider whether the target audience for the campaign will be exposed to persuasive messages of their own volition.

## HOW OLD IS THE TARGET AUDIENCE?

Another variable that may inhibit the effectiveness of fear appeals is the age of the target audience. Boster and Mongeau (1984; Mongeau, in press) reported that fear appeals are more effective for older audiences. The age of the target audience influences the audience's perceived vulnerability to the threat. Younger persons feel as though death and disease happen to elders or perhaps to other young people, but not to themselves (Irwin & Millstein, 1986). Older persons, on the other hand, perceive a greater threat to their health and well-being.

The impact of age on the persuasiveness of fear appeals also helps to explain why so many fear appeals to promote better health are ineffective. Televised public service messages to decrease driving under the influence of alcohol or drug abuse are frequently targeted at adolescents. Those messages frequently employ fear appeals, but fear appeals are unlikely to influence the young people at whom they are aimed. We can imagine living rooms across America where parents of adolescents find a public service announcement compelling, but where the target of the appeal (the child) is unaffected by it.

## HOW ANXIOUS ARE TARGETS
## AND WHAT ARE THEIR RESPONSE COSTS?

*Trait Anxiety.* Social science literature differentiates between "state" and "trait" anxiety. *State anxiety* is tension that results from a specific and localized set of circumstances. It is fleeting and changes from one context to the next. *Trait anxiety,* on the other hand, is a personality trait—a relatively enduring personal quality. There are some people who are "anxious by nature"; those people suffer from trait anxiety. There is evidence to suggest that anxious persons, also called "avoiders," respond differently to fear appeals than do their less anxious counterparts, also called copers. Specifically, for copers high fear messages are more effective than low fear messages. For avoiders, high fear messages are no more or less persuasive than low fear messages (e.g., Boster & Mongeau, 1984). Unfortunately, health campaign directors rarely have specific enough information about a target person or audience to tailor a message based on trait anxiety. It is also the case that extreme amounts of trait anxiety are uncommon, so fear appeals would be an effective strategy for a mass audience. The trait anxiety finding, however, helps to explain why some persons do not respond favorably to high fear messages.

*Response Costs.* Response costs refer to negative outcomes that result from complying with a message recommendation. In Fruin et al.'s (1992) study of exercise to reduce risks of cardiovascular disease, response costs included lost time and physical discomfort associated with exercising. In Witte's (1992b) study of risk behaviors and AIDS, response costs of wearing condoms might have included lost spontaneity. In Hale et al.'s (1993) study of risks from ultraviolet radiation, several participants would not use a sun block every day because its application was inconvenient.

There is little doubt that perceived response costs inhibit the effectiveness of fear appeals. Response costs can, however, frequently be reduced by careful planning and communication. Witte's (1992b) messages, for example, specifically refuted the notion that condom use interfered with spontaneity. The inconvenience of applying a sun block every morning can be directly refuted by suggesting that the application takes very little time. The message producer must either anticipate the response costs or carefully pretest the messages (a strategy we wholeheartedly recommend). If response costs are not anticipated or discovered and refuted, then a certain portion of fear appeals will not reach their persuasive potential.

## Summing Up

Fear appeals have enormous persuasive potential and can promote better health. Their effectiveness depends in large part on the structure of the messages. At the least, an effective fear appeal must include a severe threat, evidence suggesting the target is especially vulnerable to the threat, and solutions that are both easy to perform and effective. Additional features that should be considered are the use of a problem-solution format for the message and vivid content that is negatively framed. Finally, fear appeals do not work in every circumstance, so one should be mindful of the age of the target audience and the likelihood of voluntary message processing when deciding whether to construct a fear appeal.

Many fear appeals fail to modify unhealthy behaviors because they do not follow the maxims listed above. Recall the drug abuse prevention PSA depicting the egg, the frying pan, and the fried egg that we used as an illustration in the opening of this chapter. The verbal content of the appeal said "This is your brain. This is your brain on drugs. Any questions?" The message is a good example of a bad fear appeal. The threat, vulnerability, personal efficacy, and response efficacy of the message are nonexistent or so confusing that they are useless. Responses to that particular message have even been derisive. When one considers the poor use of fear appeal components in the message, it is no wonder that posters and T-shirts have been printed showing a fried egg and two strips of bacon, with the phrase, "This is your brain with a side of bacon."

# References

Backer, T. E., Rogers, E. M., & Sopory, P. (1992). *Designing health care campaigns: What works.* Newbury Park, CA: Sage.

Beck, K. H., & Frankel, A. (1981). A conceptualization of threat communication and protective health behavior. *Social Psychology Quarterly, 44,* 204-217.

Boster, F. J., & Mongeau, P. A. (1984). Fear-arousing persuasive messages. In R. Bostrom (Ed.), *Communication yearbook* (Vol. 8, pp. 330-375). Newbury Park, CA: Sage.

Brouwers, M. C., & Sorrentino, R. M. (1993). Uncertainty orientation and protection motivation theory: The role of individuals differences in health compliance. *Journal of Personality and Social Psychology, 65,* 102-112.

Dillard, J. P. (in press). Rethinking the study of fear appeals. *Communication Theory.*

Eagly, A., & Chaiken, S. (1993). *The psychology of attitudes.* Orlando, FL: Harcourt Brace Jovanovich.

Edgar, T., Freimuth, V. S., & Hammond, S. L. (1988). Communicating the AIDS risk to college students: The problem of motivating change. *Health Education and Research: Theory and Practice, 3,* 59-65.

Freimuth, V. S., Hammond, S. L., Edgar, T., & Monahan, J. L. (1990). Reaching those at risk: A content analytic study of AIDS PSA's. *Communication Research, 17,* 775-791.

Fruin, D. J., Pratt, C., & Owen, N. (1992). Protection motivation theory and adolescents' perceptions of exercise. *Journal of Abnormal Social Psychology, 22,* 55-69.

Gray, L. A., & Saracino, M. (1989). AIDS on campus: A preliminary study of college students' knowledge and behaviors. *Journal of Counseling and Development, 68,* 199-202.

Greene, K. L., Rubin, D., & Hale, J. L. (1993, November). *Egocentrism, message explicitness and AIDS messages directed toward adolescents: A test of the theory of reasoned action.* Paper presented at the annual meeting of the Speech Communication Association, Miami Beach, FL.

Hale, J. L., Mongeau, P. A., & Lemieux, R. (1993, November). *Trait anxiety and fear arousing messages regarding sun exposure.* Paper presented at the annual meeting of the Speech Communication Association, Miami Beach, FL.

Horowitz, I. A. (1969). Effects of volunteering, fear arousal, and number of communications on attitude change. *Journal of Personality and Social Psychology, 11,* 34-77.

Horowitz, I. A. (1972). Attitude change as a function of perceived arousal. *Journal of Social Psychology, 87,* 117-126.

Hovland, C. I., Janis, I. L., & Kelley, H. H. (1953). *Communication and persuasion.* New Haven, CT: Yale University Press.

Irwin, C. E., & Millstein, S. G. (1986). Biopsychosocial correlates of risk taking behaviors during adolescence: Can the physician intervene? *Journal of Adolescent Health Care, 7,* 82-96.

Janis, I. L., & Feshbach, S. (1953). Effects of fear-arousing communications. *Journal of Abnormal and Social Psychology, 48,* 78-92.

Kohn, P. M., Goodstadt, M. S., Cook, G. M., Sheppard, M., & Chan, G. (1982). Ineffectiveness of threat appeals about drinking and driving. *Accident Analysis and Prevention, 14,* 457-464.

Leventhal, H. (1971). Fear appeals and persuasion: The differentiation of a motivational construct. *American Journal of Public Health, 61,* 1205-1224.

Meyerowitz, B. E., & Chaiken, S. (1987). The effect of message framing on breast self-examination attitudes, intentions, and behaviors. *Journal of Personality and Social Psychology, 52,* 500-510.

Miller, G. R. (1963). Studies on the use of fear appeals: A summary and analysis. *Central States Speech Journal, 24,* 117-125.

Mongeau, P. A. (in press). Fear-arousing persuasive messages: A meta-analysis revisited. In M. Allen & R. Preiss (Eds.), *Persuasion: Advances through meta-analysis.* Thousand Oaks, CA: Sage.

Newcombe, T. M., Turner, R. H., & Converse, P. E. (1965). *Social psychology.* New York: Holt, Rinehart & Winston.

Quinley, H. (1988). The new facts of life: Heterosexuals and AIDS. *Public Opinion, 11,* 53-55.

Rogers, R. W. (1975). A protection motivation theory of fear appeals and attitude change. *Journal of Psychology, 91,* 93-114.

Rogers, R. W. (1983). Cognitive and physiological processes in fear appeals and attitude change: A revised theory of protection motivation. In J. Cacioppo & R. Petty (Eds.), *Social psychophysiology* (pp.153-176). New York: Guilford.

Rogers, R. W., & Mewborn, C. R. (1976). Fear appeals and attitude change: Effects of a threat's noxiousness, probability of occurrence, and the efficacy of coping responses. *Journal of Personality and Social Psychology, 34,* 54-61.

Sutton, S. R. (1982). Fear-arousing communication: A critical examination of theory and research. In J. R. Eiser (Ed.), *Social psychology and behavioral medicine* (pp. 303-337). London: John Wiley.

Sutton, S. R., & Eiser, J. R. (1984). The effect of fear-arousing communications on cigarette smoking: An expectancy-value approach. *Journal of Behavioral Medicine, 7,* 13-33.

Sutton, S. R., & Hallett, R. (1989). The contribution of fear and cognitive factors in mediating the effects of fear-arousing communications. *Social Behaviour, 4,* 83-98.

Taylor, S. E., & Thompson, S. C. (1982). Stalking the elusive "vividness" effect. *Psychological Review, 89,* 155-181.

Witte, K. (1992a). Putting fear back into fear appeals: The extended parallel process model. *Communication Monographs, 59,* 329-349.

Witte, K. (1992b). The role of threat and efficacy in AIDS prevention. *International Quarterly of Community Health Education, 12,* 225-249.

# 5 Thinking Positively

## USING POSITIVE AFFECT WHEN DESIGNING
## HEALTH MESSAGES

### JENNIFER L. MONAHAN

Communication campaigns play an important role in disease prevention and health promotion. Designing effective campaigns about health is a difficult task, however. As Arkin (1989) notes, "Health information is often complex and technical. In addition, the information may be inconclusive, controversial, contradictory and subject to change as new research findings are released" (p. 3). Moreover, communication specialists are often put in the unenviable position of conducting campaigns asking people to give things up, to change comfortable habits, and to refrain from pleasurable experiences. Consider messages in which the audience is asked to stop eating fatty foods, quit smoking, "Just Say No," and "Be Smart—Don't Start."

In trying to reach a broad population with messages about unhealthful practices, campaigns have often relied on two strategies: fear appeals and straightforward presentations of fact. A recent content analysis of AIDS public service announcements (PSAs) found that approximately one fourth of the PSAs used fear appeals to persuade individuals to change risky behaviors, and half of the PSAs were affectively neutral, utilizing straightforward presentations of facts (Freimuth, Hammond, Edgar, & Monahan, 1990).

Although fear appeals and affectively neutral rational appeals have long been the mainstays of public communication campaigns, the opposite is true for commercial advertising. Commercial advertisers tend to avoid negative affect and rational claims and instead focus their messages on the positive side of life. Consumer advertisers ask their audiences to "Be All That You Can Be," "Reach Out and Touch Someone," or "Be Heart Smart." The appeal of positive affect for commercial advertisers is simple: Research consistently shows advertisements that arouse positive emotions result in more positive feelings toward the product and greater intent to comply with the message (see, e.g., Batra & Ray, 1986; Thorson & Friestad, 1989).

This chapter explores the potential of simple positive affective appeals in reaching audiences important to the health communicator. Moreover, it does so from a theoretical framework that allows message designers to interpret how and when positive messages will be most appropriate. Literature is reviewed that suggests positive feelings can substantially influence social behavior and cognitive processes.

## Positive Affect

*Affect* is a generic term for a whole range of feelings and emotions. Theorists often use the term *affect* to refer to messages and responses to messages that include a *subjective* feeling component. More specific terms such as *feelings* or *emotions* are defined by the intensity and pervasiveness of the affect. Positive feelings are relatively mild subjective reactions—those that are essentially pleasant, such as attraction and liking. These feelings are called moods when they refer to global, generalized affective states that influence nonspecific affective events. Emotions refer to a more complex assortment of affects such as joy, serenity, or elation. Emotions are thought of as more intense and short-lived than are moods. In addition, emotions usually have physical as well as mental manifestations.

## Types of Affective Appeals

Affect can be conceptualized as residing within a person (i.e., something that happens to the viewer in response to a campaign), or it can be conceived of as the emotional valence of a message. The primary focus of this chapter is how best to employ affect when designing messages in order to trigger an appropriate response in the audience. Two forms of messages, emotional benefit appeals and heuristic appeals, will be examined. The chief distinction between these two forms of messages is that emotional benefit appeals incorporate both affective and rational elements whereas heuristic appeals rely primarily on affect.

Traditionally, it was assumed that messages were either rational or affective. For example, straightforward presentations of facts were envisioned as rational appeals, whereas fear appeals were supposed to solicit an emotional response. More recently, analyses find most messages utilize, or at least are *perceived* by audiences as utilizing, both rational and affective appeals (Stewart & Furse, 1986). Messages that have both affective and rational components are called *emotional benefit appeals* and include slice-of-life ads such as those emphasizing people getting over an illness (persuasion through peer influence), celebrity ads (persuasion through credibility), and certain types of fear appeals (persuasion through fear of injury or harm).

Emotional benefit appeals elicit affective responses to a message by creating emotional states that exemplify the emotional, psychological, or experiential benefits of complying with a campaign (Pechman & Stewart, 1989). Such appeals are grounded primarily in observational learning principles: It is expected that message recipients will comply with the message in order to obtain the benefits that the message promises. A campaign that shows healthy people engaging in "fun" activities with a message that tells the viewer to "live longer and live healthier by eating more fruits and vegetables" is an example of an emotional benefit appeal.

Unlike emotional benefit appeals, which rely on both rational and affective cues, *heuristic appeals* utilize a more indirect approach to target individuals who do not have the time, skill, or motivation to evaluate the attributes and benefits of a particular campaign (Pechman & Stewart, 1989). For example, AT&T's "Reach Out and Touch Someone" campaign used positive affect indirectly to influence the viewer. Instead of trying to persuade the viewer that the features of AT&T's service are good, heuristic appeals attempt to make the message recipient feel good about the product. Campaigns use music, artwork, or background to evoke positive imagery or a favorable mood, and it is the mood or feeling that is expected to sell the idea rather than the benefits one could derive from complying with the message.

## The Primacy of Affect

Positive affect induced via heuristic appeals represents a distinct campaign style that can be contrasted with straightforward presentation of facts and emotional benefit appeals. How do such heuristic appeals work? Why should mood, feelings, or image matter?

Zajonc (1980) argued that feelings matter because our responses to social stimuli are seldom emotionally neutral, and that there are few social perceptions or thoughts that do not implicate affect in some significant way. Further, he noted that:

it is entirely possible that the very first stage of the organism's reaction to stimuli and the very first elements in retrieval are affective. It is further possible that we can like something or be afraid of it before we know precisely what it is and perhaps even without knowing what it is. (p. 154)

Research has shown that affective responses are unmediated and fast initial reactions to people, events, and other stimuli (see Murphy & Zajonc [1993] for a review). After this immediate feeling response, cognitive and affective reactions interact resulting in a specific response to a message (Murphy, 1990). Affective reactions to stimuli are assumed to be primary, occurring before and influencing subsequent cognitive processing. From this perspective, researchers believe that first we feel, and then we think.

This chapter explores how to use emotional benefit and heuristic appeals to trigger positive initial feelings toward a campaign. Further, it illustrates how these initial positive reactions can be used to effect subsequent cognitive and behavioral responses such as selective attention, degree of processing, memory, attitude, and compliance.

## SELECTIVE ATTENTION

Viewers have an array of defense mechanisms to filter out information that is not salient to them or to change messages that may be troubling. Affective appeals can be quite powerful in overcoming these defense mechanisms because people pay greater attention to affective messages than to other message types (Ray, 1977). Moreover, research indicates that positive affect is an especially effective tool in overcoming filtering devices.

A person's feelings often act like a selective filter, tuned to incoming material that supports or justifies these feelings. From an affect primacy perspective, initial positive responses to any stimuli (e.g., a public service advertisement) should result in *approach* behaviors. Approach behaviors allow individuals to open up and be receptive to the external stimuli, to relax their guard.

Like affect theorists, advertising practitioners and public health researchers also find positive affect is a useful ploy to gain attention. One survey of advertising practitioners found that most advertising specialists believe humor is very effective in drawing attention to an issue (Madden & Weinberger, 1984). In addition, several studies have demonstrated that positive affect leads to greater receptiveness of messages (see Janis, Kay, & Kirschner, 1965; Reeves, Newhagen, Maibach, Basil, & Kurz, 1991). Overall, public service messages that are entertaining, engaging, humorous, or dramatic are more likely to succeed in overcoming such barriers as selective perception and selective retention than are more strictly rational messages.

Heuristic appeals such as a good-looking spokesperson, beautiful artwork, or a popular song can be especially good attention-gaining devices. For example, the California Raisin Advisory Board used a positive heuristic cue in the form of a popular song, "I Heard It Through the Grapevine," to garner immediate attention and positive feelings toward their message. Heuristic cues are very effective at garnering positive attention because the audience does not have to *think* about the cue, the positive impact is immediate.

Positive affect can be a particularly useful attention-getting device when attempting to reach individuals who consider themselves to be overly familiar with a campaign. In these cases, individuals may not pay attention to new information because they feel that they know all they need to know. The use of humor or warm and touching situations is particularly effective in getting individuals to process messages about topics that are already familiar (Ogilvy & Raphaelson, 1982).

Although positive affect within messages usually leads to greater receptiveness, there are circumstances in which this may not hold true. In particular, when individuals are threatened by an issue, using positive affect in a message may not promote receptiveness (Forest, Clark, Mills, & Isen, 1979). These findings are consistent with a primacy of affect perspective, because such a perspective assumes negative feelings evoke *avoidance* behaviors. Avoidance behaviors result in individuals blocking subsequent messages, turning away from the negative source, or processing the message through a defensive filter. In this situation, even if a positive message attracts attention, message recipients are likely to slow down their processing and examine subsequent information critically rather than acceptingly.

In summary, positive affect is a good attention-getting device. The use of positive emotions such as humor and joy can catch the audience's eye and convince individuals to watch something they might otherwise avoid. Heuristic cues such as the use of visual imagery or a popular song are the most effective attention-getters, primarily because such cues can be processed with minimum thought. An affect primacy theoretical perspective suggests that positive affect is a useful attention-getting device because positive affect invokes approach behaviors, enhancing the probability that the audience will be receptive to the forthcoming message. An exception is when the audience feels threatened by an issue. Under these circumstances, positive affect may not promote receptiveness.

## DEPTH OF PROCESSING

A second cognitive process that is influenced by affective appeals is depth of processing. Once the audience is paying attention, how much effort will they expend to process the information presented? The amount of effort individuals expend to process a message is important because it can affect what they remember, their attitudes, and their intent to comply with the message. The valence of affective appeals (positive vs. negative) appears to be related to how much effort an audience will expend to process a message.

Negative messages foster the use of more elaborate, detail-oriented, and analytical processing strategies. Negative messages result in more thoughtful processing because negative affect informs the audience that the current situation is problematic. Individuals are therefore more likely to focus their attention on aspects of the situation that elicited bad feelings and are less likely to pay attention to inconsequential information or get distracted.

Positive messages, on the other hand, foster good feelings and the use of less elaborate or more heuristic strategies. Positive affect does not activate feelings of self-protection but rather engenders feelings of ease or comfort. A message that uses positive affect informs the audience that the current situation is nonthreatening and that a high degree of attention or processing is not necessary. Positive messages thus trigger what is known as *peripheral processing* (Petty & Cacioppo, 1986). Peripheral processing occurs when individuals spend very little time thinking about a message and is a relatively mindless endeavor. This type of processing most likely occurs as the result of some simple cue in the message that induces a reaction without necessitating any scrutiny of the message. Changes that occur via peripheral processing are often short-lived effects, although systematic changes in attitudes do occur in response to such processing (Murphy, Monahan, & Zajonc, 1992).

Overall, the evidence suggests that a strength of positive affect is that it draws attention to a message; its weakness is that it encourages peripheral processing rather than more thoughtful information processing. Although positive affect is assumed to provoke minimal processing and, thus, relatively short-lived effects, there are forms of positive appeals that result in long-term effects. Recall that emotional benefit appeals combine rational and affective components to present the emotional, psychological, or experiential benefits of complying with a campaign. These messages can produce relatively permanent changes in attitudes and/or behaviors without necessarily requiring the message recipient to engage in effortful systematic processing. Emotional benefit appeals can be persuasive, regardless of the type of cognitive processing they evoke.

Positive heuristic appeals, on the other hand, are targeted at individuals who are not motivated to evaluate the benefits of a campaign. These appeals evoke an affective response that is not directly related to the campaign and are likely to result in less stable effects than are emotional benefit appeals. Although heuristic appeals usually result in short-lived attitude shifts, they can be quite useful in a campaign. For example, Cacioppo and Petty (1989) suggest that message designers might use heuristic appeals as a first step in enhancing the likelihood that individuals will engage in thoughtful processing. If the targeted audience does not have the motivation to think carefully about the merits of a campaign, then repeated presentations of a positive cue with the campaign may be one of the few ways to induce an audience to engage in processing information. Multiple exposures of a positive heuristic cue is an effective strategy, because repeated exposure to a heuristic appeal (such as the use of a popular song or visual imagery) generally leads to an increased positive feeling toward the specific message associated with the cue. This association may result in approach behaviors, facilitating a more open-minded and thoughtful consideration of an issue.

Positive affect can also be a useful strategy when it is important to help individuals reframe issues that they feel are not salient or relevant to their lives. Monahan and Collins-Jarvis (1992) evaluated the effectiveness of several AIDS PSAs from the perspective of young adults. The college students in this sample were quite familiar with the AIDS crisis, felt that their chance of becoming HIV positive was quite remote, and that HIV/AIDS had little to do with their lives. Most of the PSAs they viewed did little to change these impressions; however, those that cued empathy were effective in getting students to process the meaning in the ad.

For example, one spot entitled "Home Movies" featured three victims of AIDS: a teenager, a young woman, and a toddler. Each victim was shown in a home movie-style clip enjoying some form of family celebration. Each clip ended with a free-frame close-up on the victim and the superimposition of their birth and death dates. This spot is an example of the type of PSA that increased subjects' self-reported feelings of empathy and compassion for the victims of the disease. PSAs that elicited feelings of empathy also resulted in significant changes in the students' subjective probability ratings that they or someone they know might contract HIV. These PSAs were also more likely to stimulate the students to discuss the message afterwards and to feel thoughtful about it. These results suggest that evoking positive emotions such as empathy and compassion may result in the audience reframing an issue to consider the implications in a new light.

In summary, positive message appeals tend to provoke less thoughtful processing than do other forms of appeals. Positive affect can be usefully employed in message design when the target audience is overfamiliar with an issue or when an issue needs to be reframed for audience members. Emotional benefit appeals are likely to produce stronger, more durable effects than heuristic appeals. Heuristic appeals, however, are effective in gaining attention and in associating the campaign with good feelings.

## RECALL

Evaluations of campaigns often include a component to assess how memorable the campaign was for the intended audience. Do audience members recall seeing any campaign materials? What did the messages say? It is presumed that in order for a message to be effective, the audience must first be able to recall the message.

Studies repeatedly find that affective messages are better remembered than are nonaffective messages. Further, although affective material, regardless of valence, seems to be remembered better, the influence of positive message appeals on cognitive processes is pronounced and relatively direct, whereas the influence of negative affect is more complex and harder to predict (Crockett, 1988; Isen, 1987).

Results from memory studies indicate that issues *already* associated with good feelings may be the best issues to use in conjunction with positive affect in a campaign. Positive mood selectively promotes retrieval of positive information from memory and inhibits retrieval of negative material (see Clark & Isen, 1982; Isen, 1989). This finding implies that messages that evoke positive feelings cue material that is organized in the mind as relevant to positive affect. Consider a campaign to convince young mothers to breast-feed their infants. Young mothers most likely feel positive toward infants, and this feeling can be capitalized on in campaigns by presenting information about breast-feeding in a positive light rather than by accentuating the negatives associated with not breast-feeding. In campaigns where the audience already feels quite negatively toward an issue (e.g., breast cancer) there is little evidence to conclude that pairing the issue with positive affect will enhance memory or recall for the issue. Breast cancer prevention, on the other hand, may be facilitated by use of positive affect appeals.

The relationship between affect and memory is also confounded by involvement. Affective messages appear to be more memorable for individuals who do not feel much involvement with an issue, whereas highly involved individuals are no more likely to recall affective messages than rational ones

(Flora & Maibach, 1990). These results suggest that positive affect may be an especially useful ploy to reach the "low-involvement" audience. Again, it reinforces the point that when people do not care about a message/campaign, positive message appeals may be a tool to gain attention. For individuals who already feel strongly committed, the affective component of a message does not seem as important.

In general, the relationship between memory and positive affect is quite robust. Positive messages in the form of emotional benefit or heuristic appeals can evoke a positive mood that, in turn, facilitates recall. Positive affect is most likely to enhance memory when used in conjunction with issues that are associated with good feelings and when individuals are not highly involved with an issue.

## ATTITUDES

Although the ultimate goal of campaigns might be behavioral change, messages also focus on changing attitudes. For example, a campaign to prevent drunk driving might use messages designed to facilitate positive feelings toward designated drivers or may promote feelings of disgust toward drunk drivers. Campaigns are also used to change attitudes toward the victims of a disease (e.g., people with AIDS are not immoral) or to elicit feelings of sympathy (e.g., Jerry Lewis's Muscular Dystrophy Campaign).

There is very strong evidence to suggest that positive affect within messages can lead to positive feelings within the person that, in turn, make the person easier to persuade. One review on persuasion and positive affect concluded that persuasive impact is stronger when messages induce an individual to be happy or to smile, or when messages are combined with watching a good program (McGuire, 1985). Heuristic appeals (e.g., using pleasant music, artwork, or background to evoke positive imagery or a favorable mood) can be especially useful when attempting to get the audience "in the mood" to be persuaded.

There are at least three important factors to consider when using positive affect in a message to induce attitude change: (a) how familiar is the message/topic to the audience; (b) how strong are the arguments that are being made; and (c) how involved is the audience with the message. To begin with, the attitudes of individuals with little knowledge about a topic are often significantly influenced by positive appeals, whereas those who are very familiar with the topic are less influenced by the use of positive appeals. In one study of affective messages, Park and Thorson (1990) had participants evaluate 74 commercials. Based on their findings, they suggested that when familiarity with a campaign is low, campaigns should focus on positive affect in the form of comparisons, demonstrations, and testimonials (i.e., emotional benefit appeals). Once message recipients are familiar with a campaign or the issues related to a campaign, heuristic appeals prove useful in recapturing the audience's attention.

The influence of positive affect on attitudes is further mediated by the quality of arguments in the message. Messages that create a positive mood (as compared to a neutral state) tend to increase persuasion when arguments are weak, but tend to decrease it when arguments are strong (Batra & Stayman, 1990; Bless, Bohner, Schwarz, & Strack, 1990). Thus, if formative research indicates that the targeted audience may be skeptical toward an argument or may be difficult to persuade about the merits of an argument, positive affect should be paired with the argument in an emotional benefit appeal. If formative research indicates that the rational appeal is strong or acceptable to the audience, however, the use of positive affect may do little to enhance the likelihood of persuasion.

Finally, the amount of commitment and/or involvement the audience feels toward an issue also has implications for using positive messages to induce attitude change. Recent research finds that messages that produce a positive mood lead to more positive attitudes *regardless* of how involved the audience feels toward the message (Petty, Schumann, Richman, & Strathman, 1993). However, positive affect influenced the positivity of subjects' thoughts only under high-involvement conditions. This second finding is important because previous research indicates attitude change is more stable and long-lasting when individuals report positive thoughts about a topic. That highly involved individuals may exhibit more stable attitude change in response to a positive message than individuals who feel relatively uninvolved is not particularly surprising. After all, it is the highly involved individual who feels motivated to process both the affective and rational components of the message. The less involved individual is likely to process and retain only the positive affect, ignoring or forgetting the *content* of the message. Hence the highly involved person feels more positively toward a message and has good reasons to back up his or her feelings, whereas the less involved individual feels positive toward the message but may have no good reasons for his or her feelings.

Although the relationship between positive affect and attitude change is strong, there are issues that are not good candidates for positive messages. For example, when an issue is viewed by the intended audience as negative, campaign designers may be tempted to change that negative image through association with positive affect. The research literature, however, suggests that it may be very difficult to do so. First, positive affect does not appear to extend its influence to negative materials. Positive feelings are generally found to influence the ratings of neutral or ambiguous material rather than to influence the ratings of more clearly negatively valenced materials (Schiffenbauer, 1974). Second, positive affect is most effective when subjects are relatively uncertain as to their attitudes or when they already have some positive feelings toward the campaign. These results are consistent with a primacy of affect perspective because it is very difficult to change initial positive/negative biases toward a stimulus.

When dealing with an issue that has negative affect associated with it, researchers might consider using positive affect in a more indirect fashion. In other words, message designers would probably not change a strongly held negative feeling to a positive one, but it may be possible to shift emphasis in a campaign. The National Cancer Prevention Awareness Program is an exemplar of a campaign designed to use positive affect to change people's feelings about a negative issue. Formative research suggested that the public was "confused and skeptical about cancer, its risks, and prevention" (Romano, 1986, p. 94). Results of a 1983 survey indicated that the public's perceptions of risk and potential for personal control over cancer were overly pessimistic (NCI Cancer Prevention Awareness Survey; see Romano, 1986). For example, most people expected that only one in five persons with cancer would survive for 5 years, whereas the actual rate was nearly 50% (Romano, 1986).

There is little a campaign can do to change the negative attitudes associated with cancer. If these feelings become overwhelming, however, individuals may stop contributing to cancer research and may avoid messages designed to reduce their likelihood of contracting cancer. The National Cancer Prevention Awareness Program was designed to promote a more positive view of issues related to cancer prevention. For example, the campaign reinforced a positive, good-news theme (Cancer Prevention: The News Is Getting Better All the Time), described risk factors that individuals could control, and recommended positive steps or actions to take to prevent cancer. The press kits and promotional packets sent to doctors championed this positivity effect by using *survivors* of cancer and by showing progress. For example, consider three messages used in this campaign:

GOOD NEWS: Everyone does *not* get cancer. 2 out of 3 Americans will never get it.

BETTER NEWS: Every day more and more people with cancer are cured.

BEST NEWS: Every day you can do something to help protect yourself from cancer.

Although this campaign will probably not change the negative affect associated with cancer, it may enhance attitudes toward prevention (I can control my likelihood of getting cancer) and may enhance positive attitudes toward cancer research.

In summary, a rather substantial literature indicates that positive messages often invoke positive affect that, in turn, fosters attitude change. These effects are especially pronounced when the issue is unfamiliar or the intended audience already feels positive about it. Messages that use positive affect produce shifts in attitude regardless of how involved individuals feel toward an issue or topic. Finally, even though there is little evidence to suggest that positive affect can change strongly held negative attitudes, positive information can be used indirectly to change related attitudes.

## COMPLIANCE

Most campaign evaluators are interested in the impact of positive affective appeals on selective perception, depth of processing, memory, and attitudes because these mental processes can be predictive of behavioral outcomes. How can affect enhance behavioral modification or compliance with the goals of the campaign? Though research examining the role of affective messages on compliance is scarce, it is suggestive.

Without discriminating among positive and negative appeals, a few studies suggest that affect can be instrumental in stirring individuals toward action. For example, one study found affective appeals worked better than logical or rational appeals at motivating those who are indifferent (Atkin, 1979). Flora and Maibach (1990) also found affective messages were significantly more effective in stimulating a desire to learn more about AIDS than were primarily rational appeals.

In an interesting comparison of positive and negative appeals, McNeil and colleagues (1982) demonstrated greater compliance with a doctor's recommendation for a surgical procedure when the outcome from surgery was presented as the probability of survival (a positive gain) relative to when the outcome was presented as the probability of mortality (fear).

One study of a dental hygiene program found that although negative appeals elicited more verbal promises to comply, as well as reports of having complied, they were actually less effective than positive appeals in increasing message retention and compliance (Evans et al., 1970). Thus negative appeals may provoke a social desirability bias: Individuals may feel the need to say they understood the message and are "changing" their ways, but feel no motivation to actually change their behaviors. Though negative affect may provoke a social desirability bias, positive affect can be used to make people feel good about themselves. People have a powerful need to think positively of themselves, especially along dimensions that are important to them. Messages that promote good feelings about the self can be especially persuasive. Positive messages make people feel better about themselves and thus lead to increased benevolence toward others (Isen, 1987).

A recent example of a campaign that used positive heuristic and emotional benefit appeals to increase compliance was the 1993 campaign of the California Transportation Department and the Southcoast Air Quality Management District's "Team Rideshare." The purpose of this campaign was to encourage commuters to carpool one day a week. Formative research indicated that most commuters believed in ridesharing, were aware of their options regarding ridesharing, and felt ridesharing was a great idea . . . for someone else.

To evoke interest in a new campaign on an old issue for Californians, a heuristic affective cue in the form of a theme song "Sharin a Ride," based on an upbeat song "Hitchin a Ride," was employed. The use of this song was successful in gaining the attention of commuters.[1] Once the commuter audience's attention was captured and a positive feeling toward the campaign was established via this heuristic appeal, emotional benefit appeals were then used to present compelling reasons to change behaviors. The emotional benefit appeals focused on the benefit of ridesharing for the environment (healthier air and a cleaner environment) and the benefits to the commuter (more time and money to enjoy, less stress, and increased speeds on the freeway system). In addition, parties were set up at major employers throughout the area as a pleasant way for prospective rideshare partners to meet and become acquainted. As part of the campaign's evaluation, traffic engineers monitored carpool and vanpool lanes during the campaign and reported an approximately 25% increase in carpool activity for "Rideshare Thursday."

Finally, there are circumstances in which positive affect may hinder the likelihood of compliance. One study, for example, found people in whom positive affect had been induced were less helpful to a disliked cause than were control subjects (Forest et al., 1979): Attempts to improve the image of a disliked topic/campaign by means of attaching positive affect to it may backfire. People in whom positive feelings have been induced may demonstrate more freedom to express their thoughts and do as they please. If people are generally negatively disposed to an idea (say, wearing a condom), inducing positive affect by means of a humorous PSA campaign may cause recipients of the message to denigrate the idea even further. Importantly, these findings reinforce those based on depth-of-processing, memory, and attitude change studies: Positive affect may not be a useful ploy to gain compliance when strongly held negative attitudes already exist.

Evaluations of campaigns using positive affect to induce behavioral change are few and far between. The few results that exist suggest that positive affect might be more effective than negative affect in getting individuals to comply with a campaign. Considerable research remains to be done in this area.

To summarize: Positive affect found in emotional benefit appeals and heuristic appeals can facilitate cognitive and behavioral responses to messages. Table 5.1 summarizes the relative effectiveness of these two types of appeal.

Heuristic appeals target individuals who do not have the time, skill, or motivation to evaluate the attributes and benefits of a particular campaign. Heuristic appeals attempt to make the message recipient feel good by using music, artwork, or background to evoke positive imagery or to create a favorable mood. The strength of heuristic appeals is that they are particularly effective in capturing the audience's attention. Because such appeals rely on imagery and feeling rather than on content, however, the audience spends minimal time processing the message. Although individuals show enhanced recall for the imagery and good feelings, heuristic appeals do not result in enhanced recall for the *content* of the campaign. In addition, such messages are likely to result in short-lived or fleeting attitude change, unless message(s) are repeated several times. Little to no work has been reported that examines the effects of heuristic appeals on compliance behaviors.

Emotional benefit appeals combine rational and affective components in order to create affective responses to a message. Such messages illustrate the emotional, psychological, or experiential benefits of complying with a campaign. Positive emotional benefit appeals can be effective at capturing attention; however, they are not as effective as heuristic appeals in the attention-getting stage. Because of their combination of rational and affective components, emotional benefit appeals are more likely than heuristic appeals to provoke thoughtful processing, enhanced recall, and stable attitude shifts. Finally, a small number of studies indicate emotional benefit appeals result in increased compliance with the message of a campaign.

## Conclusions

In this chapter the benefits and perils of positive affect were briefly examined. Zajonc's theory suggests that affective responses to messages are primary: We feel, then we think. Positive affect is hypothesized to result in approach

TABLE 5.1 Effect of Positive Message Appeals on Cognitive and Behavioral Responses

| Type of Message | Attention-Getting | Depth of Processing | Recall | Attitude Change | Compliance |
|---|---|---|---|---|---|
| Positive Heuristic Appeals | Highly effective | Tends to elicit minimal processing | Recall enhanced for feelings but not message content | More likely to result in short-lived, fleeting effects | Effects unknown |
| Positive Emotional Benefit Appeals | Effective if incorporates heuristic component | Elicits more thoughtful processing | Recall for both feelings and message is enhanced | Results in more stable long-lasting effects | Increased compliance |

behaviors that enable an audience to feel open minded and positively toward an issue or campaign. Affect can be directly attached to an issue through testimonials, demonstrations, slice-of-life ads, or any other form of emotional benefit appeal. Positive affect can also be indirectly attached to an issue through the use of heuristic appeals like artwork, music, and background to create a mood or a positive uplifting feeling. Regardless of whether it is direct or indirect, positive affect has shown to encourage people to recall pleasant things, to judge things positively, to make faster decisions, to be more benevolent toward others, and to be more compliant (Isen, 1987).

Positive affect has too often been an underutilized tactic in communication campaigns. This chapter ends with a few suggestions for when and how to use positive appeals:

1. When the intended audience is unfamiliar with an issue, use emotional benefit appeals in the form of comparison, demonstration, satisfaction, and testimonials.

2. Use heuristic or indirect affective appeals once message recipients are familiar with an issue or campaign. Humor or other positive feelings are very effective in overcoming selective attention due to boredom and overexposure.

3. Use positive affect very carefully once an issue is associated with strong negative feelings. It is difficult to use positive feelings to change strongly held negative attitudes. Moreover, using positive affect in these circumstances may backfire, making the negative attitudes even more firmly entrenched.

4. Use positive affect to change the focus of a campaign. When it is important to get the audience to view an issue in a new light, positive affect may be instrumental in shifting the mental frame that audiences use to understand an issue.

5. In order to increase compliance, stress positive outcomes rather than negative ones and emphasize control over an issue rather than helplessness.

6. Whenever the intended audience is undecided or confused (as is so often the case with health issues), positive affect is an excellent strategy. The most consistent and effective findings for positive affect changing behavior and attitudes are under these circumstances.

Positive affect can be used to stress the benefits of healthy behavior, to give individuals a sense of control, and to reduce anxiety or fear. All of these tactics are likely to enhance the success of a communication campaign.

## Note

1. Early evaluations of this campaign were obtained via a personal correspondence from the account executive for Team Rideshare, Pam Hill.

# References

Arkin, E. B. (1989). *Making health communication programs work: A planner's guide* (NIH Publication No. 89-1493). Washington, DC: U.S. Department of Health and Human Services.

Atkin C. (1979). Research evidence on mass mediated health communication campaigns. In D. Nimmo (Eds.), *Communication yearbook, 3* (pp. 655-668). New Brunswick, NJ: Transaction-International Communication Association.

Batra, R. (1986). Affective advertising: Role, processes, and measurement. In R. A. Peterson, W. D. Hoyer, & W. R. Wilson (Eds.), *The role of affect in consumer behavior: Emerging theories and applications* (pp. 53-87). Lexington, MA: Lexington Books.

Batra, R., & Stayman, D. M. (1990). The role of mood in advertising effectiveness. *Journal of Consumer Research, 17,* 203-214.

Bless, H., Bohner, G., Schwarz, N., & Strack, F. (1990). Mood and persuasion: Cognitive response analysis. *Personality and Social Psychology Bulletin, 16,* 332-346.

Cacioppo, J. T., & Petty, R. E. (1989). The elaboration likelihood model: The role of affect and affect-laden information processing in persuasion. In P. Cafferata & A. Tybout (Eds.), *Cognitive and affective responses to advertising* (pp. 69-90). Lexington, MA: Lexington Books.

Clark, M. S., & Isen, A. M. (1982). Toward understanding the relationship between feeling states and social behavior. In A. Hastorf & A. Isen (Eds.), *Cognitive social psychology.* New York: Elsevier-North Holland.

Crockett, W. H. (1988). Schemas, affect and communication. In L. Donohew, H. E. Sypher, & E. T. Higgins (Eds.), *Communication, social cognition, and affect* (pp. 33-52). Hillsdale, NJ: Lawrence Erlbaum.

Evans, R. I., et al. (1970). Fear arousal, persuasion and actual versus implied behavioral change: New perspectives utilizing a real-life dental hygiene program. *Journal of Personality and Social Psychology, 16,* 220-227.

Flora, J. A., & Maibach, E. W. (1990). Cognitive responses to AIDS information: The effects of issue involvement and message appeal. *Communication Research, 17,* 759-774.

Forest, D., Clark, M. S., Mills, J., & Isen, A. M. (1979). Helping as a function of feeling state and nature of the helping behavior. *Motivation and Emotion, 3,* 161-169.

Freimuth, V. S., Hammond, S. L., Edgar, T., & Monahan, J. L. (1990). Reaching those at risk: A content-analytic study of AIDS PSAs. *Communication Research, 17,* 775-791.

Isen, A. M. (1987). Positive affect, cognitive processes, and social behavior. In L. Berkowitz (Ed.), *Advances in experimental social psychology* (Vol. 20, pp. 203-254). New York: Academic Press.

Isen, A. M. (1989). Some ways in which affect influences cognitive processes: Implications for advertising and consumer behavior. In P. Cafferata & A. Tybout (Eds.), *Cognitive and affective responses to advertising* (pp. 91-118). Lexington, MA: Lexington Books.

Janis, I. L., Kay, D., & Kirschner, P. (1965). Facilitating effects of "eating while reading" on responsiveness to persuasive communications. *Journal of Personality and Social Psychology, 1,* 181-186.

Madden, T. J., & Weinberger, M. G. (1984). Humor in advertising: A practitioner view. *Journal of Advertising Research, 24,* 23-29.

McGuire, W. J., (1985). Attitudes and attitude change. In G. Lindsey & E. Aronson (Eds.), *The handbook of social psychology* (3rd ed.) (Vol. 2, pp. 233-346). New York: Random House.

Monahan, J. L., & Collins-Jarvis, L. A. (1992). *Personalizing risk for college students: The effects of identification strategies.* Annenberg Working Paper, University of Southern California.

Murphy, S. T. (1990). *The primacy of affect: Evidence and extension.* Unpublished doctoral dissertation, University of Michigan.

Murphy, S. T., Monahan, J. L., & Zajonc, R. B. (1992, May). *The role of affect in the mere exposure paradigm.* Paper presented to the 42nd Annual Convention of the International Communication Association, Miami.

Murphy, S. T., & Zajonc, R. B. (1993). Affect, cognition, and awareness: Affective priming with suboptimal and optimal stimulus. *Journal of Personality and Social Psychology, 64*(5), 723-739.

Ogilvy, D., & Raphaelson, J. (1982, July-August). Research advertising techniques that work—and don't work. *Harvard Business Review,* pp. 14-18.

Park, C., & Thorson, E. (1990). Influences on emotional response to commercials of different executional styles. In S. J. Agres, J. A. Edell, & T. M. Dubitsky (Eds.), *Emotion in advertising: Theoretical and practical explorations* (pp. 161-174). New York: Quorum.

Pechman, C., & Stewart, D. W. (1989). The multidimensionality of persuasive communications: Theoretical and empirical foundations. In P. Cafferata & A. Tybout (Eds), *Cognitive and affective responses to advertising* (pp. 31-66). Lexington, MA: Lexington Books.

Petty, R. E., & Cacioppo, J. T. (1986). *Communication and persuasion: Central and peripheral routes to attitude change.* New York: Springer.

Petty, R. E., Schumann, D. W., Richman, S. A., & Strathman, A. (1993). Positive mood and persuasion: Different roles for affect under high and low elaboration conditions. *Journal of Personality and Social Psychology, 64,* 5-20.

Ray, M. L. (1977). When does consumer information processing research actually have anything to do with consumer information processing. In W. D. Perreault, Jr. (Ed.), *Advances in Consumer Research, 4,* 372-375.

Reeves, B., Newhagen, J., Maibach, E., Basil, M., & Kurz, K. (1991). Negative and positive television messages: Effects of message type and context on attention and memory. *American Behavioral Scientist, 34,* 679-694.

Romano, R. M. (1986). The Cancer Prevention Awareness Program: Approaching public understanding with good news. In D. S. Leathar, G. B. Hastings, K. O'Reilly, & J. K. Davies (Eds.), *Health education and the media II.* Oxford: Pergamon.

Schiffenbauer, A. (1974). Effect of observer's emotional state on judgments of the emotional state of others. *Journal of Personality and Social Psychology, 30,* 31-36.

Stewart, D. W., & Furse, D. H. (1986). *Effective television advertising: A study of 1,000 commercials.* Lexington, MA: Lexington Books.

Thorson, E., & Friestad, M. (1989). The effects of emotion on episodic memory for television commercials. In P. Cafferata & A. Tybout (Eds.), *Cognitive and affective responses to advertising* (pp. 305-326) Lexington, MA: Lexington Books.

Zajonc, R. B. (1980). Feeling and thinking: Preferences need no inferences. *American Psychologist, 35,* 151-175.

# 6 Designing Messages for Behavioral Inoculation

## MICHAEL PFAU

*A body of research dealing with the techniques for inducing resistance to change has accumulated. We view this research as a valuable, largely ignored contribution to the literature of persuasion.*

—Gerald R. Miller and Michael Burgoon,
Communication Professors
(Miller & Burgoon, 1973, p. 6)

*Inoculation [is the] best way to protect kids.*

—Ann Landers, Syndicated Advice
Columnist (Landers, 1992; Permission
granted by Ann Landers
and Creators Syndicate)

Despite the overwhelming evidence documenting the adverse consequences of cigarette smoking, alcohol consumption, drug use, and other deleterious behaviors, all too many adolescents still succumb to one or more of these behaviors, with often devastating results in terms of short- and long-term morbidity and mortality (Atkin, 1991; U.S. Department of Health and Human Services, 1989; Donovan, Jessor, & Jessor, 1983). Furthermore, once these behaviors are adopted they are extremely difficult to

AUTHOR'S NOTE: The author is grateful to Jong G. Kang, Associate Professor of Communication at Illinois State University, Julia Pachoud, Assistant Professor of Theatre at Augustana College, and Brian Sather, a former cameraman at KELO television, for creative contributions. Professors Kang and Pachoud wrote and produced the smoking prevention inoculative messages that are described in this chapter.

change (Reardon, 1988), prompting much greater emphasis among health educators and practitioners on preventive approaches targeting increasingly younger age cohorts (Einsiedel & Cochrane, 1988). This change in emphasis is consistent with a gradual shift in the overall health care system from a curative to a preventive focus (Einsiedel & Cochrane, 1988), motivated by considerations of cost and efficacy (Hunt, Barnett, & Branch, 1971).

This chapter examines the nature, potential, and use of one specific prevention strategy: inoculation. Inoculation seeks to strengthen existing attitudes, rendering them less susceptible to change. As a prevention approach, inoculation can be employed to target young children and strengthen their attitudes opposing smoking, drinking, drug use, or other deleterious behaviors, thus rendering them more resistant to subsequent pressure to engage in these risky practices. Syndicated advice columnist Ann Landers urges America's parents to make sure that their children are inoculated, thus protecting them from common physical diseases. This chapter maintains that similar concern should be extended to common "societal diseases"— particularly smoking, drinking, and drug use—that exact a much more devastating toll. Smoking prevention research supports the broader application of Ann Landers's advice that, "Inoculation [is the] best way to protect kids" (1992, p. 5B). The chapter demonstrates how health campaigners can design and implement inoculation messages to confer resistance.

## Nature of Inoculation

The inoculation approach has its origins in early research on the relative superiority of one- versus two-sided messages. One of the unexpected findings of this research was that the use of two-sided messages rendered receivers more resistant to subsequent attempts at counterpersuasion (Lumsdaine & Janis, 1953). This finding, although interesting, required a theoretical construct in order to explain why two-sided messages promoted resistance to subsequent attitude change. The theoretical rationale for this finding was provided by social psychologist William J. McGuire, who introduced the inoculation construct and supported it in a series of laboratory studies spanning nearly a decade (McGuire, 1970). Inoculation is based on a biological analogy. As McGuire (1970) describes the inoculation process:

> We can develop belief resistance in people as we develop disease resistance in biologically overprotected man or animal; by exposing the person to a weak dose of the attacking material strong enough to stimulate his defenses but not strong enough to overwhelm him. (p. 37)

The integral features of inoculation are threat and refutational preemption.

The threat component of behavioral inoculation takes the form of forewarning against an impending challenge to existing attitudes. The receiver is told of potential challenges to existing attitudes. Because threat is an internal process, a manipulation check is required in inoculation research in order to insure that the threat component takes hold (Pfau, Van Bockern, & Kang, 1992). The refutational preemption component is conducted by initially raising, and then directly refuting, one or more specific challenges to existing attitudes. The inoculation process thus consists of posing a threat then following with refutational preemption.

The threat component is particularly important, because it serves as a motivational trigger. Threat involves people's acceptance of the vulnerability of their attitudes to potential challenges. It *should not be confused with* the concept of a threatening message, which is characteristic of fear appeals. When receivers accept the vulnerability of existing attitudes, and if those attitudes are salient, they will be motivated to strengthen them (Anderson & McGuire, 1965; McGuire, 1961a, 1962, 1964, 1970; Papageorgis & McGuire, 1961). In this manner the inoculation process works by motivating receivers to bolster their attitudes, not by simply providing answers to potential counterarguments. As McGuire (1962) describes: "The resistance conferred by the refutational defense . . . derives not only from the assimilation and retention of the bolstering material . . . but also from the motivation effect of preexposure to the threatening material" (p. 248).

The threat component triggers the receiver's motivation to bolster attitudes and gives inoculation its distinctive power. "If the construct were limited to preemptive refutation, it would afford limited utility since communicators would need to prepare specific preemptive messages corresponding to each and every anticipated attack" (Pfau & Kenski, 1990, p. 75). Instead, by first motivating receivers and only then preemptively refuting one or more potential counterarguments, inoculation spreads a broad umbrella of protection, safeguarding against both those counterarguments addressed by refutational preemption and those not addressed.

Research on inoculation supports this position. Both the early laboratory research (McGuire, 1961b, 1962; Papageorgis & McGuire, 1961) and subsequent field research (Pfau & Burgoon, 1988; Pfau, Kenski, Nitz, & Sorenson, 1990; Pfau et al., 1992) found that inoculation confers resistance to both same (those specifically preempted in the pretreatments) and novel (those not specifically preempted) counterarguments. These findings affirm that the threat component of inoculation is the underlying basis of the construct's power, serving as the motivational trigger for strengthening existing attitudes, thus conferring resistance.

Inoculation differs from social inoculation, an approach with origins in Evan's social inoculation theory (Wallack & Corbett, 1987). Social inoculation theory melds McGuire's inoculation construct and Bandura's social learning theory, placing primary emphasis on the construct of refutational preemption. Social inoculation approaches typically use a combination of strategies, such as peer-led discussions, peer modeling, slide shows, and videos. A number of the programs applying social inoculation have demonstrated modest success (Flay & Burton, 1990). This chapter's focus, however, will be on the use of inoculation rather than social inoculation.

## Application to Smoking Prevention

Inoculation strategies should be considered whenever supportive prevailing attitudes are subject to serious challenges. This will often be the case when conducting primary prevention among youth, particularly when targeting prevention of smoking, drinking, drug use, violence, and accidents. As a result of the efforts of parents and teachers, most children develop strong attitudes in opposition to these harmful behaviors that extend through their elementary school years. However, the transition to the middle grades, which is characterized by "far-reaching physiological upheavals" in many youth (Hamburg, 1979, p. 1031), and the declining influence of parents and growing impact of peers (Rosenberg, 1965), is often difficult, producing an erosion of attitudes opposing smoking, drinking, and drug use.

The attitudinal pattern of children regarding smoking has been well documented. Young children's attitudes opposing smoking are often strong, so much so that many will overtly chastise their smoking parents and older siblings. Most adolescents begin the transition from primary to middle school with their strong attitudes opposing smoking intact (Pfau et al., 1992). During the transition from the primary to middle grades, however, such attitudes deteriorate (Evans & Raines, 1982; Killen, 1985; Pfau et al., 1992), which produces *in some* adolescents a growing chance of experimental and regular smoking, and *in most* an increasing tolerance of smoking by peers (Pfau & Van Bockern, 1994). During this critical transition period, adolescents develop an indifference to the health consequences of smoking (Rokeach, 1987) at the same time they become increasingly vulnerable to the influence of peer pressure (Flay, d'Avernas, Best, Kersell, & Ryan, 1983; Friedman, Lichtenstein, & Biglan, 1985; Gottlieb & Baker, 1986).

As a result, public health officials acknowledge that "smoking is a behavior that is initiated primarily during the adolescent years" (Chassin et al., 1981, p. 445), specifically, during the early adolescent years. Preventative efforts should be geared to sixth and seventh grade children because "more than half of all current young people who adopt the habit of daily smoking do so before or during their ninth grade school year" (McAlister, Perry, & Maccoby, 1979, p. 651).

This scenario carries important implications for the most appropriate approach to smoking prevention. The question is not whether health educators should be targeting younger adolescents. That question has been resoundingly answered: They should (Chassin et al., 1981; Elder & Stern, 1986; Hamburg, 1979; Johnson, 1982; Killen, 1985; Pfau et al., 1992)! Instead, the *crucial issue* is whether a persuasion or an inoculation approach should be used in prevention efforts.

A persuasion approach is appropriate in those circumstances when receiver attitudes and/or behaviors require change. The data indicate, however, that adolescents commence the transition from the primary to middle grades with strong attitudes opposing smoking. "They have *already been persuaded* that smoking is bad. The question is whether these attitudes will persist" [emphasis in original] (Pfau & Van Bockern, 1994, p. 420). In one study, the data show that these attitudes often do not persist during the 2 years following the transition from elementary school to junior high school. The large majority of adolescents began this transition with negative attitudes toward smoking, but those attitudes deteriorated during the next 2 years. Adolescents grew more positive toward smoking, more positive toward peer smoking, and less likely to overtly resist smoking (Pfau & Van Bockern, 1994). Perhaps most telling, adolescents' perception of their likelihood to smoke rose steadily during 2 two years, "from a low of 4% at the start of seventh grade to more than 22% near the conclusion of eighth grade" (Pfau & Van Bockern, 1994, p. 424). These results are consistent with behavioral data from other sources (Johnson, 1982) showing smoking rates of 4%-8% prior to ages 12 and 13, and 22% by high school.

These findings support the use of an inoculation approach to smoking prevention. The inoculation strategy is the appropriate choice because, at the point of transition from the primary to middle school grades, adolescents possess reasonably established attitudes opposing smoking. What is needed at this point is a strategy to protect these antismoking attitudes from deterioration during the turbulent middle school years.

## Inoculation Versus "Social Inoculation"

Because studies on smoking onset identify peer pressure as the most powerful predictor of adolescent smoking (Gordon, 1986; McCaul, Glasgow, O'Neill, Freeborn, & Rump, 1982; Mettlin, 1976), a number of researchers have examined the potential of what is termed a "social inoculation" strategy to foster resistance to adolescent smoking. "Social inoculation" features a permutation of McGuire's inoculation construct, which emphasizes resistance, and Bandura's social learning theory, "which emphasizes the role of the social context and the relevance of social skills to smoking behavior" (Wallack & Corbett, 1987, p. 235). "Social inoculation," however, employs only one of two essential components of the inoculation construct: namely, refutational preemption.

"Social inoculation" typically relies on a smorgasbord of tactics—teacher- and peer-led discussion, peer modeling, slide shows, videos, school-wide campaigns, and others. Despite the modest success of "social inoculation" approaches (see Flay & Burton, 1900), they offer limited utility to health campaigners.

The extensiveness and variability of the varied components included under the rubric "social inoculation" undermine their usefulness, because it is difficult to discern the specific tactics that are responsible for the success of these campaigns (Foon, 1986). This prompted Flay (1985) to conclude, following his extensive review of the "social inoculation" research, that, "we really know very little at this time about which of these program components are necessary for program effectiveness or how other components . . . might or might not add to program effectiveness" (p. 378).

Further compounding the problem, these studies failed to operationalize and confirm threat, the component that truly distinguishes inoculation from other resistance approaches. As noted previously, threat is an intrinsic feature of inoculation, providing the motivational catalyst for receivers to strengthen existing attitudes (McGuire, 1962; Papageorgis & McGuire, 1961). This raises a distinct possibility that tactics other than the preemptive component of "social inoculation" may have actually accounted for their results. This concern has motivated some scholars to question the potential of this approach in smoking prevention (Flay, 1985; Foon, 1986; McCaul & Glasgow, 1985).

## Inoculation Message Construction

Inoculation message construction techniques employed in a longitudinal study of inoculation and smoking prevention (Pfau et al., 1992; Pfau & Van Bockern, 1994) can inform health educators and practitioners who seek to use this strategy in health campaigns. This investigation of smoking prevention employed videotapes as the communication modality, although inoculation has been operationalized in other applied studies using print and direct mail modalities (Pfau, 1992; Pfau & Burgoon, 1988; Pfau et al., 1990). No matter what modality is chosen, the basic approach to message design is basically the same, although the messages need to be adapted to the channel characteristics of the chosen modality for optimal efficacy.

Two steps should be taken as a prelude to message design. First, existing health messages designed for late primary and early middle grade students should be previewed. These may include pamphlets, books, videotapes, and films. This assists message designers in appreciating both the language level and communication styles appropriate for the age cohort, which determines adolescent message expectations. Second, a panel of experts, late primary and early middle grade health educators, should be assembled. They are in a unique position to provide valuable advice during the message design process. In addition, they can provide an ongoing check against the natural tendency of many health campaigners to overestimate younger adolescent language capabilities and message involvement levels.

### INOCULATION MESSAGE DESIGN

Inoculation message design requires two message types: a set of initial inoculation messages as well as follow-up reinforcing materials. The initial inoculation messages require two components: threat plus refutational preemption.

In the threatening component of the messages, adolescents are cautioned that, in spite of their present attitudes opposing smoking and although they may not be able to imagine themselves as smokers, as a result of significant peer pressure during the coming weeks and months, many of them will become increasingly uncertain about smoking, and some of them will actually change their minds and try smoking. The threat component needs to be handled realistically, causing adolescents to experience some degree of anxiety about the future stability of their current attitudes.

In the peer-video, *Why Start? It's Your Choice*, threat was embedded early in the message. During the opening segment, an adolescent speaks of her older sister's smoking habit. After a largely visual lead, the teenager laments:

> My sister smokes and I hate it! I tell her that all the time, but I keep finding her stupid cigarettes everywhere. She says nobody cares, but I do. It stinks up the house and makes my eyes water. I think it's a gross habit.
>
> My parents smoke too, but if they found out about her, I bet they'd kill her. She doesn't care; she says she's hooked. . . . And she used to complain that *they* smoked. What happened? Junior high is what happened.
>
> Did you know that of all kids who enter junior high, almost three out of every four will try smoking at least once. No matter how you feel about smoking *now*, no matter how bad you think it is, or even if you *swear* you'll never start, almost a third of you will become experimental smokers, and many of you will end up as regular smokers! Federal officials say that 3,000 teens start smoking each day, and you can count on the fact that most of them thought smoking was a stupid habit to pick up. But something or someone convinced them otherwise.

This opening scene is designed to cause adolescents to experience involvement with, and some anxiety about, the beliefs they now hold dear in the face of future challenges.

In the adult-led video, *Up in Smoke*, following an opening scene designed to introduce the character, the actor playing the role of a teacher warns:

> Stupid habit! I don't know why people waste their breath on these things—literally. We used to call them "cancer sticks." I know that you think that smoking is a messy habit, right? It stinks, it's bad for you, and it costs bucks. As they say in baseball, "three strikes and you're out." (Pitches cigarette in the trash)
>
> No matter how much you want to stay a nonsmoker, the truth is that the pressure to smoke in junior high is greater than it will be at any other time of your life. Three out of four young adults (points to camera)—and *that's you*—will pick up a cigarette and let curiosity take over.
>
> Think about it. No matter how you feel about smoking *now*, no matter how bad you think it is, or even if you *swear* you'll never start, three of every four of you will try it at least once. Almost a third of you will become experimental smokers, and many of you will end up with a pack and a lighter full time. Research tells us that 3,000 teens start smoking each day, and you can count

on the fact that most of them, like you, once thought that smoking was something that they'd never do. But something or someone convinced them otherwise.

These segments were designed to convince nonsmokers that they will face serious threats to existing attitudes opposing smoking. In order to assess whether or not messages attain this goal, message designers must pretest their messages on adolescents. A threat manipulation, consisting of five 7-interval semantic differential scales designed to assess perceptions of the video (safe/dangerous, not risky/risky, nonthreatening/threatening, unintimidating/intimidating, and unharmful/harmful), has been employed in past inoculation research. This particular threat manipulation instrument has achieved excellent reliability ratings in past studies (Pfau, 1992; Pfau et al., 1990; Pfau et al., 1992).

The threat manipulation employed in the smoking prevention investigation was effective in that adolescents perceived the video to be threatening. The first- and second-year results indicated that those adolescents who reported highest perceived threat following administration of the pretreatments were most resistant to smoking onset during each of the assessments over the following 2 years (Pfau et al., 1992; Pfau & Van Bockern, 1994).

The refutational preemption aspect of inoculation messages is more obvious on its face. Message designers need to examine already published research and conduct some formative study to identify the counterarguments that message recipients will encounter. The process of refutational preemption involves identifying and refuting as many of these counterarguments as possible within the constraints of time and receiver attention span.

The messages employed in the inoculation pretreatments in the smoking prevention videotapes featured the three most common counterarguments, including:

smoking is "cool";
experimental smoking is not addicting; and
smoking won't harm me.

For example, the video *Up in Smoke* addressed the counterargument that smoking is "cool." The actor, playing the role of a young, attractive teacher explains:

Half of all smokers say they started between sixth and ninth grades, most because they thought it might bring acceptance; like maybe, if you smoke people won't make fun of you, or at least they won't look down on you.

Hey, nobody wants to be left out. Those feelings are normal. What isn't normal is risking your life for other peoples' acceptance. It is definitely *not cool* for friends to expect you to do something stupid. Real friends will respect your decision to live a healthy life, because they will want what's best for you. What is "cool" is knowing your mind and doing what you feel is right for you—and nobody else but you.

So, how do you stick to your guns when the odds are against you? Well, you might run into this crowd [Shot of kids hanging out, smoking, being "cool"]. Do they look cool to you? Putting a lit stick up to your mouth is not cool. It's extremely unattractive—What you might call "gross." It causes bad breath, yellow teeth, and smelly clothes and hair [a male, smoking a cigarette, walks by an attractive female, waves at her, and coughs. He looks for a response, but realizes that he struck out because of the cigarette. Others, looking on, flick out their cigarettes, looking down].

Try asking someone out after you've smoked. They *might say no* because you smell. And how about kissing? You might as well lick an ashtray. The distant look may be "a ten," but the "close-up and personal" rates "a zero."

Notice the absence of hard data in support of the refutational claim in the preceding message segment. Effective messages are tailored to targeted receivers (Atkin & Freimuth, 1989; Flay & Burton, 1990; Kotler & Roberto, 1989; Pfau & Parrott, 1993), and formative data in this case indicated that adolescents respond to the counterargument that "smoking is cool" emotionally, not cognitively. Hence, the refutational responses were grounded with emotionals rather than facts, at both the verbal and visual levels.

It is not necessary to refute all potential counterarguments. As discussed previously, the strength of the inoculation approach is that it confers resistance to both same and novel counterarguments. Health message designers may be successful even with a limited number of counterarguments. The most common and most persuasive counterarguments should be refuted first. Other considerations for counterarguments selected for refutation include optimal message length, which is a function of receiver attention, and modality expectations (e.g., shorter public service announcements [PSAs] typically receive more radio and television air time), such as the particular source to be used to deliver the message.

## SOURCE CONSIDERATIONS

The issue of most appropriate spokesperson has generated much attention in past inoculation and "social inoculation" research. Peer and adult spokespersons have been employed in past research, and the two compared. The peer-led approach has been more common in "social inoculation" efforts. However, the results comparing the relative superiority of the two approaches has proven equivocal (Best, Thompson, Santi, Smith, & Brown, 1988).

Some "social inoculation" research indicates that peer-led spokespersons are superior (Botvin, Baker, Renick, Filazzola, & Botvin, 1984; Luepker, Johnson, Murray, & Pechacek, 1983; Murray, Luepker, Johnson, & Mittelmark, 1984). One of the first studies comparing program providers, however (Irwin, Creswell, & Stauffer, 1970), reported the peer-led approach was least effective, whereas other studies revealed that spokesperson approach interacts with receiver gender (Clarke, MacPherson, Holmes, & Jones, 1986; Fisher, Armstrong, & de Klerk, 1985). The results of the 2-year inoculation study described in this chapter supports the Best et al. (1988) conclusion: First- and second-year findings indicate that *both* peer and adult approaches proved moderately effective, with no main or interaction effects for spokesperson evident (Pfau et al., 1992; Pfau & Van Bockern, 1994).

## BOOSTER MESSAGE APPROACH

As with all messages, it should be expected that the impact of an inoculation message will deteriorate over time. Although past inoculation research suggests considerable persistence for inoculative materials (Pfau & Burgoon, 1988; Pfau et al., 1990; Pfau & Van Bockern, 1994) and suggests minimal efficacy for reinforcement (McGuire, 1961b; Tannenbaum, Macaulay, & Norris, 1966; Pfau et al., 1990; Pfau & Van Bockern, 1994), message designers are advised to prepare and utilize a second message type consisting of reinforcing materials. The timing of the administration of the reinforcing materials in previous research may have diminished their effect by presenting the messages too soon after the inoculative pretreatments (Pfau et al., 1992).

The reinforcing messages should focus on the content covered in the inoculation pretreatments, employing the same design in terms of length, language use, and arrangement of arguments. If the initial inoculation pretreatments used both peer and adult spokespersons, reinforcing materials could also utilize a combination approach. The smoking prevention study described in this chapter employed a combined approach in the reinforcement video by featuring an interaction of the peer and adult spokespersons. More research is required to pinpoint the optimal use of reinforcing materials.

## Conclusion

Preliminary research indicates that inoculation is a viable strategy in smoking prevention campaigns targeting youngsters at the point of transition from primary to middle grades, precisely because they possess attitudes opposing smoking, which are under increasing pressure during adolescence. The initial inoculation pretreatments should include threat and refutational preemption components, may feature peer or adult spokespersons, and can be delivered via any number of communication media, although videos may prove the most cost effective. Initial pretreatments should be reinforced, using messages similar in design to the originals. Questions about timing and efficacy of the reinforcing materials remain unresolved, however.

In addition to its use in smoking prevention campaigns, health message designers should consider the use of inoculation in other health campaign contexts, including those involving prevention of adolescent drug and alcohol use, violence and conflict resolution, and accident prevention. The circumstances dictate the appropriate message strategy. When attitudes need to be strengthened, inoculation is a promising but often overlooked approach (Miller & Burgoon, 1973).

## References

Anderson, L. R., & McGuire, W. J. (1965). Prior reassurance of group consensus as a factor in producing resistance to persuasion. *Sociometry, 28,* 44-56.

Atkin, C. K. (1991). Be smart, don't start. In R. E. Rice & C. K. Atkin (Eds.), *Public communication campaigns* (2nd ed.) (pp. 224-226). Newbury Park, CA: Sage.

Atkin, C., & Freimuth, V. (1989). Formative evaluation research in campaign design. In R. E. Rice & C. K. Atkin (Eds.), *Public communication campaigns* (2nd ed.) (pp. 131-150). Newbury Park, CA: Sage.

Best, J. A., Thompson, S. J., Santi, S. M., Smith, E. A., & Brown, K. S. (1988). Preventing cigarette smoking among school children. *Annual Review of Public Health, 9,* 161-201.

Botvin, G. J., Baker, E., Renick, N. L., Filazzola, A. D., & Botvin, E. M. (1984). A cognitive-behavioral approach to substance abuse prevention. *Addictive Behavior, 9,* 137-147.

Chassin, L., Corty, E., Presson, C. C., Olshavsky, R. W., Bensenberg, M., & Sherman, S. J. (1981). Predicting adolescents' intentions to smoke cigarettes. *Journal of Health and Social Behavior, 22,* 445-455.

Clarke, J. J., MacPherson, B., Holmes, D. R., & Jones, R. (1986). Reducing adolescent smoking: Comparison of peer-led, teacher-led, and expert interventions. *Journal of School Health, 56,* 102-106.

Donovan, J. E., Jessor, R., & Jessor, L. (1983). Problem drinking in adolescents and young adulthood: A follow-up study. *Journal of Studies on Alcohol, 44,* 189-237.

Einsiedel, E. F., & Cochrane, K. (1988, June). *Using social marketing and theoretical perspectives for health comparisons to adolescents.* Paper presented to the annual meeting of the International Communication Association, New Orleans.

Elder, J. P., & Stern, R. A. (1986). The ABCs of adolescent smoking prevention: An environment and skills model. *Health Education Quarterly, 13,* 181-191.

Evans, R. I., & Raines, B. E. (1982). Control and prevention of smoking in adolescents: A psychosocial perspective. In T. J. Coates, A. C. Petersen, & C. Perry (Eds.), *Promoting adolescent health: A dialogue on research and practice* (pp. 101-136). New York: Academic Press.

Fisher, D. A., Armstrong, B. K., & de Klerk, N. H. (1985). A randomized-controlled trial of education for prevention of smoking in 12-year-old children. In W. F. Forbes, R. C. Frecker, & D. Nostbakken (Eds.), *Proceedings of the 5th World Conference on Smoking and Health* (pp. 263-270). Ottawa: Canadian Council on Smoking and Health.

Flay, B. R. (1985). Prosocial approaches to smoking prevention: A review of findings. *Health Psychology, 4,* 449-488.

Flay, B. R., & Burton, D. (1990). Effective mass communication strategies for health campaigns. In C. Atkin & L. Wallack (Eds.), *Mass communication and public health: Complexities and conflicts* (pp. 129-146). Newbury Park, CA: Sage.

Flay, B. R., d'Avernas, R. J., Best, J. A., Kersell, M. W., & Ryan, K. B. (1983). Cigarette smoking: Why young people do it and ways of preventing it. In P. J. McGrath & P. Firestone (Eds.), *Pediatric and adolescent behavioral medicine* (pp. 132-183). New York: Springer.

Foon, A. E. (1986). Smoking prevention programs for adolescents: The value of social psychological approaches. *The International Journal of the Addictions, 21,* 1017-1029.

Friedman, L. S., Lichtenstein, E., & Biglan, A. (1985). Smoking onset among teens: An empirical analysis of initial situations. *Addictive Behaviors, 10,* 1-13.

Gordon, N. P. (1986). Never smokers, triers, and current smokers: Three distinct groups for school-based antismoking programs. *Health Education Quarterly, 13,* 163-179.

Gottlieb, N., & Baker, J. (1986). The relative influence of health beliefs, parental and peer behaviors and exercise program participation on smoking, alcohol use and physical activity. *Social Science and Medicine, 22,* 915-927.

Hamburg, D. A. (1979). Disease prevention: The challenge of the future. *American Journal of Public Health, 69,* 1026-1033.

Hunt, W., Barnett, L., & Branch, L. G. (1971). Relapse rates in addiction programs. *Journal of Clinical Psychology, 27,* 455-456.

Irwin, R. P., Cresswell, W., Jr., & Stauffer, D. J. (1970). The effect of the teacher on three different classroom approaches on seventh grade students' knowledge, attitudes and beliefs about smoking. *Journal of School Health, 40,* 355-359.

Johnson, C. A. (1982). Untested and erroneous assumptions underlying antismoking programs. In T. J. Coates, A. C. Petersen, & C. Perry (Eds.), *Promoting adolescent health: A dialogue on research and practice* (pp. 149-165). New York: Academic Press.

Killen, J. D. (1985). Prevention of adolescent tobacco smoking: The social pressure resistance training approach. *Journal of Child Psychology and Psychiatry, 26,* 7-15.

Kotler, P., & Roberto, E. L. (1989). *Social marketing: Strategies for changing public behavior.* New York: Free Press.

Landers, A. (1992, March 18). Inoculation best way to protect kids. *Sioux Falls Argus Leader,* p. 5B.

Luepker, R. V., Johnson, C. A., Murray, D. M., & Pechacek, T. F. (1983). Prevention of cigarette smoking: Three-year follow-up of an education program for youth. *Journal of Behavioral Medicine, 6*, 53-62.

Lumsdaine, A. A., & Janis, I. L. (1953). Resistance to "counterpropaganda" produced by one-sided and two-sided "propaganda" presentations. *Public Opinion Quarterly, 17*, 311-318.

McAlister, A. L., Perry, C., & Maccoby, N. (1979). Adolescent smoking: Onset and prevention. *Pediatrics, 63*, 650-658.

McCaul, K. D., & Glasgow, R. E. (1985). Preventing adolescent smoking: What have we learned about treatment construct validity? *Health Psychology, 4*, 361-387.

McCaul, K. D., Glasgow, R., O'Neill, H. K., Freeborn, V., & Rump, B. S. (1982). Predicting adolescent smoking. *The Journal of School Health, 52*, 342-346.

McGuire, W. J. (1961a). The effectiveness of supportive and refutational defenses in immunizing and restoring beliefs against persuasion. *Sociometry, 24*, 184-197.

McGuire, W. J. (1961b). Resistance to persuasion conferred by active and passive prior refutation of the same and alternative counterarguments. *Journal of Abnormal and Social Psychology, 63*, 326-332.

McGuire, W. J. (1962). Persistence of the resistance to persuasion induced by various types of prior belief defenses. *Journal of Abnormal and Social Psychology, 64*, 241-248.

McGuire, W. J. (1964). Inducing resistance to persuasion. Some contemporary approaches. In L. Berkowitz (Ed.), *Advances in experimental social psychology* (Vol. 1, pp. 191-229). New York: Academic Press.

McGuire, W. J. (1970, February). A vaccine for brainwash. *Psychology Today, 3*, pp. 36-39, 63-64.

Mettlin, C. (1976). Peer and other influences on smoking behavior. *The Journal of School Health, 46*, 529-536.

Miller, G. R., & Burgoon, M. (1973). *New techniques of persuasion.* New York: Harper & Row.

Murray, D. M., Luepker, R. V., Johnson, C. A., & Mittelmark, M. B. (1984). The prevention of cigarette smoking in children: A comparison of four strategies. *Journal of Applied Social Psychology, 14*, 274-288.

Papageorgis, D., & McGuire, W. J. (1961). The generality of immunity to persuasion produced by pre-exposure to weakened counterarguments. *Journal of Abnormal and Social Psychology, 62*, 475-481.

Pfau, M. (1992). The potential of inoculation in promoting resistance to the effectiveness of comparative advertising messages. *Communication Quarterly, 40*, 26-44.

Pfau, M., & Burgoon, M. (1988). Inoculation in political campaign communication. *Human Communication Research, 15*, 91-111.

Pfau, M., & Kenski, H. C. (1990). *Attack politics: Strategy and defense.* New York: Praeger.

Pfau, M., Kenski, H. C., Nitz, M., & Sorenson, J. (1990). Efficacy of inoculation strategies in promoting resistance to political attack messages: Application to direct mail. *Communication Monographs, 57*, 25-43.

Pfau, M., & Parrott, R. (1993). *Persuasive communication campaigns.* Boston: Allyn & Bacon.

Pfau, M., & Van Bockern, S. (1994). The persistence of inoculation in conferring resistance to smoking initiation among adolescents: The second year. *Human Communication Research, 20*, 413-430.

Pfau, M., Van Bockern, S., & Kang, J. G. (1992). Use of inoculation to promote resistance to smoking initiation among adolescents. *Communication Monographs, 59*, 213-230.

Reardon, K. K. (1988). The role of persuasion in health promotion and disease prevention: Review and commentary. In J. A. Anderson (Ed.), *Communication yearbook 11* (pp. 277-297). Newbury Park, CA: Sage.

Rokeach, M. (1987). *Health values.* Paper presented to the Institution for Health Promotion and Disease Prevention, Pasadena, CA.

Rosenberg, M. (1965). *Society and adolescent self-image.* Princeton, NJ: Princeton University Press.

Tannenbaum, P. H., Macaulay, J. R., & Norris, E. L. (1966). Principle of congruity and reduction in persuasion. *Journal of Personality and Social Psychology, 2,* 223-238.

U.S. Department of Health and Human Services. (1989). *1989 Surgeon General's report: Reducing the health consequences of smoking: 25 years of progress* (DHHS Publication No. CDC 89-8411). Washington, DC: Government Printing Office.

Wallack, L., & Corbett, K. (1987). Alcohol, tobacco and marijuana use among youth: An overview of epidemiological, program and policy trends. *Health Education Quarterly, 14,* 223-249.

# 7 Reaching Young Audiences

## DEVELOPMENTAL CONSIDERATIONS IN DESIGNING HEALTH MESSAGES

### ERICA WEINTRAUB AUSTIN

Children and adolescents welcome health information they perceive as substantive, provided that information is presented in a relevant, comprehensible, and realistic form. Unfortunately, too many campaigns geared to young people have offered only simplistic, short-term assistance that leaves children who are seeking effective solutions to difficult problems to lose hope of finding real help. This chapter will argue that to avoid encouraging children to settle for trying to "live fast, die young and leave a good looking corpse" (Kassebaum, 1990, p. 88), health communication campaigns need to adopt broader and more aggressive strategies than has been the case historically. Specifically, effective health campaigns must (a) target children younger than has been the norm; (b) microtarget strategies to the needs and interests of different ages and environments; (c) provide consistent messages from a variety of sources and over a long period of time; and (d) emphasize giving children control and ownership of their own destinies.

## General Principles for Targeting Children and Adolescents

A common mistake in campaign design has been to assume that portraying a behavior as bad or unhealthy (such as binge drinking or unprotected sex) will cause children to reject it. This fails to recognize that some of the appeal of certain behaviors may lie in their forbiddance (McGuire, 1989). Knowledge-based campaigns thus rarely affect young people's attitudes and behaviors and often just serve as primers on how to do the dangerous behavior (Goodstadt & Mitchell, 1990; Kassebaum, 1990). Not coincidentally, public

114

service announcements (PSAs) showing behaviors such as smoking and drinking as "only for adults"—some produced by industry—make them even more appealing (DiFranza & McAfee, 1992).

In general, health message designers need to do more listening to children and less preaching to them. Children—especially older children—respond best when involved in their own decision making. They respect rules they have a part in making and get more out of programs they have had a part in producing. Thus, instead of viewing children and adolescents only as the campaign target, planners should view them also as one of their most potent resources.

Fortunately, campaigns based on moralizing, scare tactics, and knowledge-only approaches are beginning to be recognized as counterproductive or of limited effectiveness. More promising and comprehensive health communication strategies with an emphasis on social influences and social and cognitive skills are being developed in their place. The driving force in this evolution in campaign strategy is the recognition that effective prevention efforts must address both individuals and the environments in which they live. To motivate behavior change, campaigns need to address both the internal (personal) and external (environmental) forces that guide a child's behavior (McGuire, 1989).

To target internal or personal factors, campaign designers must understand and respect the child's perspective, explaining specific effects of risk taking and showing both physical and social consequences relevant to the child (Baumrind, 1985). It is better to emphasize short-term negative effects rather than long-term abstract dangers, because children and adolescents striving for physical attractiveness and social power care more that smoking will make their breath smell bad than that they could develop cancer (Kutner, 1991). One well-received poster developed by the National Council on Alcoholism, for example, showed Brooke Shields declaring that "alcohol is fattening" (Kassebaum, 1990). It is both ineffective and unethical, however, to put all of the responsibility or blame for risk taking on the child, whose resistance skills can break down under extreme social pressure (Wallack & Corbett, 1990). Thus, campaigns also need to target external or environmental factors.

To do so, campaigns must consider how a particular problem relates to a child's resources, needs, goals, and conflicting interests. Mixed messages from the community frequently leave children confused, skeptical, and disillusioned. In one town, for example, parents, community, and law enforcement tell children that substance abuse is bad but have annually taken up a collection to sponsor a graduation all-night keg party monitored by the sheriff's department (Free, 1993). When the social norm is to drink, 75% of students will be drinking by the time they are high school seniors (Johnston, O'Malley, & Bachman, 1991). This makes it incumbent on campaign designers to cultivate partnerships among community groups.

One campaign attempting to address the interplay of internal and external forces is the STAR (Students Taught Awareness and Resistance) program, which corrects children's misperceptions and acknowledges media, family, and peer influences. Students are encouraged to talk about effects of substance use that seem positive, not just those that seem negative. They then role play how to respond to situations, and they receive a five-session booster program the following year (Falco, 1992; Johnson, Pentz, & Weber, 1990; Pentz, Dwyer, & Mackinnon, 1989; Pentz, Trebow, & Hansen, 1990). The program also emphasizes school and community involvement, such as convincing convenience store owners not to sell alcohol to high school students (Falco, 1992).

The following sections focus on four principles that can guide the design of comprehensive health campaigns geared to young people. Each section discusses a variety of considerations involved in taking a developmental approach to message design, which have been summarized for quick reference in the Appendix following this chapter. Important issues affected by the age of the message recipient include: relevant risk factors to target; children's orientations toward health; the credibility of various information sources; the relative influence of parents, peers, media, and others; important sources of motivation; effective teaching strategies, tactics, and media channels; understanding of the motives behind broadcast programming and advertising; techniques for attracting children's and adolescents' attention; how and how well young people understand campaign messages; the development of inferential abilities; the development of skepticism toward messages; and the ability to integrate elements of a message.

## PRINCIPLE 1: BEGIN
## PREVENTION EARLIER

Generally, health campaigns focus on one or more of three goals. The first (prevention) aims to delay or prevent experimentation and promote wellness; the second (moderation) strives to develop strategies that limit health-endangering behavior to a safer level, such as the designated driver concept; and the third (intervention) focuses on reducing habitual actions that are health endangering, such as drinking and smoking together (Jessor, 1982). Although prevention can be the least costly campaign, both in economic and social terms (Falco, 1992), it needs to begin surprisingly early, because children begin learning about health issues from birth.

Well before children can drive a car, swig a beer, or smooch in a movie theater, they learn how and why people do these things by observing family, peers, other individuals, and the media (Bandura, 1986; Christiansen, Goldman, & Inn, 1982; McCarthy, 1985; Roberts, 1989; Wallack, Cassady, & Grube, 1990). By 4 months of age, for example, they already perceive cigarettes in their environment (Barie & Fischer, 1979). They cannot choose nutritious foods or reach for a cigarette, but even infants imitate televised models (Bandura, 1986; Hollenbeck & Slaby, 1979). By 18 months, children learn "strategically" (Gelman & Brown, 1986), and by age 2 they watch television purposefully, including an estimated 3 hours of advertising per week (Adler et al., 1979). As a result, a few prevention programs target infants as young as 3 months (e.g., Steele, 1989), focusing on self awareness, communication and bonding, problem solving, and the development of healthy perspectives.

As children become aware of needs, they seek ways of resolving them, developing attitudes surprisingly early that can predict later behavior (Glynn, Leventhal, & Hirschman, 1985; Kandel & Logan, 1984; Kandel & Yamaguchi, 1985). Expectancies for alcohol, "if-then" beliefs concerning the perceived physical and social consequences of drinking, have been found as early as first grade (Miller, Smith, & Goldman, 1989). Moreover, these expectancies have been shown to predict alcohol use (Christiansen & Goldman, 1983; Goldman, Brown, & Christiansen, 1987). Because earlier use of mind-altering substances creates a more dangerous and difficult problem (Barringer, 1990; Conroy, 1988), it is important to delay initial use (Robins & Pryzbeck, 1985).

Fortunately, well before children begin experimenting with dangerous substances and unprotected sex, prevention programs can identify and target predictive risk factors. As summarized in the Appendix, danger signs include underachievement as early as first grade and markedly antisocial behavior such as "acting out" before age 10 (Gordon & McAlister, 1982; National Institute on Drug Abuse [NIDA], 1988). Other factors include male aggressiveness, especially combined with shyness (Kellam & Brown, 1982); low expectations; low resistance to peer influences; a lack of parental support; and a generally deprived environment (Dryfoos, 1990).

Unfortunately, intervention also needs to begin early. One national study (PRIDE, 1992) reported 15% of sixth grade children used beer before age 10. The Mokulele Elementary School in Hawaii launched a comprehensive program after a student survey showed that 66% of the sixth graders had consumed alcohol and 23% had tried other drugs ("Solutions," 1993). More than half of the children who become daily smokers do so before or during ninth grade (McAlister, 1981). Attitudes toward drinkers are established by age 6 (Spiegler, 1983), although still in flux. Six-year-olds who know the signs of drunkenness (Jahoda & Cramond, 1972) and understand social norms about drinking (Zucker, 1979) do not yet have strong personal opinions. Because children may not view drinkers negatively, great potential exists for both positive and negative influences, creating a need and an opportunity for early intervention (Spiegler, 1983).

The likelihood of improving a child's environment also is higher when addressed early. As Kassebaum (1990) notes, parents of young children often are more hopeful and flexible, whereas parents may have given up on an older, difficult child. In addition, by adolescence many risk factors and peer groups are well entrenched and many young people difficult to reach. This does not mean the campaigner should give up on the older child, of course, but it does mean that strategies will need to change and improvements likely will be more gradual.

## PRINCIPLE 2: MICROTARGET TO
## AGE AND ENVIRONMENTAL DIFFERENCES

As children develop cognitive and physical skills, they learn new things in new ways. Stage theories of child development have been largely rejected, but scholars still point to possible "critical periods" when major skills come into place and new kinds of decisions are being made. Thus, to assist the design of developmentally appropriate messages, this chapter and the Appendix are organized by age ranges identified as critical periods in development. Each period represents a distinct context for health promotion, consisting of changes in motivations, information processing, and interactions with environmental influences. As the Appendix shows, for example, we all strive for rewards (Bandura, 1986), which we can receive from others, experience vicariously by watching others such as on television, or award ourselves from within (Heath & Bryant, 1992). But younger children are less able to reward themselves, seeking instead rewards from others and striving to avoid negative, often physical, consequences (Kohlberg, 1976).

### The Age Groups

*Preschoolers (0-5).* It is in the preschool period that a child begins to become aware of health attitudes and behaviors. Children do not yet understand health as a concept but nevertheless are learning and imitating what they see, particularly at home. A warm and stimulating environment is their most basic need, to help them develop a positive self-image and basic social and cognitive skills.

*Early School Age (5-7).* The jump from preschool to school age marks one critical period of concern. At this age children begin to develop peer groups and must deal with new sources of influence (e.g., teachers), new roles, and pressure to fit sex roles (Higgins & Parsons, 1983). They are beginning to understand that perspectives other than their own exist (Flavell, Miller, & Miller, 1993) and can take another's perspective with help (Gelman & Brown, 1986). As a result, they can understand other people's intentions when described clearly, such as through pictures instead of words (Chandler, Greenspan, & Barenboim, 1973). They have developed a keen interest in cause and effect (Gelman & Brown, 1986) and respond well by age 5-7 to morality labels and conventional rules (Kohlberg, 1976).

*Middle Childhood (7-10).* Another possibly critical age occurs around 7-10. At this point children no longer automatically accept parental authority, increasingly accept peer values and those of slightly older children perceived as role models, better understand symbols and metaphors in messages, and can better express themselves (Miller et al., 1989; Worth & Gross, 1974). They also begin to establish friendships based on admiration of another's dispositions or traits (Higgins & Parsons, 1983).

*Early Adolescence (10-13).* A third critical period occurs around the transition from middle school or junior high school to high school. Now adolescents are thrown into situations that expose them to a wider variety of people. By this time they are good at understanding perspective and intent (Christenson & Roberts, 1990; Flavell et al., 1993; Higgins & Parsons, 1983), which makes their world infinitely more complicated. They must negotiate their way through a period of enormous uncertainty that leads to intense information seeking, media use, and experimentation (Baumrind, 1985; Roberts, 1971, 1973; Schramm, 1965).

*Mid- to Late Adolescence (13-16, 16+).* From mid-adolescence on, children focus on achieving independence by forming an identity, developing a positive body image, developing an inner conscience, defining sex roles and learning about cross-sex relationships, preparing for future family and civic roles, and developing more sophisticated problem-solving capabilities

(Christenson & Roberts, 1990; Kohlberg, 1976). In the meantime, they still realize that ultimately teachers, counselors, parents, and other adults are still in charge. To avoid seeming dependent or controlled by adults, they tend to reject explicit acceptance or approval of adult-sponsored interests (Baumrind, 1985). Now beyond simple physical rewards and punishments but not yet fully able to reward themselves from within, adolescents seek social rewards and strive to avoid social threats (Pfau & Van Bockern, 1993; Schoenbachler, 1993).

## Targeting Different Age Groups

*Targeting the Preschooler.* Although attitudes and risk factors already are developing in preschoolers, children this young are not ready for campaign messages emphasizing abstractions such as cause, hypothetical dangers, inferences, or personal feelings as motivations for health behavior (Baumrind, 1985). Failing to see good and ill health as a continuum (Hawkins, Lishner, & Catalano, 1985), young children focus more on wellness than on illness (Bush & Ianotti [1985] discussing paper by Vogt, Lieberman, Iverson, & Walter, 1983). Campaigns for preschool children need to emphasize the positive, such as what kinds of things are good to put into our bodies, general skill development, and the development of a supportive environment.

Programs for young children need to be experiential rather than "academic." BABES (1978)—Beginning Alcohol & Addictions Basic Education Studies—for example, teaches cognitive and interpersonal problem-solving skills (Spivak & Shure, 1982) via game playing, songs, and puppets. The program helps children identify problems, helps them learn about self-image and feelings, teaches coping skills, and shows them how to get help.

Because young children are so dependent on their caregivers, parent and teacher training is especially important to include. Many scholars recommend helping parents develop good family communication skills, positive parenting styles, and knowledge about risk factors and protective factors (Kassebaum, 1990; Kumpfer & DeMarsh, 1984). The BABES program, for example, provides special assistance to families with current problems and provides training and support groups for parents. Although long-term evaluation is difficult to perform, this type of program shows much promise. The Perry Preschool Program, which helps parents with family management and includes weekly home visits, has successfully predicted fewer adolescent pregnancies (Berrueta-Clement, Schweinhart, Barnett, & Weikhard, 1983).

*Targeting in Early School Age and in Middle Childhood.* During the early school age and middle childhood period children begin to develop patterns of success or failure, both academically and socially. As a result, campaigns must begin by assisting with cognitive and social skill development and by including stress reduction training to teach children how to handle frustration (Murray & Perry, 1985). Until children can master basic skills, such as starting a conversation and how to act when someone is rude to them, the health educator cannot begin to address tougher issues such as how to "say no" to sexual overtures or pressure to use drugs (Botvin, 1990).

Children believe this is a good period for classroom-based instruction, recommending presentations, counselors, and outside speakers (Billings, Burton, Mertens, & Strong, 1993). An informal teaching style is best, featuring a gradual transfer of responsibility to students through "natural tutoring" (Palincsar & Brown [1984] as reviewed by Gelman & Brown, 1986). As children become comfortable with each challenge presented and modeled by a teacher and then practiced by the children, the responsibility for learning is transferred to the student, instilling both the new skill and a sense of confidence and control. By taking turns as a discussion leader, for example, children can help model refusal strategies or pinpoint weaknesses in a persuasive message, increasing their own confidence in the skill.

Although the home environment remains an important factor at this age, and families are still frequently cited as a resource by sixth graders (Billings et al., 1993), peers are gaining in influence. As a result, peer leaders—who can be the same age—also are a useful tool (Perry & Jessor, 1985). Peer discussion, for example, has helped students reduce smoking (Peterson & Clark, 1986). The danger of discussion techniques, however, is that children can be hesitant to appear unknowledgable or vulnerable in front of their peers. A less threatening discussion format, such as watching similar children asking the difficult questions via the mass media, as well as interactive media in a more private setting such as by video game, can prove helpful as a result.

By middle childhood, children voraciously consume mass media, including television, radio, and—by about age 9 or 10—magazines. By third or fourth grade, children are quite interested in radio, which is peer centered (Christenson, DeBenedittis, & Lindloff, 1985), by adolescence they are listening 2-5 hours a day. Children at this age also are at their peak of television watching (Lyle & Hoffman, 1972; Van der Voort, 1986), which they tend to do more with family (Christenson et al., 1985). As a result, as the Appendix shows, campaigns can make good use of the mass media to teach facts and social norms, but they also need to address the counter-messages present in much programming and advertising. Children appear to be vulnerable to televised portrayals of norms surrounding health issues.

Young children, especially those younger than about age 8, for example, are not as good at understanding the persuasive intent of commercials (Blosser & Roberts, 1985), and children younger than 5 or 6 often confuse ads and programs (Ward & Wackman, 1973). But learning the intentions behind ads and progressing toward disbelief may not be enough to protect children from alcohol ads' appeals (Austin & Nach-Ferguson, 1995; Jeffrey, McLellarn, & Fox, 1982). Teenagers overwhelmingly report that even though they know ads make drinking look better than it really is they nevertheless respond to the advertisements (Billings et al., 1993), a self-diagnosis supported by other research (e.g., Atkin, Hocking, & Block, 1984; Austin & Meili, in press). Thus, media literacy skills need to be included in campaigns (e.g., Austin & Nach-Ferguson, 1995; Grube, 1993).

*Targeting the Early Adolescent.* Middle school and junior high represent a last chance for campaign designers to reach many at-risk youth in a traditional setting, because at-risk youth tend to begin dropping out of school. At this time, cognitive skills are fairly sophisticated and most at-risk children have not yet given up and dropped out (Falco, 1992). *At-risk* generally refers to a child from a disadvantaged environment, such as low income, crime-ridden areas, or from a family in which a member abuses a substance (Kassebaum, 1990), factors that tend to contribute to a loss of hope in the future (Ezekoye, Kumpfer, & Bukosi, 1985; Hurst-Palermo, 1992). Among 10- to 17-year-olds, Dryfoos (1990) has estimated one in four to be at risk for multiple problem behaviors.

The message designer, however, must remember that the other three of each four also may experiment with risky behaviors such as drug use but will not continue past about age 23 (Kumpfer, 1986; Yamaguchi & Kandel, 1984). As Baumrind (1985) notes, mere experimentation is typical and developmentally normal. Campaigns implying that risk takers are deviant can produce a self-fulfilling prophecy, especially among those who already have lost hope for themselves (Baumrind, 1985). Thus, overreaction by adults can backfire (Kumpfer, 1986; Tobler, 1986; Yamaguchi & Kandel, 1984). Kassebaum (1990) also recommends avoiding heterosexism, because higher risk behavior is more common among homosexual populations; campaigns need to combat, not exacerbate, cultural stereotypes that contribute to their feelings of failure.

In early adolescence, children still turn to family, but they overwhelmingly credit school with teaching them the most about drugs and drinking

(Billings et al., 1993). Adolescents tend to overestimate the prevalence of drug use and rarely discuss it with each other (Falco, 1992). As a result, campaigns need to teach facts; correct misperceptions; and address the myriad of media, family, and peer influences faced by the adolescent. The STAR (Students Taught Awareness and Resistance) program, for example, teaches resistance skills in junior high via 13 sessions that include discussion, role playing, and a five-session booster program the following year (Falco, 1992; Johnson et al., 1990; Pentz et al., 1989; Pentz et al., 1990).

Long-term reinforcement becomes especially important as societal pressures to take risks become more intense. Even with the STAR program, lauded as one of the most successful programs in the country, gains tend to shrink with time. One way to reinforce lessons over a longer period of time is to give teachers "ownership" of the program by training them to introduce discussion of alcohol and other drugs into daily activities. Teachers thus can reinforce lessons over time and in a variety of contexts (Fagin & Sauer [1990] as reviewed by Falco, 1992). Decision-making skill development, for example, which helps young people weigh options, goals, and uncertainty, can be applied to nearly any topic. Helping children develop good decision-making skills is of the utmost importance because they will find that prevention messages often provide conflicting advice (Fischhoff, 1993). Media messages for this age group should make use of radio, television, and teen or sports magazines, focusing on teaching facts, disproving myths, and advocating moderation.

*Targeting the Mid- to Late Adolescent.* By mid- to late adolescence a great deal of experimentation is taking place, so campaigns need to emphasize moderation and intervention more than prevention. Adolescents seek solutions, not preaching, and they want to be part of the solution rather than viewed only as the problem (Washington State Association of Broadcasters [WSAB], 1990). They need to hear messages frequently to counterbalance the frequent pressures they face, but they think news stories exaggerate and most PSAs are silly (WSAB, 1990).

Mass media become a more important tool for this age group, because the most at-risk youth are already out of school and on the streets. Mass media that may reach them include heavy metal radio stations, afternoon soap operas, *Oprah,* MTV and micro-targeted cable, teenage radio stations, subway ads, and posters at hangouts such as video arcades and malls (Christenson & Roberts, 1990; Kassebaum, 1990). Hawkins and colleagues (1985) recommend using local sports heroes, popular drug-free celebrities, and older peers, but exploitation of celebrities can backfire: Teenagers report that celebrities' motives are suspect, that rock stars are hypocritical, and that too many athletes have "messed up" (WSAB, 1990).

Some adolescents respond to their need for "sensation," or excitement, by using more drugs and using them earlier (Donohew, 1988; Donohew, Lorch, & Palmgreen, 1993). Unhealthy or risky behavior for 14- to 16-year-olds also correlates with more radio use, more use of music video, and more TV movies. As a result, use of these media to produce novel, dramatic, and stimulating messages can motivate sensation seekers to call a hot line (Palmgreen et al., 1993), which—after peers—is the most preferred source of information for this age group (Billings et al., 1993). Effective messages acknowledge the natural appeals of dangerous health behaviors ("you probably think you'll seem more grown up or adventurous") and then refute them, showing how to achieve similar goals via realistic and appealing behavioral alternatives (Tobler, 1986).

A mass media campaign, however, serves more as a catalyst to direct adolescents to sources of help (such as 1-800 numbers) than as a solution to any problem. The major effect of mass media tends to be more communication (Chaffee, 1982; Christenson & Roberts, 1990). A competition for song writers in Latin America to promote sexual abstinence among teenagers, for example, encouraged teens to talk more freely and openly about sex-related issues. The campaign reinforced teens who already wanted to use restraint and sensitized younger teens to the importance of the topic (Singhal & Rogers, 1989). A similar American campaign (Rock Against Drugs [RAD], 1988) also may prove effective in this way.

## PRINCIPLE 3: MAKE SURE CONSISTENT MESSAGES COME FROM A VARIETY OF SOURCES AND OVER A LONG PERIOD OF TIME

Despite the many differences in strategy required for targeting children at various developmental periods, the common thread is that no one-shot message from any single source can do the job. Interpersonal sources ultimately are more important than the media, but the relative power of each primary influencer—mass media, family, and peers—will change, as will strategies that maximize their influence.

At adolescence, for example, children move away from parents toward peers as sources of attitudes and values (Glynn, 1981; Lull, 1985). At no point are children wholly influenced by peers or family, however, and acceptance of one influence does not mean rejection of the other. Sources of influence can differ depending on the situation (Kandel, Kessler, & Margulies, 1978) and across types of substances (Glynn, 1981). Where strong interpersonal sources do not exist, mass media fill the gap.

*Mass Media as an Influence.* Children tend to learn from what they see but imitate only what they see rewarded (Bandura, 1986; Bandura, Ross, & Ross, 1963). Thus, despite society's frequent condemnations of television, prosocial media messages tend to have a stronger effect than antisocial ones (Hearold, 1986). Because television selectively amplifies and reinforces tendencies already present in society (Gitlin, 1989), it is not unreasonable for 9- to 15-year-olds to report learning about things and themselves as their most common reason for liking to watch TV (Greenberg, 1974). How and what they learn, however, changes greatly with age.

A mature understanding of mass media messages requires the ability to pay attention selectively, to understand implicit as well as explicit information, to understand the perspective and intentions of program developers and characters, and to understand the meaning behind techniques such as slow motion and flashbacks (Dorr, 1980; Miller et al., 1989). Anderson and Collins (1988) surmise that young children have trouble understanding television messages because programming often is geared to adults or older children and contains unfamiliar language, situations, ideas, and actions. As the Appendix illustrates, adult levels of understanding—including comprehension and inferential abilities—may not be not reached until about eighth grade (Collins, 1982), and even adolescents often misinterpret (or at least interpret in myriad ways) popular music lyrics (Christenson & Roberts, 1990). As a result, message designers need to understand a child's skills and perspective in order to prepare media messages the child will understand as intended.

Preschoolers, for example, pay more attention to dialogue with immediate (here-and-now) referents (Anderson, Lorch, Field, & Sanders, 1981). They are attracted to animation, striking voices, lively music, rhyming, sound effects, rapid pacing, repetition, alliteration, women, children, and puppets (Anderson & Levin, 1976; Calvert & Gersh, 1987). They tend to pay less attention to men, animals, inactivity, and still drawings. PSAs on good nutrition, for example, were better understood by young children when they included animation, sprightly voices, and lively background music instead of live photography of real people and narration by adult males in a serious tone (Campbell, Wright, & Huston [in press] as discussed by Anderson & Collins, 1988). Older children learn to pay attention for interesting information (Wright & Huston, 1981) as opposed to merely provocative visual and sound effects. Production values, however, remain an important draw (Basil, 1993).

Children tend to understand better when settings and characters seem familiar (Newcomb & Collins, 1979). Because they have difficulty seeing beyond the surface meaning of a message, young children will depend more on stereotypes to predict likely outcomes if the context is less familiar (Collins & Wellman, 1982). In addition, as the Appendix illustrates, young children are less able to make inferences and integrate disparate pieces of information separated by time or context. As a result, they have trouble sifting out irrelevant information (Collins, 1975). For the message designer, this means that what characters say and what they do must be clearly consistent for the intended message to be learned (Liss, Reinhardt, & Fredriksen, 1983). Children will more likely remember actions than utterances (Gibbons, Anderson, Smith, Field, & Fischer, 1986), which can lead them to focus more on portrayed conflict than on its resolution (Silverman & Sprafkin, 1980; Singer, 1980). Young children may thus think things other than the main message are the most important aspects (Collins, 1982, 1983b; Cullingsford, 1984). An adult will realize that *Winnie the Pooh and the Honey Tree* teaches that being piggish can get you stung by bees and make you too fat to fit through doorways. To a young child, however, it may teach merely that being piggish is cute and funny.

Preschoolers can understand a central message and make some inferences if programs are short and direct (Anderson & Collins, 1988). But young children are less able to understand cause and effect, particularly when separated by commercials or subplots (Collins, 1981, 1983b). Fast pacing can further interfere with their understanding (Wright et al., 1984). They remember verbal messages better without the interference of visual effects (Meringoff, 1980). They can cope with some cuts and edits, which the campaign targeting more than one age group needs to use to attract older children. But fancy production techniques will fail with a younger audience if the effects get too complex, such as with changes in time, distortion to convey drunkenness, or instant replays (see Anderson & Collins, 1988).

Redundancy can help young children understand more complex material. A verbal label, for example, helps them understand a complex visual (Ball & Bogatz, 1970; Watkins, Calvert, Huston-Stein, & Wright, 1980), and congruence of audio and visual information helps them remember a message (Anderson & Collins, 1988; Sadowski, 1972). Redundancy also helps young children make predictions about cause and effect (Winick & Winick, 1979).

Momentous advances in understanding take place by about age 8 and can be traced to changes in children's abilities to engage in controlled, deliberate information processing. They learn how to reflect on language and thinking processes—enabling them to understand metaphors, consider motives, and appreciate irony and sarcasm. As a result, as shown in the Appendix, a big jump occurs between second and fifth grade in children's understanding of implicit information (i.e., the ability to go beyond the information given) (Collins, 1983a). Before this skill develops, their understanding of messages can be "exotically different" from adults' (Collins, 1983a; Young, 1990).

One way they change is to become more skeptical about television realism as they grow older. Preschoolers tend to believe TV characters are real (Dorr, 1980) and may even think that "Barney the Dinosaur" lives in the TV set. Kindergartners use appearances such as animation to determine realism, although even young children realize that fantastic forms such as cartoons can provide real-life information (Dorr, 1983). By about age 8 they make a big jump in understanding that television is fabricated and with age use increasingly more content-related cues to judge realism (Dorr, 1983; Young, 1990). Overall, children begin by checking whether a portrayal is "physically possible" to whether it is "probable" or "representative" by about sixth grade (Dorr, 1983).

Thus even young children do not accept or act on everything they see, and they apply more weight to real-world impressions gained from personal experience than to conflicting portrayals seen only via the media world. As a result, structured, direct experiences and information campaigns can be used to educate children to be more skeptical of unhealthy media portrayals (Austin, Roberts, & Nass, 1990; Young, 1990). Message characteristics that predict imitation include perceptions of realism (Hawkins & Pingree, 1982; Reeves, 1978), similarity, and identification with characters (Austin et al., 1990; Reeves & Garramone, 1982); frequent exposure to consistent messages (Gerbner, Gross, Morgan, & Signorielli, 1986); messages seen as reinforced in real life (Austin et al., 1990; DeFleur & Ball-Rokeach, 1982) and by significant others (Austin et al., 1990); and for topics about which children get little information from other sources (Miller & Reese, 1982; Rosengren & Windahl, 1972). Overall, children tend to imitate portrayals seen frequently and that seem relevant, useful, realistic, and rewarding (Bandura, 1988).

Adults can help children interpret more critically what they see in media portrayals (Austin, 1993a; Corder-Bolz, 1980; Salomon, 1981). Issues such as perceived realism, fantasy, stereotypes, violence, and aggression on television have been put into lessons for children from kindergarten through fifth grade (Singer, Zuckerman, & Singer, 1980). In 1983, for example, Huesman, Eron, Klein, Brice, and Fischer successfully used critical viewing skills training to help children recognize and deal with televised violence. As a result, adults may be able to help children see alcohol ads as less relevant, useful, realistic, and rewarding. The Scott Newman Center, for example, has been developing an AdSmarts campaign to teach media literacy and action skills to middle school children for alcohol and tobacco ads. Creative tactics to get children involved include newsletters with articles and cartoons created by children, mixed with statistics on substance use gathered by adults; making PSAs, learning models, and videotapes for in-school use; and role playing. Ideally, the program should be expanded to target even younger children, because those who have the most to learn tend to benefit the most from such training (Roberts, Christenson, Gibson, Mooser, & Goldberg, 1980).

*Family as an Influence.* On the whole, family influences are the most enduring. Family communication begins to exert its influence early, and good communication patterns improve the chances that familial support will endure when adolescents face tough decisions (Glynn, 1981). In the absence of strong family or other significant adult influences, children turn to media messages or appealing role models. Ironically, health campaigns have rarely targeted or involved parents (Barnea, Teichman, & Rahav, 1992).

How a family interrelates is more important than family structure (Baranowski & Nader, 1985). Parents influence the ways children develop strategies to seek and analyze information in general (Austin, 1993a; McLeod & Chaffee, 1972), and parents also influence how children approach information about serious topics (Austin, in press). The ability to communicate openly with a parent, for example, can help a child develop confidence in the ability to resist social pressures and predicts information seeking about drugs and AIDS (Austin, in press; Jessor & Jessor, 1975).

Strict controls and parental disagreement about discipline increase children's risk (Glynn, 1981). Sharp increases in parental control at the onset of adolescence also can be counterproductive (Glynn, 1981). Permissive strategies—warm but noncontrolling approaches to parenting—also place a child at risk (Baumrind, 1985). A parenting style emphasizing reasoning rather than strict rules is most successful, especially when developed *before* adolescence (Baumrind, 1985; Glynn, 1981). Responsive and negotiated control succeeds because children view it as legitimate.

When it comes to exerting control over other information sources rather than over the child directly, parents too frequently miss an important opportunity. Parents generally do not talk often about television with their children (Austin et al., 1990; Ward, Wackman, & Wartella, 1977). This lack of familial communication about television content gives television messages greater influence than they might otherwise have. As a result, health campaigns need to persuade parents to talk with their children about difficult issues, to talk about what their children see on television, and to do so early. Such conversations may increase skepticism (Austin, 1993a), keep the parent's influence ahead of the TV's (Austin et al., 1990; Corder-Bolz, 1980), help children understand content (Corder-Bolz, 1980), and provide opportunities to practice better ways of interrelating with each other. A Washington State campaign, for example, targets the need for parental discussion of television and alcohol via a comprehensive campaign, launched by coordinating the support of state agencies, community groups, broadcaster groups, the Governor's Office, academicians, and schools. Targeting parents of 3- to 10-year-olds, it features slogans such as "Make sure the most important messages about alcohol come from you."

Besides recommending discussion, however, campaigners need to provide parents with realistic and nonthreatening opportunities to develop their own knowledge and communication skills. Parents appear inadvertently to reinforce the wrong things (Austin, 1993a; Austin & Nach-Ferguson, 1995; Desmond, Singer, & Singer, 1990), and unclear messages from a parent can be perceived differently by the child than the parent intends (Austin, 1993b). Parents tend to explain their views more than they try to understand the adolescent's views (Hunter, 1985). They also are more future oriented than their children are, which can make communication more difficult.

Future orientation makes parents better suited to communicate about prevention, which is future oriented, than intervention, which addresses the present. Direct parental influence on at-present issues wanes by adolescence, with the majority of the parents' influence on their children becoming more indirect (Lull, 1985). This does not make it less important for children's well-being; children's long-term attachment to their parents remains a more powerful influence than children's more transitional relationships with peers (Burke & Weir, 1978, 1979; Greenberg, Siegel, & Leitch, 1983). Thus, although indirect, parental support remains crucial.

*Peer Influence.* By preadolescence, peers emerge as critical influences for (present-oriented) intervention. Peers can be a positive as well as a negative influence (Clasen & Brown, 1985), and they are perceived as credible (WSAB, 1990). Peer pressure has been called the pivotal force for an adolescent on the edge (Oetting & Beauvais, 1988).

Adolescents adjust their present values and style to match those that represent the status toward which they aspire, with involvement in certain teen groups and music styles providing a symbolic expression of those values (Roe, 1985). As a result, adolescents may strive to imitate "elite" peers more than their own peers. In addition, because they may be desperately longing to be a part of a group, loners actually may be more influenced by the perceived norms of others than those already in peer groups (Clasen & Brown, 1985). The campaign designer, as a result, needs to find out whom children admire, not just with whom they associate.

Peer influence does not appear to vary by SES (socioeconomic status) but does vary by gender, age, and family structure. Boys are more susceptible to negative influences than are girls. Early adolescents are more susceptible than preadolescents or older adolescents. Children from single-parent households and stepparent households are more susceptible to peer influence (probably due to the variety of stresses on the family relationship), as are latchkey children (Steinberg, 1986; Steinberg & Silverberg, 1986).

## PRINCIPLE 4: EMPHASIZE GIVING CHILDREN CONTROL AND OWNERSHIP OF THEIR OWN DESTINIES

Because the goal of growing up is to become self-reliant, health promotion campaigns should facilitate that process by building confidence and skills. Someday, after all, the campaign will end, leaving children to control their own behavior. Promoting the development of skills in nonthreatening ways and providing appealing alternatives to risk taking can help put children in control of some aspect of their lives, perhaps for the first time (Tobler, 1986). As the Appendix suggests, giving young people some input or control over the campaign designed to accomplish this can help campaigners develop a realistic and well-received intervention even while it encourages children and adolescents to take responsibility for themselves.

The first step is to listen carefully to young people's needs and desires. Children say they want help early, believing more in the effectiveness of prevention than intervention. More than 40% of Washington State 6th to 12th graders, for example, favor substance abuse education by third grade, with one in five also favoring sex education this early (Billings et al., 1993). By 12th grade, however, nearly one quarter (of those still in school) seem to have lost hope that any intervention programs can help them.

The next step is to include young people in program planning. Increasingly, locally based programs are making use of peer leaders, often including adolescents on the program advisory board (Office of Substance Abuse Prevention [OSAP], 1989). In the Peer Leaders Program in Maine, for example, students have contributed to program decision making, survey design, and data collection, as well as attended workshops on substance abuse prevention and helping skills (OSAP, 1989). Inviting at-risk teenagers to help another, such as a younger sibling, rather than just portraying them as victims or problems, can instill purpose, hope, and self-confidence (Kassebaum, 1990). In some cases programs have been initiated by teenagers to overcome denial among adults in the community (e.g., Teens Are Concerned, 1989).

Children can help guide the selection of message sources, channels, content, and supporting activities. Television, for example, has been cited as a source of information for alcohol by 37% of 8- and 9-year-olds, more than parents or peers (Aitken, Leathar, & Scott, 1988). Despite the plethora of celebrities eager to lend their names to a good cause, adolescents—delighted to have been asked—have suggested using people more like themselves, with whom they more likely identify (WSAB, 1990). They also suggest striving for realism, using facts, and relating them to things adolescents care deeply about, such as family and friends. Because current slang and popular activities change quickly, children themselves are bound to be the planner's best sources for successful ideas, such as all-night alcohol-free parties bursting with activities that seem attractive instead of silly. Children want help, but they want and deserve to be treated with respect as partners in prevention and intervention efforts.

## Summary

Early prevention and intervention can be remarkable investments—both in social and in monetary terms—when done properly. Life Skills Training and STAR, two of the most effective programs as reviewed by Falco (1992), cost $15 to $25 per pupil, including classroom materials and teacher training. By contrast, drug treatment in prisons can cost $4,000 to $8,000 per year per inmate, with the cost of keeping drug-related criminals behind bars estimated at least $10 billion (Falco, 1992). To be effective, however, health promotion must address problems rather than focus on isolated symptoms. Well-meaning but misguided programs risk abandoning children to hopelessness.

Campaign designers have earned much criticism for underresearching, underevaluating, and overplaying the success of programs such as those in the "Just Say No" genre (e.g., Bangert-Drowns, 1988; Elliott, 1993; Falco,

1992; Goodstadt & Mitchell, 1990; Wallack, 1986). The Media-Advertising Partnership for a Drug-Free America, for example, has been rightly criticized for identifying problems but offering no resolutions; portraying improbable rather than most probable consequences; narrowly focusing on less commonly abused substances (e.g., cocaine) instead of gateway drugs (alcohol, tobacco, and marijuana); and making use of shock-value techniques, which can backfire (Tortu, 1990). The Partnership's tactics have had some value, however, apparently helping to overcome complacency and denial in communities, which increasingly are getting involved in campaign partnerships (Falco, 1992).

To achieve success among the children themselves, however, campaigns should be designed to be comprehensive, long term, and begun early. Effective tactics microtarget the needs and interests of children of different ages and environments and are realistic, credible, and balanced. Effective messages come from a variety of sources and over a long period of time. Effective campaign planning acknowledges and works with these various, often conflicting, sources of information. In addition, effective campaigns make the target part of the solution by including young people in program development. The inescapable conclusion is that children and adolescents make challenging targets for health promotion; fortunately, they also provide some of the most promising opportunities. The message designer's reward is that a developmental approach to health promotion can help children gain control of their own destinies, ultimately instilling in them the power to develop a healthy future for themselves.

# References

Adler, R. P., Friedlander, B. Z., Lesser, G. S., Meringoff, L., Robertson, T. S., Rossiter, J. R., & Ward, S. (1979). *Research on the effects of television advertising on children.* Washington, DC: National Science Foundation.

Adler, R. P., Lesser, G. S., Meringoff, L. K., Robertson, T. S., Rossiter, J. R., & Ward, S. (1980). *The effects of television advertising on children: Review and recommendations.* Lexington, MA: Lexington Books.

Aitken, P., Leathar, D., & Scott, A. (1988). Ten- to sixteen-year-olds' perceptions of advertising for alcoholic drinks. *Alcohol and Alcoholism, 23,* 491-500.

Anderson, D., & Collins, P. (1988). *The impact on children's education: Television's influence on cognitive development* (Working Paper No. 2). Washington, DC: U.S. Department of Education, Office of Educational Research and Improvement.

Anderson, D., & Levin, S. (1976). Young children's attention to "Sesame Street." *Child Development, 47,* 806-811.

Anderson, D., Lorch, E., Field, D., & Sanders, J. (1981). The effects of TV program comprehensibility on preschool children's visual attention to television. *Child Development, 52,* 151-157.

Atkin, C., Hocking, J., & Block, M. (1984). Teenage drinking: Does advertising make a difference? *Journal of Communication, 34,* 157-167.

Austin, E. W. (1993a). Exploring the effects of active parental mediation of television content. *Journal of Broadcasting & Electronic Media,* (Spring), 147-158.

Austin, E. W. (1993b). The importance of perspective in parent-child interpretations of family communication patterns. *Journalism Quarterly, 70,* 558-568.

Austin, E. W. (in press). Direct and indirect influences of parent-child communication norms on adolescents' tendencies to take preventive measures for AIDS and drug abuse. In G. Kreps & D. O'Hair (Ed.), *Relational communication and health outcomes.* Creskill, NJ: Hampton Press.

Austin, E. W., & Meili, H. K. (in press). Effects of interpretations of televised alcohol portrayals on children's alcohol beliefs. *Journal of Broadcasting & Electronic Media.*

Austin, E. W., & Nach-Ferguson, B. (1995). Sources and influences of young school-age children's general and brand-specific knowledge about alcohol. *Health Communication, 7,* 1-20.

Austin, E. W., Roberts, D. F., & Nass, C. I. (1990). Influences of family communication on children's television-interpretation processes. *Communication Research, 17,* 545-564.

BABES. (1978). *Beginning alcohol & addictions basic education studies.* National Council on Alcoholism and Other Dependencies in the Greater Detroit, MI, area.

Ball, S., & Bogatz, G. (1970). *The first year of "Sesame Street": An evaluation.* Princeton, NJ: Educational Testing Service.

Bandura, A. (1986). *Social foundations of thought & action: A social cognitive theory.* Englewood Cliffs, NJ: Prentice Hall.

Bandura, A. (1988). Social cognitive theory of mass communication. In J. Groebel & P. Winterhoff (Ed.), *Empirische medienpsychologie.* Munich: Psychologie Verlags Union.

Bandura, A., Ross, D., & Ross, S. (1963). Vicarious reinforcement and imitative learning. *Journal of Abnormal and Social Psychology, 67,* 601-607.

Bangert-Drowns, R. (1988). Effects of school-based substance abuse education—A meta-analysis. *Journal of Drug Education, 18,* 243-264.

Baranowski, T., & Nader, P. R. (1985). Family health behavior. In D. C. Turk & R. D. Kerns (Ed.), *Health, illness & families: A life-span perspective* (pp. 51-80). New York: John Wiley.

Barie, L., & Fischer, C. (1979). Acquisition of the smoking habit. *Health Education Journal, 38,* 71-76.

Barnea, Z., Teichman, M., & Rahav, G. (1992). Personality, cognitive, and interpersonal factors in adolescent substance use: A longitudinal test of an integrative model. *Journal of Youth and Adolescence, 21,* 187-200.

Barringer, F. (1990, August). What is youth coming to? *WSCADD Newsletter.* (Available from the Washington State Council on Alcoholism and Drug Dependence)

Basil, M. D. (1993, May). *Targeting: Ethnic match and production quality effects on the evaluation of drug abuse messages.* Paper presented at the 1993 International Communication Conference, Washington, D.C.

Baumrind, D. (1985). Familial antecedents of adolescent drug use: A developmental perspective. In C. L. Jones & R. J. Battjes (Eds.), *Etiology of drug abuse: Implications for prevention* (NIDA Research Monograph 56, pp. 13-44). Washington, DC: Government Printing Office.

Berrueta-Clement, J. R., Schweinhart, L. J., Barnett, W. S., & Weikhard, D. P. (1983). *The effects of early education intervention on crime and delinquency in adolescence and early adulthood.* Ypsilanti, MI: Center for the Study of Public Policies for Young Children.

Billings, J. A., Burton, W., Mertens, B., & Strong, C. R. (1993). *Substance use among public school students in Washington state.* Olympia, WA: Superintendent of Public Instruction.

Blosser, B. J., & Roberts, D. F. (1985). Age differences in children's perceptions of message intent: Responses to TV news, commercials, educational spots, and public service announcements. *Communication Research, 12,* 455-484.

Botvin, G. J. (1990). Substance abuse prevention: Theory, practice, and effectiveness. In M. Tonry & J. Q. Wilson (Eds.), *Drugs and crime* (pp. 461-520). Chicago: University of Chicago Press.

Burke, R. J., & Weir, T. (1978). Benefits to adolescents of informal helping relationships with parents and peers. *Psychology Reports, 42,* 1175-1184.

Burke, R. J., & Weir, T. (1979). Helping responses of parents and peers and adolescent well-being. *Journal of Psychology, 102,* 49-62.

Bush, P. J., & Ianotti, R. (1985). The development of children's health orientations and behaviors: Lessons for substance abuse prevention. In C. L. Jones & R. J. Battjes (Eds.), *Etiology of drug abuse: Implications for prevention* (NIDA Research Monograph 56, pp. 45-74). Rockville, MD: National Institute on Drug Abuse.

Calvert, S. L., & Gersh, T. L. (1987). The selective use of sound effects and visual inserts for children's television story comprehension. *Journal of Applied Developmental Psychology, 8,* 363-375.

Campbell, T., Wright, J., & Huston, A. (in press). Form cues and content difficulty as determinants of children's cognitive processing of televised educational messages. *Journal of Experimental Child Psychology.*

Chaffee, S. H. (1982). Mass media and interpersonal channels: Competitive, convergent, or complementary? In J. Gumpert & R. Cathcart (Eds.), *Inter/media* (pp. 57-75). New York: Oxford University Press.

Chandler, M. J., Greenspan, S., & Barenboim, D. (1973). Judgements of intentionality in response to videotaped and verbally presented moral dilemmas: The medium is the message. *Child Development, 44,* 315-320.

Christenson, P., DeBenedittis, P., & Lindloff, T. (1985). Children's use of audio media. *Communication Research, 12,* 327-343.

Christenson, P. G., & Roberts, D. F. (1990). *Popular music in early adolescence.* Washington, DC: Carnegie Council on Adolescent Development.

Christiansen, B. A., & Goldman, M. S. (1983). Alcohol related expectancies vs. demographic/ background variables in the prediction of adolescent drinking. *Journal of Consulting and Clinical Psychology, 51,* 249-257.

Christiansen, B. A., Goldman, M. S., & Inn, A. (1982). The development of alcohol-related expectancies in adolescents: Separating pharmacological from social learning influences. *Journal of Consulting and Clinical Psychology, 50,* 336-344.

Clasen, D. R., & Brown, B. B. (1985). The multidimensionality of peer pressure in adolescence. *Journal of Youth and Adolescence, 14,* 451-468.

Collins, W. A. (1975). The developing child as viewer. *Journal of Communication, 25,* 35-44.

Collins, W. A. (1981). Schemata for understanding television. In H. Kelly & H. Gardner (Eds.), *Viewing children through television* (pp. 31-45). San Francisco: Jossey-Bass.

Collins, W. A. (1982). Cognitive processing in television viewing. In D. Pearl, L. Bouthilet, & J. Lazar (Ed.), *Television and behavior: Ten years of scientific progress and implications for the eighties* (pp. 9-23). Washington, DC: Government Printing Office.

Collins, W. A. (1983a). Interpretation and inference in children's television viewing. In J. Bryant & D. R. Anderson (Eds.), *Children's understanding of television: Research on attention and comprehension* (pp. 125-150). New York: Academic Press.

Collins, W. A. (1983b). Social antecedents, cognitive processing, and comprehension of social portrayals on television. In E. T. Higgings, D. N. Ruble, & W. W. Hartup (Eds.), *Social cognition and social development: A sociocultural perspective* (pp. 110-133). New York: Cambridge University Press.

Collins, W., & Wellman, H. (1982). Social scripts and developmental changes in representations of televised narratives. *Communication Research, 9,* 380-398.

Conroy, M. (1988, May). Is your child an alcoholic? *Better Homes and Gardens,* p. 72.

Corder-Bolz, C. R. (1980). Mediation: The role of significant others. *Journal of Communication,* (Summer), 106-118.

Cullingsford, C. (1984). *Children and television.* England: Gower.

DeFleur, M. L., & Ball-Rokeach, S. (1982). *Theories of mass communication* (4th ed.). New York: David McKay.

Desmond, R. J., Singer, J. L., & Singer, D. G. (1990). Family mediation: Parental communication patterns and the influences of television on children. In J. Bryant (Ed.), *Television and the American family* (pp. 293-310). Hillsdale, NJ: Lawrence Erlbaum.

DiFranza, J. R., & McAfee, T. (1992). The tobacco institute: Helping youth say "yes" to tobacco. *Journal of Family Practice, 34,* 694-696.

Donohew, L. (1988). *Effects of drug abuse message styles: Final report* [A report of a study conducted under a grant from the National Institute on Drug Abuse, Rockville, MD].

Donohew, L., Lorch, E., & Palmgreen, P. (1993). Sensation seeking and targeting of televised anti-drug PSAs. In L. Donohew, W. J. Bukoski, & H. E. Sypher (Eds.), *Persuasive communication and drug abuse prevention* (pp. 209-226). Hillsdale, NJ: Lawrence Erlbaum.

Dorr, A. (1980). When I was a child, I thought as a child. In S. Withey & R. Abeles (Eds.), *Television and social behavior: Beyond violence and children.* Hillsdale, NJ: Lawrence Erlbaum.

Dorr, A. (1983). No shortcuts to judging reality. In J. Bryant & D. Anderson (Eds.), *Children's understanding of television: Research on attention and comprehension.* New York: Academic Press.

Dryfoos, J. G. (1990). *Adolescents at risk: Prevalence and prevention.* New York: Oxford University Press.

Elliott, J. (1993). Just say nonsense. *The Washington Monthly, 25,* 18-21.

Ezekoye, S., Kumpfer, L., & Bukoski, W. (1985). *Children and chemical abuse: Prevention and intervention.* New York: Hawthorn Press.

Fagin, J., & Sauer, R. (1990). *Evaluation report: Project healthy choices.* New York: Special Consulting Services.

Falco, M. (1992). *The making of a drug-free America: Programs that work.* New York: Times Books.

Fischhoff, B. (1993). Decisions about alcohol: Prevention, intervention and policy. *Alcohol Health & Research World, 16,* 257-266.

Flavell, J. H., Miller, P. H., & Miller, S. A. (1993). *Cognitive development* (3rd ed.). Englewood Cliffs, NJ: Prentice Hall.

Free, C. (1993, July 14). All-night kegger may help save teenager's lives. *Spokesman Review,* p. B1.

Gelman, R., & Brown, A. L. (1986). Changing views of cognitive competence in the young. In N. J. Smelser & D. R. Gerstei (Ed.), *Behavioral and social science: Fifty years of discovery* (pp. 175-207). Washington, DC: National Academy Press.

Gerbner, G., Gross, L., Morgan, M., & Signorielli, N. (1986). Living with television: The dynamics of the cultivation process. In J. Byrant & D. Zillmann (Eds.), *Perspectives on media effects* (pp. 17-40). Hillsdale, NJ: Lawrence Erlbaum.

Gibbons, J., Anderson, D. R., Smith, R., Field, D. E., & Fischer, C. (1986). Young children's recall and reconstruction of audio and audiovisual narratives. *Child Development, 57,* 1014-1023.

Gitlin, T. (1989). On drugs and mass media in America's consumer society. In H. Resnik (Ed.), *Youth and drugs: Society's mixed messages* (OSAP Prevention Monograph 6, pp. 31-52). Rockville, MD: U.S. Department of Health and Human Services.

Glynn, T. J. (1981). From family to peer: Transitions of influence among drug-using youth. In D. J. Lehiehi & J. P. Ludford (Ed.), *Drug abuse and the American adolescent* (NIDA Research Monograph 38, pp. 57-81). Washington, DC: Government Printing Office.

Glynn, K., Leventhal, H., & Hirschman, R. (1985). A cognitive developmental approach to smoking prevention. In C. S. Bell & R. Battjes (Eds.), *Prevention research: Deterring drug abuse among children and adolescents* (NIDA Research Monograph 63, pp. 130-152). Rockville, MD: U.S. Department of Health and Human Services.

Goldman, M., Brown, S., & Christiansen, B. (1987). Expectancy theory: Thinking about drinking. In H. Blane & D. Leonard (Eds.), *Psychological theories of drinking and alcoholism* (pp. 181-220). New York: Guilford.

Goodstadt, M. S., & Mitchell, E. (1990). Prevention theory and research related to high-risk youth. In E. N. Goplerud (Ed.), *Breaking new ground for youth at risk: Program summaries* (pp. 7-23) (Tech. Rep. 1). Washington, DC: Office of Substance Abuse Prevention.

Gordon, N., & McAlister, A. (1982). Factors related to the onset of drinking and problem drinking. In T. J. Coates, A. C. Petersen, & C. Perry (Eds.), *Promoting adolescent health: A dialog on research and practice.* New York: Academic Press.

Greenberg, B. S. (1974). Gratifications of television viewing and their correlates for British children. In J. Blumer & E. Katz (Eds.), *Annual review of communication research* (Vol. 3). Beverly Hills, CA: Sage.

Greenberg, M. T., Siegel, J. M., & Leitch, C. J. (1983). The nature and importance of attachment relationships to parents and peers during adolescence. *Journal of Youth and Adolescence, 12,* 373-386.

Grube, J. W. (1993). Alcohol portrayals and alcohol advertising on television: Content and effects on children and adolescents. *Alcohol Health & Research World, 17,* 61-66.

Hawkins, J. D., Lishner, D., & Catalano, R.F.J. (1985). The development of children's health orientations and behaviors: Lessons for substance use prevention. In C. L. Battjes & R. J. Jones (Eds.), *Etiology of drug abuse: Implications for prevention* (NIDA Research Monograph 56, pp. 75-126). Washington, DC: Government Printing Office.

Hawkins, R., & Pingree, S. (1982). *Television's influence on social reality. Television and behavior: Ten years of scientific progress and implications for the eighties* (Technical Reviews 2). Rockville, MD: National Institute of Mental Health.

Hearold, S. (1986). A synthesis of 1043 effects of television on social behavior. In G. Comstock (Ed.), *Public communications and behavior* (Vol. 1, pp. 65-133). New York: Academic Press.

Heath, R. L., & Bryant, J. (1992). *Human communication theory and research: Concepts, contexts and challenges.* Hillsdale, NJ: Lawrence Erlbaum.

Higgins, E. T., & Parsons, J. E. (1983). Social cognition and the social life of the child: Stages as subcultures. In E. T. Higgins, D. N. Ruble, & W. W. Hartup (Eds.), *Social cognition and social development: A socio-cultural perspective* (pp. 15-61). Cambridge: Cambridge University Press.

Hollenbeck, A., & Slaby, R. (1979). Infant visual and vocal responses to television. *Child Development, 50,* 41-45.

Huesman, L. R., Eron, L. D., Klein, R., Brice, P., & Fischer, P. (1983). Mitigating the imitation of aggressive behaviors by changing children's attitudes about media violence. *Journal of Personality and Social Psychology, 44*(5), 899-910.

Hunter, F. T. (1985). Adolescents' perception of discussions with parents and friends. *Developmental Psychology, 21,* 443-440.

Hurst-Palermo, K. (1992, February). *Speech communication at LeMoore High School.* Paper presented at the annual meeting of the Western Speech Communication Association, Boise, ID.

Jahoda, G., & Cramond, J. (1972). *Children and alcohol.* London: HMSO.

Jeffrey, D. B., McLellarn, R. W., & Fox, D. T. (1982). The development of children's eating habits: The role of television commercials. *Health Education Quarterly, 9,* 78-93.

Jessor, R. (1982). Critical issues in research on adolescent health promotion. In T. J. Coates, A. C. Perry, & C. L. Peterson (Ed.), *Promoting adolescent health: A dialog on research and practice* (pp. 447-465). New York: Academic Press.

Jessor, R., & Jessor, S. L. (1975). Adolescent development and the onset of drinking: A longitudinal study. *Journal of Studies on Alcohol, 36,* 27-51.

Johnson, C. A., Pentz, M. A., & Weber, M. (1990). Relative effectiveness of comprehensive community programming for drug abuse prevention with high-risk adolescents. *Journal of Consulting and Clinical Psychology, 58,* 447-456.

Johnston, L. D., O'Malley, P. O., & Bachman, J. G. (1991). *Drug use among American high school seniors, college students, and young adults, 1975-1990.* Rockville, MD: National Institute on Drug Abuse.

Kandel, D. B., & Logan, J. A. (1984). Patterns of drug use from adolescence to young adulthood-I. Periods of risk for initiation, stabilization and decline in use. *American Journal of Public Health, 74,* 660-666.

Kandel, D., Kessler, R. C., & Margulies, R. Z. (1978). Adolescent initiation into stages of drug use: A developmental analysis. In D. Kandel (Ed.), *Longitudinal research on drug use: Empirical findings and methodological issues* (pp. 73-99). New York: John Wiley.

Kandel, D. B., & Yamaguchi, K. (1985). Developmental patterns of the use of legal, illegal and medically prescribed psychotropic drugs from adolescence to young adulthood. In C. L. Jones & R. J. Battjes (Eds.), *Etiology of drug abuse: Implications for prevention* (NIDA Research Monograph 56, pp. 193-235). Washington, DC: Government Printing Office.

Kassebaum, P. (1990). Reaching families and youth from high-risk environments. In E. B. Arkin & J. E. Funkhouser (Eds.), *Communicating about alcohol and other drugs: Strategies for reaching populations at risk* (OSAP Prevention Monograph 5, pp. 11-120). Rockville, MD: Office of Substance Abuse Prevention.

Kellam, S., & Brown, H. (1982). *Social adaptational and psychological antecedents of adolescent psychopathology ten years later.* Baltimore, MD: Johns Hopkins University Press.

Kohlberg, L. (1976). Moral stages and moralization: The cognitive-developmental approach. In T. Lickona (Ed.), *Moral development and behavior: Theory, research and social issues* (pp. 31-53). New York: Holt, Rinehart & Winston.

Kumpfer, K. L. (1986). Special populations: Etiology and prevention of vulnerability to chemical dependency in children of substance abusers. In B. S. Brown & A. R. Mills (Eds.), *Youth at high risk for substance abuse* (pp. 1-72). Rockville, MD: National Institute on Drug Abuse.

Kumpfer, K. L., & DeMarsh, J. P. (1984). Genetic and family environmental influences on children's future chemical dependency. *Journal of Children in Contemporary Society, 3,* 117-151.

Kutner, L. (1991, December 19). Holiday drinking opens adolescents' eyes to alcohol. *The New York Times,* p. C9. (Available from National Council on Alcoholism and Drug Dependence)

Liss, M. B., Reinhardt, L. C., & Fredriksen, S. (1983). TV heroes: The impact of rhetoric and deeds. *Journal of Applied Developmental Psychology, 4,* 175-187.

Lull, J. (1985). On the communicative properties of music. *Communication Research, 12,* 363-372.

Lyle, J., & Hoffman, H. R. (1972). Children's use of television and other media. In E. A. Rubinstein, G. A. Murphey, & J. P. Comstock (Eds.), *Television and social behavior: Vol. 4. Television in day-to-day life: Patterns of use* (pp. 129-256). Washington, DC: Government Printing Office.

McAlister, A. (1981). Antismoking campaigns: Progress in developing effective communications. In R. E. Rice & W. J. Paisley (Eds.), *Public communication campaigns* (pp. 91-103). Beverly Hills, CA: Sage.

McCarthy, W. J. (1985). The cognitive developmental model and other alternatives to the social skills deficit model of smoking onset. In C. S. Bell & R. Battjes (Eds.), *Prevention research: Deterring drug abuse among children and adolescents* (NIDA Research Monograph 63, pp. 153-169). Rockville, MD: U.S. Department of Health and Human Services.

McGuire, W. J. (1989). Theoretical foundations of campaigns. In R. E. Rice & C. K. Atkin (Eds.), *Public communication campaigns* (pp. 43-65). Newbury Park, CA: Sage.

McLeod, J. M., & Chaffee, S. H. (1972). The construction of social reality. In J. Tedeschi (Ed.), *The social influence process* (pp. 50-59). Chicago: Aldine-Atherton.

Meringoff, L. K. (1980). Influence of the medium on children's story apprehension. *Journal of Educational Psychology, 72,* 240-249.

Miller, M. M., & Reese, S. D. (1982). Media dependency as interaction: Effects of exposure and reliance on political activity and efficacy. *Communication Research, 9,* 227-248.

Miller, P. M., Smith, G. T., & Goldman, M. S. (1989). Emergence of alcohol expectancies in childhood: A possible critical period. *Journal of Studies on Alcohol, 51,* 343-349.

Murray D. M., & Perry, C. L. (1985). The prevention of adolescent drug abuse: Implications of etiological, developmental, behavioral, and environmental models. In C. R. Jones & R. J. Battjes (Eds.), *Etiology of drug abuse: Implications for prevention* (NIDA Research Monograph 56, pp. 236-256). Washington, DC: Government Printing Office.

Newcomb, A., & Collins, W. A. (1979). Children's comprehension of family role portrayals in televised drama: Effects of socioeconomic status, ethnicity, and age. *Developmental Psychology, 15,* 417-423.

National Institute on Drug Abuse. (1988). *Highlights of a national adolescent school health survey on drug and alcohol use.* (Available from U.S. Department of Health and Human Services, Alcohol, Drug Abuse and Mental Health Administration, Rockville, MD)

Oetting, E. R., & Beauvais, K. L. (1988). Peer cluster theory, socialization characteristics, and adolescent drug use: A path analysis. *Journal of Counseling Psychology, 34,* 205-213.

Office for Substance Abuse Prevention. (1989). *Stopping alcohol and other drug use before it starts: The future of prevention* (OSAP Monograph 1). Rockville, MD: U.S. Department of Health and Human Services.

Palincsar, A. S., & Brown, A. L. (1984). Reciprocal teaching of comprehension-fostering and monitoring activities. *Cognition and Instruction, 1,* 117-175.

Palmgreen, P., Lorch, E. P., Donohew, L., Harrington, N. G., Dsilva, M., & Helm, D. (1993, May). *Reaching at-risk populations in a mass media drug abuse prevention campaign: Sensation seeking as a targeting variable.* Paper presented at the 1993 International Communication Association Annual Conference, Washington, DC.

Pentz, M. A., Dwyer, J. H., MacKinnon, D. P., Flay, B. R., Hansen, W. B., Wang, E.Y.I., & Johnson, C. A. (1989). A multi-community trial for primary prevention of adolescent drug abuse: Effects on drug use prevalence. *Journal of the American Medical Association, 261,* 3259-3266.

Pentz, M. A., Trebow, E. A., & Hansen, W. B. (1990). Effects of program implementation on adolescent drug use behavior: The Midwestern prevention project (MPP). *Evaluation Review, 14,* 264-289.

Perry, C., & Jessor, R. (1985). The concept of health promotion and the prevention of adolescent drug abuse. *Health Education Quarterly, 12,* 169-184.

Peterson, A. J., & Clark, A. W. (1986). Using group decision to reduce adolescent girls' smoking. *Psychological Reports, 58,* 179-185.

Pfau, M., & Van Bockern, S. (1993, May). *The persistence of inoculation in conferring resistance to smoking initiation among adolescents: The second year.* Paper presented at the annual meeting of the International Communication Association Annual Conference, Washington, DC.

PRIDE, I. (1992). *High school student drug use rose in '91 for most drugs; in junior high usage climbed in all drug types* (1991-1992 National Summary Report 4-6). Atlanta, GA: Parents' Resource Institute for Drug Education.

Reeves, B. (1978). Perceived reality as a predictor of children's social behavior. *Journalism Quarterly, 55,* 682-689, 695.

Reeves, B., & Garramone, G. (1982). Children's person perception: The generalization from television people to real people. *Human Communication Research, 8,* 317-326.

Roberts, D. (1971). The nature of communication effects. In W. Schramm & D. F. Roberts (Eds.), *The process and effects of mass communication* (2nd ed.). Urbana: University of Illinois Press.

Roberts, D. F. (1973). Communication and children: A developmental approach. In I. deSola Pool, W. Schramm et al. (Eds.), *Handbook of communication* (pp. 174-215). Chicago: Rand McNally.

Roberts, D. (1989). The impact of media portrayals of risky driving on adolescents: Some speculation. *Alcohol, Drugs and Driving, 4,* 13-20.

Roberts, D. F., Christenson, P., Gibson, W. A., Mooser, L., & Goldberg, M. E. (1980). Developing discriminating consumers. *Journal of Communication, 30,* 94-105.

Robins, L. N., & Pryzbeck, T. R. (1985). Age of onset of drug use as a factor in drug and other disorders. In C. L. Jones & R. J. Battjes (Eds.), *Etiology of drug abuse: Implications for prevention* (NIDA Research Monograph 56, pp. 178-192). Washington, DC: Government Printing Office.

Rock Against Drugs. (1988). *Rock Against Drugs (RAD) foundation kicks-off 1988 public service campaign with mini-video by Siedah Garrett* [Press Release, January 26, as reported in

Christenson, P. G., & Roberts, D. F. (1990). *Popular music in early adolescence.* Washington, DC: Carnegie Council on Adolescent Development].

Roe, K. (1985). Swedish youth and music: Listening patterns and motivations. *Communication Research, 12,* 353-362.

Rosengren, K. E., & Windahl, S. (1972). Mass media as a functional alternative. In D. McQuail (Ed.), *Sociology of mass communications* (pp. 166-194). Middlesex, England: Penguin.

Sadowski, R. P. (1972). Immediate recall of TV commercial elements—revisited. *Journal of Broadcasting, 16,* 277-287.

Salomon, G. (1981). Introducing AIME: The assessment of children's mental involvement with television. In H. Kelly & H. Gardner (Eds.), *Viewing children through television* (pp. 89-102). San Francisco: Jossey-Bass.

Schoenbachler, D. (1993, May). *The effectiveness of varying levels of physically and socially threatening fear appeals in anti-drug public service announcements.* Paper presented at the 1993 International Communication Association, Washington, D.C.

Schramm, W. (1965). Communication in crisis. In W. Schramm & E. B. Parker (Eds.), *The Kennedy assassination and the American public: Social communication in crisis.* Stanford, CA: Stanford University Press.

Silverman, L. T., & Sprafkin, J. N. (1980). The effects of Sesame Street's prosocial spots on cooperative play between young children. *Journal of Broadcasting, 24,* 135-147.

Singer, D. G., Zuckerman, D. M., & Singer, J. L. (1980). Helping elementary school children learn about TV. *Journal of Communication, 30*(3), 84-93.

Singer, J. L. (1980). The power and limitations of television: A cognitive-affective analysis. In P. H. Tannenbaum (Ed.), *The entertainment functions of television* (pp. 31-65). Hillsdale, NJ: Lawrence Erlbaum.

Singhal, A., & Rogers, R. (1989). Prosocial television for development in India. In R. Rice & C. Atkin (Eds.), *Public communication campaigns* (pp. 331-350). Newbury Park, CA: Sage.

Solutions: Six schools that got it right. (1993, September). *Parenting,* pp. 80-85.

Spiegler, D. (1983). Children's attitudes toward alcohol. *Journal of Studies on Alcohol, 44,* 545-552.

Spivak, G., & Shure, M. B. (1982). The cognition of social adjustment: Interpersonal cognitive problem-solving thinking. In B. B. Lahly & A. E. Kazdin (Eds.), *Advances in child psychology.* New York: Plenum.

Steele, C. (1989). *Early beginnings. An early years substance abuse prevention curriculum for infants, toddlers ' n twos.* Rensselaer County [New York] Department of Mental Health.

Steinberg, L. (1986). Latchkey children and susceptibility to peer pressure: An ecological analysis. *Developmental Psychology, 22,* 433-439.

Steinberg, L., & Silverberg, S. (1986). The vicissitudes of autonomy in early adolescents. *Child Development, 57,* 841-851.

Teens Are Concerned. (1989). Teens are concerned. In *Prevention plus II: Tools for creating and sustaining drug-free communities* (pp. 256-257). Rockville, MD: Office for Substance Abuse Prevention.

Tobler, N. (1986). Meta-analysis of 143 adolescent drug prevention programs: Quantitative outcome results of program participants compared to a control or comparison group. *Journal of Drug Issues, 16,* 537-67.

Tortu, S. (1990). *The utility of drug research.* Paper presented at Narcotic & Drug Research, Inc., New York.

Van der Voort, T.H.A. (1986). *Television violence: A child's eye view.* Amsterdam: North-Holland.

Vogt, K., Lieberman, L. R., Iverson, D., & Walter, H. (1983). *What it means to be healthy: Concepts and constructs of children ages 6-8.* Paper presented at the annual meeting of the American Public Health Association, Dallas, TX.

Wallack, L. (1986). Mass media, youth and the prevention of substance abuse: Towards an integrated approach. In *Childhood and chemical abuse* (pp. 153-180). New York: Haworth.

Wallack, L., Cassady, D., & Grube, J. (1990). *TV beer commercials and children: Exposure, attention, beliefs and expectations about drinking as an adult.* Washington, DC: AAA Foundation for Traffic Safety.

Wallack, L., & Corbett, K. (1990). Illicit drug, tobacco, and alcohol use among youth: Trends and promising approaches in prevention. In H. Resnik (Ed.), *Youth and drugs: Society's mixed messages* (OSAP Prevention Monograph 6, pp. 5-29). Rockville, MD: U.S. Department of Health and Human Services.

Ward, S., & Wackman, D. B. (1973). Children's information processing of television advertising. In P. Clarke (Ed.), *New models for mass communication research* (pp. 119-146). Beverly Hills, CA: Sage.

Ward, S., Wackman, D., & Wartella, E. (1977). *How children learn to buy: The development of consumer information-processing skills.* Beverly Hills, CA: Sage.

Washington State Association of Broadcasters. (1990). *Community outreach handbook: Tough choices: Tackling the teen alcohol problem.* Olympia: Washington State Association of Broadcasters, Alcohol Task Force.

Watkins, B., Calvert, S., Huston-Stein, A., & Wright, J. C. (1980). Children's recall of television material: Effects of presentation mode and adult labeling. *Developmental Psychology, 16,* 672-679.

Winick, M. P., & Winick, C. (1979). *The television experience: What children see.* Beverly Hills, CA: Sage.

Worth, S., & Gross, L. L. (1974). Symbolic strategies. *Journal of Communication, 24,* 27-39.

Wright, J. C., Huston, A. C., Ross, R. P., Calvert, S. L., Rolandelli, D., Weeks, L. A., Raeissi, P., & Potts, R. (1984). Pace and continuity of television programs: Effects on children's attention and comprehension. *Developmental Psychology, 20,* 653-666.

Wright, J. C., & Huston, A. C. (1981). Children's understanding of the forms of television. In H. Kelly & H. Gardner (Eds.), *Viewing children through television* (pp. 73-88). San Francisco: Jossey-Bass.

Yamaguchi, K., & Kandel, D. B. (1984). Patterns of drug use from adolescence to young adulthood. *American Journal of Public Health, 74,* 668-681.

Young, B. M. (1990). *Television advertising and children.* Oxford: Clarendon Press.

Zucker, R. A. (1979). Developmental aspects of drinking through the young adult years. In H. T. Blane & M. E. Chafetz (Eds.), *Youth, alcohol and social policy* (pp. 91-140). New York: Plenum.

Appendix  Reasonable Generalizations About Developmental Considerations in Campaign Design and Message Understanding

| | Preschool 0-5 | Early School Age 5-7 | Middle Childhood 7-10 | Early Adolescence 10-13 | Mid-Adolescence 13-16 | Late Adolescence 16+ |
|---|---|---|---|---|---|---|
| Factors placing them at risk | Deprived environment... Family problems... | Under-achievement... Antisocial behavior... | Low expectations... Substance use Low resistance to peers | Enormous uncertainty | Drop out of school More difficult to reach | |
| | | | Risk factors well entrenched... | | | |
| Orientations to health | Awareness, Imitation | Attitudes established; still in flux, know social norms | Attitudes still developing May experiment | Experimentation... | Much experimentation... Habitual use... | Gender differences in place |
| Most credible info sources | All are credible | | Peers, older role models, TV, parents | School, family, peers | 1-800 numbers Everyday role models | |
| Directly influenced by | Parents, significant caregivers | | Parents, peers | Elite peers, parental influence declining | Peers for present-oriented topics... Parents for support, future-oriented topics... | |
| Motivated by | Tangible rewards from others Avoid punishment | Rewards, moral labels Conventional rules | Social norms Need for acceptance Parental authority no longer automatic | Physical attractiveness Social power | Beyond simple rewards and punishments, reject explicit adult authority Strive for social rewards Avoid social threats Boredom, need for excitement, Idealism | Inner conscience still developing |
| Appropriate strategies | Parent & teacher training... | Cognitive and social skills... | Stress reduction training | Emphasize facts moderation... | Don't overreact, avoid preaching, avoid | Provide alternatives to risk taking |

| | | | | | |
|---|---|---|---|---|---|
| **Tactics** | Basic cognitive and problem-solving skills / How to get help / Game playing, puppets, songs, stories | Hands-on activities / Media literacy... / Decision-making skills... / Informal classroom instruction... | Teach facts, norms, consequences | Involve them in planning / Role playing, class presentation, guest speakers / Frequency... / Interactive media... | heterosexism... / Emphasize community support / Mass media as catalyst... / Peer workshops... / Novelty, drama / Guest speakers |
| **Type of media to gain access** | | Kids' TV / Programs parents watch | TV, radio | Radio & TV / Magazines (esp. *Seventeen, Teen, Sports Illustrated*)... | Radio more than TV... / Posters / Billboards / Street theater / Microcable / Soaps, MTV |
| **Why think programs broadcast** | To entertain and inform... | | | To manipulate: skeptical of news, PSAs | To make money... |
| **Understanding of advertising** | May confuse ads & programs / Separators help / Visual & sound effects such as animation, songs, puppets / Immediacy / Simplicity | Can ID an ad / Know ads sell | Understand intent behind ads | Skeptical but still respond... | |
| **Especially pay attention to** | Labels help / Can get short & direct messages / Redundancy helps / Consistency between visual | | More complexity in production... / Real characters | Relevance, importance | Production values still important... |
| **Understanding of messages** | | Visual presentations help | Understand symbols, metaphors, irony, sarcasm... / Can handle longer programs / Can handle more | | Adults levels of comprehension / Still interpret lyrics in myriad ways |

(continued)

Appendix  Continued

| | Preschool 0-5 | Early School Age 5-7 | Middle Childhood 7-10 | Early Adolescence 10-13 | Mid-Adolescence 13-16 | Late Adolescence 16+ |
|---|---|---|---|---|---|---|
| | and audio important | | complexity . . . Order of plot elements matters | | | |
| Inferential abilities | Learning conventions Respond to OVERT behavior, appearances, can miss the intended point | Understand surface meaning, may rely on stereotypes Notice consequences more than motivations Can take another's perspective with help | Interest in motives, internal responses; Make associations, may lack logical connections | Very interested in motives, good at understanding perspective and intent, can infer missing content | | |
| Skepticism toward messages | Characters are real, animation is fantasy | Portrayal is possible? More skeptical if familiar | TV is made up Use more content cues to analyze | Portrayal is probable or representative? | | |
| Integration of message elements | Can do one thing at a time Can handle a few visual effects | | Retain more information Recall more incidental information Interruptions in plot sequence still hurt understanding | Better at sorting central and incidental information | | |

NOTES: Adapted, updated, and extended from Dorr, 1980.
Age differences are merely estimates—many children will be ahead of or behind these estimates on various characteristics.
. . . Indicates characteristics relevant well past the age initially labeled.

# 8 Fishing for Success

## USING THE PERSUASIVE HEALTH MESSAGE
## FRAMEWORK TO GENERATE EFFECTIVE
## CAMPAIGN MESSAGES

### KIM WITTE

> *Give a person a fish, and he will eat supper.*
> *Teach a person to fish, and he will eat for a lifetime.*
> —Chinese Proverb

Bridging the gap between theory and practice is an increasingly important but elusive goal. One impediment to the use of theory by practitioners is that theories appear formidable and difficult to use. Indeed, some theories are so complex as to prevent their use in practical settings. In addition, the sheer number of available theories is confusing in and of itself. Many practitioners see theories as ivory-tower creations with little relevance to the real world. However, theories have the capacity to simplify and systematize the development of health education interventions. In fact, they can make the development of a health campaign easier and less time-consuming than a campaign that starts from scratch without any guiding principles. But, how does one keep all of the theories straight? How does one choose a single theory from the array of available options? Which is the most appropriate theory for a given health problem? Unfortunately, no single theory can explain everything.

AUTHOR'S NOTE: Kim Witte (Ph.D., University of California, Irvine) is Assistant Professor at Michigan State University. Kelly Morrison and Steve Robbins are gratefully acknowledged for their helpful comments on an earlier draft of this chapter, and Michael Stephenson and Melissa Becktold are thanked for developing some of the campaign messages presented in this chapter.

Theories provide explanations for limited, finite phenomena. In light of these perceived complexities, it is little wonder that practitioners throw up their hands in frustration when faced with a multitude of theories, each relevant only to limited situations.

One way to cut confusion surrounding the selection of a theory for a campaign is to combine *parts* of successful and well-tested theories into a single framework. A framework differs from a theory in that it does not attempt to explain human behavior, it simply outlines what one should do to develop the most effective and persuasive campaign possible. A framework pools the best available knowledge about a multitude of factors into a simple guide for campaign development. That is what the framework outlined here attempts to do. It takes the best of three prominent persuasion theories, combines them, and outlines step-by-step procedures for developing an effective health education program. This chapter presents a "cookbook" for busy practitioners desiring to develop theory-based campaigns that work. First, the framework will be outlined (see Witte [1992a] for full rationale and explication), then two examples will be given to illustrate how to use the framework. The goal of outlining this theoretical framework is analogous to teaching someone to fish—the framework can be used over and over as a guide to developing health campaigns.

## The Persuasive Health
## Message (PHM) Framework

Researchers and practitioners alike have argued that messages must be culturally, demographically, and geographically appropriate if they are to influence the audience as intended (Atkin & Freimuth, 1989; Fishbein & Ajzen, 1981; Flora & Thoreson, 1988). The Persuasive Health Message (PHM) Framework, comprised of elements from the theory of reasoned action (Fishbein & Ajzen, 1975), the elaboration likelihood model (Petty & Cacioppo, 1986), and protection motivation theory (Rogers, 1983), offers an integrated approach to generating effective campaigns.

In brief, the PHM framework states that two separate factors, the *constant* and the *transient* factors, must be addressed prior to the development of campaign messages (see Figure 8.1). The content and features of a persuasive message are structured by the constant components of the framework. For example, a persuasive health message should contain a *threat* message, an *efficacy* message, various *cues,* and should be targeted toward a specific audience—regardless of the topic, type of message, or environment. The threat portion of the message tries to make the audience feel *susceptible* to a *severe* threat. The efficacy portion of the message tries to convince individuals they are *able* to perform the recommended response (i.e., self-efficacy) and that the recommended response *effectively* averts the threat (i.e., response efficacy). The available evidence from fear appeal research suggests that when individuals perceive high levels of threat (e.g., "I'm at risk for developing skin cancer and could die from it") *and* high levels of efficacy (e.g., "But if I wear sunscreen and get my doctor to perform skin examinations I can prevent serious harm and perhaps prevent the disease"), then they are motivated to protect themselves against the threat (Witte, 1992b, 1992c). Thus, to motivate audiences into action, a persuasive health message should convince individuals (a) they are susceptible to a severe threat and that (b) adopting an easy and feasible recommended response would effectively avert the threat. Recent theoretical and empirical work on fear appeals offers important caveats to keep in mind when designing threatening or fear-arousing persuasive health messages. Specifically, perceptions of threat must be sufficiently balanced by strong response and self-efficacy perceptions. That is, the recommended response must be perceived by the audience as efficacious enough to eliminate or substantially reduce the threat before individuals will change their behaviors (Rogers, 1975, 1983; Witte, 1992b, 1992c). If a threat is perceived as too high, such that individuals believe no response would effectively deter it, the message will backfire. For instance, when perceived threat is high and perceived efficacy is *low* (e.g., "Skin cancer is unavoidable; I can't do anything that'll prevent it"), people become frightened and defensive motivation is elicited, resulting in maladaptive responses such as denial or defensive avoidance (Witte, 1992b, 1992c). Fear appeals can thus be effective persuasive messages, but only when *both* threat and efficacy are high.

The *cues* constant component refers to those variables that can influence the persuasive process in an indirect manner. For example, a person may accept a persuasive message simply because it was delivered by a high credibility person, not because she or he believed the arguments. Thus, people can be persuaded by peripheral cues such as credibility or attractiveness of the source or by the arguments or content of a message (Petty & Cacioppo, 1986). When people are persuaded by peripheral cues, they are said to have processed the message peripherally. That is, they have not thoughtfully considered the arguments in the message and have used cues to guide their decisions. People process a message peripherally when they have little interest, ability, and/or motivation to evaluate the message. For example, messages persuade people via the peripheral route by providing

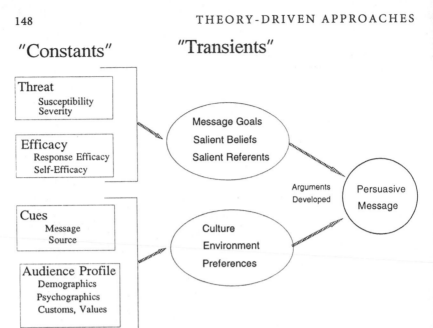

**Figure 8.1.** A Framework for Developing Culturally Specific Persuasive Health Messages

simple associations or heuristics (e.g., "If my doctor uses Bayer aspirin, then I should, too"). In contrast, when people believe a topic to be relevant to them and important, they process the message centrally by carefully listening to and evaluating the content of the message (Petty & Cacioppo, 1986). Because processing a message via the central route takes much cognitive work, however (one has to think!), messages are processed centrally only when they are very important or relevant to a person.

Two variables act as cues—source and message variables. Variables related to the source of a message, such as credibility, attractiveness, similarity, or power, can have subtle but significant impacts on whether the audience takes the message seriously and is motivated to act (McGuire, 1984). Similarly, the manner in which a message is organized, the type of appeal given (i.e., emotional or logical), the number of repetitions in a message, the vividness of language used, and more, can all influence the persuasive process (McGuire, 1984). Although source and message variables can be thoughtfully considered in a central route manner, they are believed to act more often as variables that cue a person to accept a message, and thus tend to be processed peripherally.

The final constant component is the *audience profile*. The audience profile is an important constant component because it makes the message "fit" the audience. For example, demographic and psychographic information gathered about the audience, as well as cultural beliefs and values, make the message relevant and appropriate for the targeted audience. If a targeted audience speaks Vietnamese, has a low literacy level, and holds a collectivist worldview (i.e., family concerns placed above self-concerns), then a message should be in Vietnamese, easy to read or comprehend, and frame the recommended response in a manner that helps the family or group.

The parts of a message that change given different populations and message goals are the *transient* components of the PHM framework. Transient or changeable elements of a campaign—such as salient beliefs, salient referents, culture, environment, and message goals—determine the actual message content and features of the constant components. There are two categories of transient information to gather. First, information relevant to the threat and efficacy of the recommended response must be determined. The goals of the message must be clearly stated. What exactly is the threat and what exactly is the recommended response to avert or minimize harm from the threat? As well, salient beliefs about the threat and efficacy of the recommended response need to be determined. Finally, salient referents and salient referents' beliefs about the targeted audience member's risk of experiencing the threat, the severity of the threat, the efficacy of the recommended response in averting the threat, and the targeted audience member's ability to perform the recommended response, must be gathered. (The rationale for determining these beliefs is based on the theory of reasoned action and is explained below.)

The second category of transient information—culture/environment and preferences—is used to develop cues and the audience profile. Source and message preferences will aid in the production of cues (e.g., Who do you want to hear about safer sex from?). The audience profile is developed from cultural (demographics, psychographics) and environmental (potential barriers, e.g., lack of services, lack of transportation) information. In addition, channel (e.g., radio, TV, newspaper) preferences should be determined to achieve maximum reach of the message (these are not cues per se, but they can be part of the audience profile).

To determine the transient information needed for the framework, an audience analysis needs to be conducted where information specified by the constant components is determined. Fishbein and Ajzen (1975, 1981) argue in their theory of reasoned action that the only way to effectively induce behavior change in a persuasive message is to change the underlying set of salient beliefs that are causing a specific behavior. (Salient beliefs are one's primary beliefs on a topic or issue.) For instance, if a farmer believes "I am invulnerable to skin cancer," "only city folk get the disease," "wearing a hat and a long-sleeved shirt makes me hot," "real men don't wear sunscreen," "there's nothing you can do to prevent skin cancer," and "I don't have time to go see a doctor," then changing only a single belief is unlikely to influence his overall skin cancer risk behavior because the other extant beliefs promote the same risky behavior. In addition to determining the target audience's salient beliefs about a health threat, the theory of reasoned action also suggests that salient referents be determined (e.g., individuals who influence how the farmer behaves), and beliefs about what the targeted audience thinks salient referents think about the advocated behavior change be assessed (e.g., "My wife thinks I should use sunscreen"). For example, the theory of reasoned action's subjective norm component is comprised of (a) what the targeted individual thinks salient referents think about the targeted individual performing Behavior X, and (b) the targeted individual's motivation to comply with the salient referent. Applying this concept of subjective norm to the PHM framework, it is important to determine what targeted individuals think salient referents believe about the health threat and recommended response (as well as finding out how motivated the targeted audience member is to comply with salient referents). For example, if targeted audience members are heavy smokers, salient referents will influence whether or not targeted audiences do in fact quit smoking. That is, if a significant other doesn't really think the targeted audience member is at risk for lung cancer (because he or she comes from good genetic stock), doesn't think lung cancer is severe (after all, we have two lungs), thinks it's too late to quit smoking anyway (the damage is done), and doesn't believe that the targeted audience member would actually be able to quit, then it is unlikely that the target audience members will quit.

In sum, to maximize the odds of achieving behavior change, (a) the *whole set* of salient beliefs toward an advocated behavior must be uncovered, and (b) salient beliefs that inhibit the behavior should be countered while salient beliefs that encourage the behavior should be supported (Fishbein & Ajzen, 1975, 1981). Once this transient information (i.e., salient beliefs and referents) for each of the constant components is determined, then the messages can be developed.

The integration of the "transient" information into the "constant" components of the framework serves an important function. First, the targeting of an audience's specific salient beliefs about the threat and efficacy of the recommended response increases involvement in and personal relevancy of the message. Increased involvement in a message leads to central processing of the message, which is desirable because it leads to lasting and stable attitude change (Petty & Cacioppo, 1986). If salient beliefs are targeted in the message then motivation and/or ability of audience members to process the message should increase because the message is relevant to them and they can understand it. Sometimes, however, audiences are simply too tired or preoccupied to process a message centrally, even though the integration of the transient salient beliefs should motivate them to care and to think about the health threat and recommended response. Thus, cues are important to an effective health campaign. As many of the cues (e.g., source credibility, source attractiveness, message form) as possible should be addressed in the persuasive mass media message, because people who are unable or unmotivated to process the health communication centrally can still be persuaded by appropriate cues via the peripheral route. Transient cultural, environmental, and demographic factors influence the selection of which cues to emphasize. In short, developing a persuasive health message according to this framework should enhance the likelihood of developing messages that influence both audience members who care about the topic and process the message centrally, and those who could care less about the topic and process the message peripherally.

## Using the PHM
## Framework to Develop Campaigns

Developing persuasive messages with the framework requires a three-step process. The first two steps involve determining transient information. As stated previously, first, information about the threat and efficacy of the recommended response must be determined. Second, cultural and environmental characteristics and preferences must be assessed to develop the audience profile and cues. In the third step, this transient information for each of the constant components is used to generate the persuasive message.

In Step 1, salient beliefs and salient referents must be determined and the precise campaign behavioral goal must be specified (i.e., the campaign goal is to prevent Threat X in Target Audience Y by promoting response and self-efficacy of recommended Response Z). Table 8.1 gives an example of how to determine specific goals with the case of AIDS prevention. Note that not only must the threat be specified (HIV transmission) but more importantly, the specific behavior (i.e., recommended response) that will be advocated to prevent or avert the threat (e.g., condom use). In any campaign the

TABLE 8.1 Message "Transients"

| | |
|---|---|
| **I. Message Goals** | |
| Overall | What is the threat to be prevented? |
| | → HIV infection |
| Behavior | How will this threat be prevented? |
| | → By advocating condom use |
| Population | Define target audience |
| | → Hispanic men, age 15-44 |
| **II. Salient Beliefs ("attitudes")** | |
| Susceptibility | "Will you contract the AIDS virus? Why or why not?" |
| Severity | "What will happen to you if you get the virus?" |
| Self-efficacy | "Can you use condoms to prevent HIV infection? Why or why not? Will you use condoms to prevent HIV infection? Why or why not? What are the advantages or disadvantages of using condoms?" |
| Response efficacy | "Do you think condoms prevent HIV infection? Why or why not?" |
| **Salient referents** ("**subjective norms**") | "Are there any people or groups important to you who would approve or disapprove of you using condoms to prevent pregnancy or HIV infection? Are there any people or groups important to you who would approve or disapprove of you using condoms to prevent HIV infection? Who are these people or groups?" |
| Susceptibility | "Do you think your (specific referent) thinks you are at risk for being infected with the AIDS virus? Why or why not?" |
| Severity | "What does (specific referent) think happens to people when they get infected with the AIDS virus?" |
| Self-efficacy | "Does (specific referent) think you can or should use condoms to prevent HIV infection? Why or why not? Does (specific referent) use condoms to prevent HIV infection? Why or why not? What does (specific referent) think are the advantages or disadvantages of using condoms?" |
| Response efficacy | "Does (specific referent) think condoms prevent HIV infection? Why or why not?" |

recommended response is the immediate goal or focus of the campaign (e.g., condom use), with the belief that the ultimate goal (e.g., AIDS prevention) can be achieved through adoption of this recommended response (i.e., prevent AIDS by advocating condom use). In addition to determining the campaign goals in Step 1, the target audience must be clearly identified.

There are two ways to determine salient beliefs and salient referents. Either existing research may be used or original research can be conducted. Table 8.1 shows the kinds of questions one would ask in original research, and Table 8.2 shows how existing published survey data can be used to

TABLE 8.1 Continued

| III. Culture/Environment Variables and Preferences | |
|---|---|
| Source | Who would you believe the most in an HIV/AIDS prevention message? Who do you want to hear talk about HIV/AIDS prevention? |
| Channel | Where do you prefer to get your information about HIV/AIDS prevention? |
| Message | Determine appropriate colloquialisms. Present the message in culturally appropriate manner (e.g., watch for embarrassment, respect privacy). |
| Receiver | Define target population according to demographic variables (e.g., socioeconomic status, literacy level, age, employment, residence, primary language, etc.). Survey target population for source, channel, and message type preferences, as well as for values (e.g., what are the key values this population holds), customs (e.g., any particular habits or customs?), and health beliefs (e.g., "Is it possible to carry a virus without being sick?"). |

determine salient beliefs with the example given of Hispanic men's salient beliefs toward AIDS and condoms. Salient beliefs about the threat, the efficacy of the recommended response, and beliefs about what the audience members think salient referents think about the threat and recommended response need to be determined. First, the target audience should be queried about their perceived susceptibility to the threat as well as the perceived severity of the threat (see Tables 8.1 and 8.2). Next, the target audience's salient beliefs about the effectiveness of the recommended response in averting the threat (i.e., response efficacy) and their perceived ability to use or not use the recommended response (i.e., self-efficacy and barriers to self-efficacy) need to be determined. Barriers to self-efficacy are important to determine because these act as obstacles to adoption of the recommended response. Thus, if a targeted audience member believes that condoms reduce pleasure and decrease virility, this belief acts as a barrier to his or her perceived ability to use condoms. Barriers thus decrease perceptions of self-efficacy. In the case of condoms and Hispanic men (Table 8.2), it appears that Hispanic men think that using condoms will reduce their virility and pleasure, as well as make them suspect for "loose" or dangerous behavior. It is therefore important to uncover these sensitive beliefs so that the persuasive campaign can address these issues directly. Third, salient referents must be solicited. The individuals or groups that have the most influence on the targeted audience with reference to the specified threat and the recommended response should be determined. For example, the audience should be asked whether "there are any people or groups important to you who would approve or disapprove of you using condoms to prevent AIDS?" (i.e., salient referents for the recommended response) as well as whether "there are any people or groups important to you who would approve or disapprove of you using condoms?" (i.e., salient referents for the threat). Notice that these questions may prompt different answers, so both are important. The targeted audience's beliefs about what salient referents think are important to uncover, too. In other words, a practitioner needs to ascertain what the target audience member believes his or her salient referent believes about the threat (both susceptibility and severity) and the recommended response (both response efficacy and self-efficacy) with reference to the target audience member (e.g., "My wife thinks I am at risk for contracting HIV"). Ideally, Ajzen and Fishbein's (1980, chap. 6) techniques for gathering salient beliefs and referents should be used. The Appendix to this chapter gives a prototype of a closed-ended questionnaire practitioners can use as well as an example of a questionnaire focusing on diabetes (the threat) prevention through a low-fat, low-sugar diet (the recommended response). Although a face-to-face or telephone interview may yield more in-depth information (Table 8.1), an anonymous survey or mail questionnaire (as outlined in the Appendix) may be a more efficient means to gather the information needed for the framework.

In Step 2, the audience profile is developed, and information for the cues is gathered. Demographic information available from census records and data from survey research can be used to create a profile. It is also useful to gather information directly from a sample of the targeted audience regarding their cultural values, perceived barriers, and health-related customs to flesh out the profile. Finally, channel, message, and source preferences must be determined from the target audience (e.g., "Who would you prefer to get AIDS prevention information from?").

In Step 3, the persuasive message is constructed. There are at least three types of arguments that can be made in the persuasive message. A message can try to change beliefs, reinforce existing beliefs, or introduce new beliefs (Burgoon, 1989; McGuire, 1985). It is far easier to introduce, reinforce, or build on existing beliefs in a campaign than it is to try to change existing and entrenched attitudes (Atkin, 1993). The best campaigns are those that are framed to fit within acceptable beliefs, attitudes, and behaviors (i.e., reinforcement). It is therefore helpful to frame the recommended response as already fitting within the target audience's current belief and behavioral system. Table 8.3 shows how the salient beliefs gathered from existing research about

TABLE 8.2  Message "Transients" for Targeted Population of Hispanic Men

| | |
|---|---|
| **I. Message Goals** | |
| Overall | To Prevent AIDS |
| Behavior | by Using Condoms |
| Population | Hispanic men, age 15-44 |
| **II. Salient Beliefs** | |
| Susceptibility | Perceive little susceptibility to AIDS (Navarro, 1989; Peterson & Marin, 1988). Do not think they engage in risky behaviors—even if they have unprotected anal intercourse with other men (Carrier, 1976; Marin, 1989; Peterson & Marin, 1988). |
| Severity | Perceived severity of AIDS is unknown. Hispanics in general know less about AIDS and its prevention than non-Hispanics (Marin, 1989). |
| Barriers to self-efficacy | Condoms used infrequently by Hispanics (Marin, 1989). Associate condoms with uncleanliness and prostitution, believe condoms reduce pleasure, virility, and are inconvenient and uncomfortable to use (Carrier, 1989; Marin, 1989; Marin & Marin, 1987). Using condoms may be seen as an admission that one is at risk for AIDS (Marin, 1989). Instructions typically difficult and in English only (Richwald, Schneider-Munoz, & Valdez, 1989). |
| Response efficacy | Perceived response efficacy of condoms in preventing AIDS is unknown. |
| **Salient referents** | Other Hispanic men, significant others, family members, the Roman Catholic church (Carrier, 1976; Navarro, 1989; Thompson, 1987). |
| Susceptibility | Undetermined |
| Severity | Undetermined |
| Barriers to self-efficacy | Roman Catholic church strongly disapproves of condom use. Other referent groups' beliefs undetermined (Navarro, 1989). |
| Response efficacy | Undetermined |
| **III. Culture/Environment Variables and Preferences** | |
| Source | Undetermined, Peers? |
| Channel | Radio, television |
| Message | Use appropriate colloquialisms (the "pasivo" sexual role for receptive anal intercourse; the "activo" sexual role for anal insertive role; etc.) (Carrier, 1989). |
| Audience profile | Spanish-speaking, low literacy level, lives in the Southwest, median age 22.8, retains Hispanic values and customs (e.g., machismo, familialism, *respeto, simpatía, personalismo, cooperación*), strong cultural and religious taboos against homosexuality (Carrier, 1976; Marin, 1989), economically and medically disadvantaged. |

TABLE 8.3  Salient Beliefs and Cues to Address in the Persuasive Message for
Hispanic Men

| Beliefs to CHANGE | Beliefs to REINFORCE | Beliefs to INTRODUCE | CUES TO ADDRESS |
|---|---|---|---|
| Low perceived susceptibility | Family values important (use these values in prevention message) | HIV infection is severe (even though AIDS won't appear for years) | Cultural values |
| Condoms are admission of risk | | | Colloquialisms Radio, TV channels best |
| | | Condoms prevent HIV infection if used correctly | Source preferences |
| Condoms unclean and uncomfortable | | | Literacy level |
| Condoms decrease virility, desirability, pleasure | | | Customs relating to "sexual discussions" |
| "Activo" partner not at risk | | | |

Hispanic men and HIV can be placed into each of these categories. The persuasive message, therefore, should frame the message as promoting and protecting important cultural values of Hispanic men, as well as increasing their perception of susceptibility of contracting the virus. In addition, a substantial portion of the message needs to focus on the acceptability and ease with which Hispanic men can use condoms (i.e., self-efficacy). Because we do not know whether AIDS is perceived as severe or whether condoms are seen as effective by Hispanic men, these beliefs should be introduced with HIV infection being presented as a severe and serious condition, and condoms being presented as an effective way to prevent HIV transmission. In sum, for Hispanic men, it appears that susceptibility and self-efficacy beliefs need to be targeted for change, and that severity and response efficacy beliefs need to be either introduced or reinforced.

   To maximize effectiveness, the arguments in the persuasive message need to correspond specifically to the goals of the persuasive message. In other words, the threat arguments must specifically address the audience's salient beliefs about their susceptibility and the severity of AIDS. Likewise, the efficacy arguments must specifically address their salient beliefs about response and self-efficacy of using condoms to prevent AIDS. Arguments should be supported by factual evidence. For instance, Hispanic men's beliefs that they are not at risk for HIV contraction must be countered with the fact that they are at increased risk according to many experts (Marin, 1989; Navarro, 1989). Likewise, because Hispanic men believe that condoms reduce virility, arguments must be generated to counter this misconception. Arguments may be developed using members of salient referent groups as advocates of condom use to prevent AIDS (if the audience analysis shows this is accurate). Ideally, each salient belief described in Table 8.2 should be reinforced (ideally) or refuted (if necessary) in the persuasive message. If the persuasive message is limited by space or time, however, only the most salient beliefs might be targeted for change.

As a final caveat, it is important to note that with any topic great cultural sensitivity must be used in formulating and asking questions—especially those of a sensitive nature (e.g., sexual behaviors, drug use behaviors). Surveyors or interviewers must ask questions using appropriate language (e.g., appropriate colloquialisms or slang) and it is best to match the gender, age, and ethnicity of interviewers/surveyors with members of the target population. By considering these issues up front, the chances for a successful health campaign are increased dramatically.

The example discussed here (promoting condom use among Hispanic men) used existing research to determine salient beliefs, references, and cue preferences. Following is an example where original research was conducted to uncover salient beliefs, and actual campaign messages were developed according to the framework.

## Using Original
## Research to Develop a Campaign

The other method of collecting the transient information needed for the framework is to conduct original research. This task is far easier than it might seem. The Appendix provides a questionnaire that can be used to survey for salient beliefs and Table 8.1 gives examples of questions that can be asked of the target audience. Practitioners should simply plug in their health promotion or disease prevention topic and the recommended response into the questions in the Appendix. Following is a description of the development of a campaign to prevent farm-equipment-related injuries and fatalities. Original research was conducted with farmers and ranchers in Texas to determine their salient beliefs about tractor accidents and safety procedures using the PHM framework as a guide (Witte et al., 1993).

Although the most deadly and dangerous occupation in the United States is agriculture (National Safety Council, 1992), little is known about what farmers think about farm-equipment-related accidents and safety practices and current safety interventions are typically atheoretical (Witte et al., 1993). The PHM framework was used to develop a theory-based campaign that addressed farmers' and ranchers' salient beliefs about equipment-related accidents and safety practices. First, the campaign goals and target audience were specified. The goals of the campaign were to prevent farm-equipment-related injuries and deaths (the threat) by promoting established safety procedures (the recommended response) for East Texas farmers and ranchers (the target audience). East Texas farmers and ranchers were chosen for the study because of the high number of farm-equipment-related fatalities in this area (Frerich & Valco, 1991).

To solicit salient beliefs, salient referents, and preferences, farmers and ranchers were interviewed with one of three different methods—face-to-face interviews, telephone interviews, and mailed questionnaires. The results indicated that farmers believe farm equipment injuries to be severe and serious, but do not believe themselves to be susceptible to injuries or accidents. They also believe that safety measures are effective in averting accidents and preventing injuries from farm equipment accidents. Finally, they believe they are able to carry out those safety measures to avert accidents and/or prevent injuries from accidents. In other words, they had high levels of perceived severity, response efficacy, and self-efficacy, and low levels of perceived susceptibility (see Figure 8.2). In terms of cues (Figure 8.3), the manufacturer's safety manual was the preferred message form and channel and the manufacturer was the preferred source for tractor safety information. Similarly, farmers' and ranchers' most common salient referent regarding farm-equipment-related injuries and safety procedures was the equipment company (spouses also ranked high as a salient referent). An audience profile based on demographics and self-reported experiences revealed that the target audience was primarily male (92.1%) with some college education and averaged 55 years of age. Most of the target audience was white (87.3%), with 1.9% African Americans, 0.8% Hispanics, and 10% of diverse ethnic backgrounds. Respondents farmed an average of 592 acres; and half (49.8%) owned older tractors (built before 1980), which have fewer safety features. Most farmers had no employees (72.2%), indicating that most farms were family or hobby farms (the site of most equipment accidents). Sixteen percent of the farmers reported injuries on their farms ranging from lost fingers to severe multiple injuries; 70% knew of someone who had had a severe injury caused by farm equipment; more than half (51.5%) knew someone who had died from injuries resulting from a farm equipment accident. This information gathered from the sample was used to develop an audience profile.

Step 3 was to take this information and develop persuasive messages for the campaign. First, farmers' salient beliefs were placed in the categories outlined earlier: beliefs (a) to change, (b) to reinforce, or (c) to introduce. Based on the survey, it is clear that perceived susceptibility is the belief in greatest need of change. Farmers need to be convinced of their mortality and that they are at risk for farm equipment accidents. Several of the farmers' beliefs are in the desired direction and should be reinforced in the persuasive message. Specifically, farmers need to hear that farm equipment accidents are severe (reinforce this belief), that persistent and habitual use of safety measures prevents injuries and accidents, and that the habitual and consistent use of safety measures is something that anyone can easily do. An interesting finding that emerged from the survey was that although farmers reported they consistently use safety measures, most of the more significant safety measures were not being used. For example, the majority of farmers reported they did not use seat belts even though many agricultural workers are killed when their tractor or attached equipment runs over them after they have been jolted off the vehicle. Findings such as this one indicate that a persuasive message cannot target safety in general—because farmers already believe themselves to be safe. Instead, persuasive messages must target *specific* safety behaviors, such as the use of seat belts, or having a "1 rider at a time" rule for their tractor. Because farmers' attitudes were already positive toward safety, and they intended to be safe in a general sense, the focusing of a persuasive message on specific safety behaviors is the appropriate strategy. In addition, because equipment manufacturers and spouses have the most influence on farmers' safety practices, the most effective campaign would be one that used them as the sources and channels of information. Finally, as many of the cues variables as possible should be addressed in the persuasive messages. For example, it is important to take farmers' average age (55 years), educational level (some college), and size of farm (592 acres on average) into account when developing the persuasive campaign in order to make the message appropriate and understandable.

Figure 8.3 gives examples of persuasive messages developed with information gathered according to the PHM framework. These messages are designed (a) to increase perceptions of susceptibility about farm equipment accidents (farmers already believe accidents lead to severe injuries), as well as (b) to emphasize the effectiveness of safety measures in averting accidents, and how easy and feasible it is to use safety measures consistently. In addition, because significant numbers of farmers reported not using their seat belts

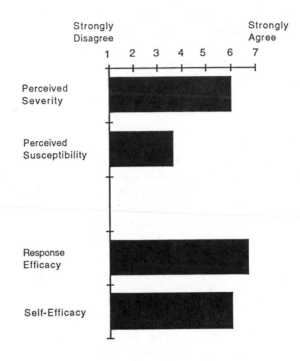

Farmers' salient referents.

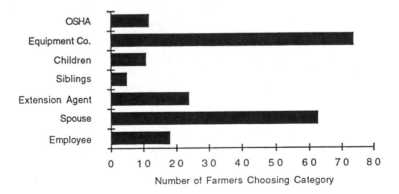

**Figure 8.2.** East Texas Farmers' and Ranchers' Salient Beliefs About the Threat of Farm Equipment Accidents and the Efficacy of Safety Procedures in Averting Farm Equipment Accidents, and Salient Referents

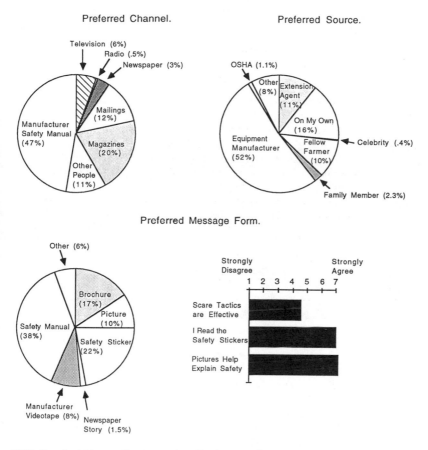

Preferred Channel.

Preferred Source.

Preferred Message Form.

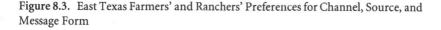

NOTE: Proportion totals may add up to more than 100% due to rounding error.

**Figure 8.3.** East Texas Farmers' and Ranchers' Preferences for Channel, Source, and Message Form

and not having a roll bar on their tractor, these specific safety practices were the focus of the persuasive messages. Finally, farmers' preferred sources of information were used (manufacturer, fellow farmer, extension agent) in addition to their preferred modes (brochure, safety stickers) and channels (magazine advertisements, mailings) of information dissemination (Figure 8.3).

<<Sound of tractor running>>

| | |
|---|---|
| JACK | Hey Bill. |
| BILL | Good mornin' Jack, Susan. |

<<Tractor sounds stop.>>

| | |
|---|---|
| JACK | We just came by to give you an update on Hank. |
| BILL | Oh thanks—isn't it a shame. I guess we're lucky he just lost his arm, he could have died like ol' Ted Rogers down the road. |
| SUSAN | Yeah, that was terrible. I always *knew* an uncovered PTO shaft is dangerous, but so many farmers—including us—don't replace the safety cover each and every time, and now look what's happened, Hank lost his arm and Ted was killed. |
| JACK | Well, you can bet that I replace my safety cover on my PTO shaft each and every time I grease it now. It's just plain stupid and lazy not to. It doesn't take but two minutes to put it back on and my and my family's peace-of-mind is worth it. |
| BILL | You're right. I have to admit that I've been kind of lax about replacing my safety cover too but now I'm going to start doing it. |
| SUSAN | You know what we did? After hearing about all of these accidents around here and the rest of the state, Jack called John Deere to come and tell us what kinds of safety upgrades our tractor needed. If your tractor was built 1980 or before, it might be missing some important safety features. The John Deere Representative came out and gave us a free safety inspection. He also gave us a special reduced price to install a roll bar and seatbelt. |
| JACK | The rep said that most farm-equipment injuries happen when you get tangled up in a PTO or when you get bounced off a tractor after hitting a ditch or a bump. |
| BILL | Hmmm, well, I better give them a call today and have them come out and look at my tractor. You say it's free for them to inspect the equipment? |
| JACK | Yeah, and they'll make you a good deal if you need to upgrade any safety features. |
| SUSAN | I bet Emma and Sophie wish Hank and Ted had done the same. |
| ANNOUNCER | Call 1-800-123-FARM for your free safety inspection by a local John Deere representative. Your safety and livelihood is important to us. Please call 1-800-123-FARM. |

**Figure 8.4.** Public Service Announcement, Tractor Safety, 45 seconds

## Conclusion

With limited funds and time, public health practitioners need quick and easy methods to develop campaigns that work. The PHM framework outlined here attempts to offer a quick and easy "cookbook" approach to developing effective and targeted persuasive messages that address specific audience beliefs and behaviors. Using a theory-based framework such as the one presented here should decrease the chances for campaign failures and increase the chances of campaign success.

# References

Ajzen, I., & Fishbein, M. (1980). *Understanding attitudes and predicting social behavior.* Englewood Cliffs, NJ: Prentice Hall.

Atkin, C. K. (1993, November). *Perspectives on health campaign persuasion strategies.* Paper presented at the annual meeting of the Speech Communication Association, Miami.

Atkin, C. K., & Freimuth, V. (1989). Formative evaluation research in campaign design. In R. E. Rice & C. K. Atkin (Eds.), *Public communication campaigns* (2nd ed.) (pp. 131-150). Newbury Park, CA: Sage.

Burgoon, M. (1989). Messages and persuasive effects. In J. J. Bradac (Ed.), *Message effects in communication science* (pp. 129-164). Newbury Park, CA: Sage.

Carrier, J. M. (1976). Cultural factors affecting urban Mexican male homosexual behavior. *Archives of Sexual Behavior, 5,* 103-124.

Carrier, J. M. (1989). Sexual behavior and the spread of AIDS in Mexico. *Medical Anthropologist, 10,* 129-142.

Fishbein, M., & Ajzen, I. (1975). *Belief, attitude, intention, and behavior: An introduction to theory and research.* Reading, MA: Addison-Wesley.

Fishbein, M., & Ajzen, I. (1981). Acceptance, yielding and impact: Cognitive processes in persuasion. In R. E. Petty, T. M. Ostrom, & T. C. Brock (Eds.), *Cognitive responses in persuasion* (pp. 339-359). Hillsdale, NJ: Lawrence Erlbaum.

Flora, J. A., & Thoreson, C. E. (1988). Reducing the risk of AIDS in adolescents. *American Psychologist, 43,* 965-970.

Frerich, S. J., & Valco, T. D. (1991, October). *Ten year summary of Texas farm and ranch fatalities for 1980-1989.* Paper presented at the annual meeting of the Texas Section of the American Society of Agricultural Engineers, Temple, TX.

Marin, G. (1989). AIDS prevention among Hispanics: Needs, risk behaviors, and cultural values. *Public Health Reports, 104,* 411-415.

Marin, B. V., & Marin, G. (1987). Attitudes and expectancies regarding AIDS among Hispanics. In *Psychology and AIDS* (pp. 46-47). Washington, DC: American Psychological Association.

McGuire, W. J. (1984). Public communication as a strategy for inducing health-promoting behavioral change. *Preventive Medicine, 13,* 299-319.

McGuire, W. J. (1985). Attitudes and attitude change. In L. Gardner & E. Aronson (Eds.), *Handbook of social psychology* (3rd ed.) (Vol. 2, pp. 233-346). New York: Random House.

National Safety Council. (1992). *Accident facts* (1992 ed.). Itasca, IL: Author.

Navarro, M. (1989, December 29). AIDS in Hispanic community: Threat ignored. *The New York Times,* pp. B1, B10.

Peterson, J. L., & Marin, G. (1988). Issues in the prevention of AIDS among black and Hispanic men. *American Psychologist, 43,* 871-877.

Petty, R. E., & Cacioppo, J. T. (1986). *Communication and persuasion: Central and peripheral routes to attitude change.* New York: Springer.

Richwald, G. A., Schneider-Munoz, M., & Valdez, R. B. (1989). Are condom instructions in Spanish readable? Implications for AIDS prevention activities for Hispanics. *Hispanic Journal of Behavioral Sciences, 11,* 70-82.

Rogers, R. W. (1975). A protection motivation theory of fear appeals and attitude change. *Journal of Psychology, 91,* 93-114.

Rogers, R. W. (1983). Cognitive and physiological processes in fear appeals and attitude change: A revised theory of protection motivation. In J. Cacioppo & R. Petty (Eds.), *Social psychophysiology* (pp. 153-176). New York: Guilford.

Thompson, L. (1987, August 11). AIDS and minorities. *The Washington Post,* p. 7.

Witte, K. (1992a). Preventing AIDS through persuasive communications: A framework for constructing effective, culturally-specific, preventive health messages. *International and Intercultural Communication Annual, 16,* 67-86.

Witte, K. (1992b). Putting the fear back into fear appeals: Reconciling the literature. *Communication Monographs, 59,* 329-349.

Witte, K. (1992c). The role of threat and efficacy in AIDS prevention. *International Quarterly of Community Health Education, 12,* 225-249.

Witte, K., Peterson, T. R., Vallabhan, S., Stephenson, M. T., Plugge, C. D., Givens, V. K., Todd, J. D., Becktold, M. G., Hyde, M. K., & Jarrett, R. (1993). Preventing tractor-related injuries and deaths in rural populations: Using a persuasive health message (PHM) framework in formative evaluation research. *International Quarterly of Community Health Education, 13,* 219-251.

# Appendix

Example of a Generic and Specific Questionnaire to Determine
Campaign Goals and Audience Salient Beliefs

*Questions for Practitioner:*

1. What is the health threat? _____

2. What is the recommended response to avert the health threat (the *specific*
   goal of the campaign)? _____

3. Who is the target audience? _____
   (describe in demographic, psychographic, cultural terms)

*Questions for the Target Audience:*

4. How serious is <HEALTH THREAT>?

   | 1 | 2 | 3 | 4 | 5 | 6 | 7 |
   |---|---|---|---|---|---|---|
   | Not At All Serious | | | | Extremely Serious | | |

5. How likely is it that <HEALTH THREAT> will happen to you?

   | 1 | 2 | 3 | 4 | 5 | 6 | 7 |
   |---|---|---|---|---|---|---|
   | Not At All Susceptible | | | | Extremely Susceptible | | |

6. <RECOMMENDED RESPONSE> will keep me from getting <HEALTH
   THREAT>.

   | 1 | 2 | 3 | 4 | 5 | 6 | 7 |
   |---|---|---|---|---|---|---|
   | Strongly Disagree | | | | Strongly Agree | | |

7. I am easily able to follow <RECOMMENDED RESPONSE> to prevent my
   getting <HEALTH THREAT>.

   | 1 | 2 | 3 | 4 | 5 | 6 | 7 |
   |---|---|---|---|---|---|---|
   | Strongly Disagree | | | | Strongly Agree | | |

8. My <SALIENT REFERENT> thinks <HEALTH THREAT> is a serious
   disease.

   | 1 | 2 | 3 | 4 | 5 | 6 | 7 |
   |---|---|---|---|---|---|---|
   | Strongly Disagree | | | | Strongly Agree | | |

9. My <SALIENT REFERENT> thinks I am at risk for <HEALTH THREAT>.

| 1 | 2 | 3 | 4 | 5 | 6 | 7 |
|---|---|---|---|---|---|---|
| Strongly Disagree | | | | | Strongly Agree | |

10. My <SALIENT REFERENT> thinks <RECOMMENDED RESPONSE> will prevent <HEALTH THREAT>.

| 1 | 2 | 3 | 4 | 5 | 6 | 7 |
|---|---|---|---|---|---|---|
| Strongly Disagree | | | | | Strongly Agree | |

11. My <SALIENT REFERENT> thinks I am able to <RECOMMENDED RESPONSE> to prevent <HEALTH THREAT>.

| 1 | 2 | 3 | 4 | 5 | 6 | 7 |
|---|---|---|---|---|---|---|
| Strongly Disagree | | | | | Strongly Agree | |

12. WHAT IS THE PREFERRED CHANNEL?

13. WHAT IS THE PREFERRED MESSAGE FORM (E.G., LOGICAL, EMOTIONAL)?

14. WHAT IS THE PREFERRED SOURCE?

PART II

# Audience-Centered Strategies for Health Message Design

Health message design is an audience-centered process. This is the single most obvious and most important lesson from several decades of collective experience in health communication. It is a lesson communicated to us by experts working in virtually every major genre of health communication, including information campaigns, social marketing, entertainment-education, clinical (i.e., provider-patient) communication, and even media advocacy.

What does it mean to be an audience-centered process? It means that health messages are designed primarily to respond to the needs and situation of the target audience, rather than to the needs and situation of the message designers or sponsoring organizations. Social marketers refer to this as adopting a consumer orientation. To adopt a consumer orientation successfully, however, entails a major commitment to a process of getting to know the target audience. That process is the focus of this section.

Although the ordering of chapters in this section is somewhat arbitrary, Nowak and Siska were selected to lead off with Chapter 9 because their topic is critical to the establishment of an audience-centered approach. They discuss the notion that, under an audience-centered approach, evaluation occurs throughout the life span of a health communication activity. They illustrate this point with formative, process, impact, and outcome evaluation research conducted in service of the Centers for Disease Control and Preventions's "America Responds to AIDS" campaign.

In Chapter 10, Slater refines the notion of audience-centered communication by establishing the need to define an audience as a relatively homogenous group of people. Without relative homogeneity among target audience members on characteristics of relevance to the communication objectives, health message designers would be unable to adopt their orientation, because members of the target audience would not share an orientation. This quandary necessitates segmentation of large heterogeneous audiences into smaller, more homogeneous audiences. The result of such segmentation is that communication planners may then examine the audience segments, rationally determine which one(s) will be selected as the target audience(s), and proceed with subsequent data collection activities that will allow them to establish the orientation shared by members of the audience segment selected. Slater provides recommendations for the conduct of audience segmentation analyses under a variety of conditions.

In Chapter 11, McGrath further refines the notion of audience-centered communication by presenting the case that target audience members are not the sole audience of importance. Media gatekeepers—including reporters, editors, public service directors, and others—are also an important audience in that their cooperation is, in many cases, vital to the success of health communication programs. McGrath describes both the gatekeeper's and the message designer's perspective, and makes a number of practical recommendations on how to include gatekeepers in the message design process for the purpose of ensuring their cooperation in providing access to the target audience.

In Chapter 12, Lefebvre and his colleagues illustrate the use of marketing databases in their design of the National Cancer Institute's 5 A Day for Better Health program. Marketing databases are an important recent development that are now available to support audience-centered approaches to health message design. Commercial marketing critics of social marketing have contended that social marketing successes will be inherently limited by the dearth of available data to support audience-centered planning decisions. This chapter is evidence that a major barrier to successful social marketing is beginning to crumble, thanks to the proliferation of health-related marketing databases. In addition, this chapter is an excellent example of audience-centered message design, or in the words of the authors, consumer-based health communication.

# 9 Using Research to Inform Campaign Development and Message Design

## EXAMPLES FROM THE "AMERICA RESPONDS TO AIDS" CAMPAIGN

GLEN J. NOWAK

MICHAEL J. SISKA

As the primary federal government agency responsible for educating the public about the human immunodeficiency virus (HIV) and acquired immunodeficiency syndrome (AIDS), the Centers for Disease Control and Prevention (CDC) established the National AIDS Information and Education Program (NAIEP) in 1987 to direct the Public Health Service's AIDS media campaigns and social marketing efforts. These duties involve designing and disseminating health communication materials that (a) educate and inform the general public about behaviors that place individuals at risk for being infected with HIV, (b) educate and motivate infected individuals to avoid transmitting HIV to non-infected individuals, and (c) support social norms consistent with no- or low-risk behaviors (Kroger, 1991; Marchman & Jason, 1991; Salmon & Kroger, 1992). Drawing primarily from experiences in the history of the six-phased "America Responds to AIDS" campaign, this chapter illustrates how NAIEP has integrated recommendations from the National Academy of Science with mass communication, marketing, and advertising research methods to formulate, develop, and evaluate the HIV/ AIDS education and prevention messages.

## The "America Responds to AIDS" Campaign

The "America Responds to AIDS" (ARTA) public information-prevention campaign, directed at the general public as well as at more specific audiences (e.g., parents and youth), has been one of the most prominent and visible means of accomplishing the objectives outlined above (Keiser, 1991). Initially a response to an immediate crisis, ARTA evolved into an ongoing multiphased, multimedia campaign whose objectives were based on the evolving needs of the general public and of specific audiences (Woods, Davis, & Westover, 1991).

From its launch in 1987 through July 1993, the ARTA campaign went through six distinct phases (i.e., releases of a specific body of education and prevention material) and made available 83 television public service announcements (PSAs), 68 radio PSAs, 62 posters, 53 print PSAs, and 20 brochures (including the nationally mailed "Understanding AIDS" booklet) (Woods et al., 1991). From October 1987 through January 1991, ARTA PSAs received an estimated 59,113 television airings, with 47% of those airings occurring during daytime hours and 9% during prime time (Gentry & Jorgensen, 1991). The CDC National AIDS Hotline, an HIV/AIDS information and referral service often promoted by ARTA materials, has received an average of about 1.4 million calls per year since 1987, or about 3,300 calls a day (Waller & Lisella, 1991). The CDC National AIDS Clearinghouse, established along with the Hotline, disseminated more than 60 million copies of publications related to HIV and AIDS between 1987 and 1991 (Sinnock, Murphy, Baker, & Bates, 1991).

## Uses of Research in the ARTA Campaign

Given that poor conceptualizations of audience, message, and media have limited the success of many mass media-based health campaigns (Atkin & Freimuth, 1989; O'Keefe, 1985; Wallack, 1981), CDC commissioned the National Academy of Science (NAS) in 1987 to recommend research and evaluation approaches for its HIV/AIDS education and prevention activities, including the ARTA media campaign. The NAS expert review panel recommended using four types of communication research to increase the likelihood of developing materials and messages that would have meaningful effects: formative evaluation to identify which concepts and strategies "work better"; efficacy trials to assess if the campaign "*could* make a difference"; process evaluation to find out what information is actually delivered;

and outcome evaluation to determine if the campaign *did* make a difference (Evaluating AIDS Prevention Programs, 1989). From this perspective, formative evaluation typically has two distinct phases: preproduction research and production testing (Atkin & Freimuth, 1989; Palmer, 1981). Preproduction research involves accumulating data on audience characteristics "that relate importantly to the medium, the message, and situation within which the desired behavior will occur," whereas production testing obtains audience reactions to prototypes or pilot messages (Palmer, p. 227).

Thanks to the scope and magnitude of NAIEP's social marketing efforts, the actual roles of research and evaluation evolved in the course of developing, implementing, and evaluating the ARTA campaign. Formative evaluation research most directly informed campaign and message design, but as Table 9.1 shows (and defines), seven other types of research also have served in a "formative" capacity by influencing the materials and messages that were created and disseminated under the ARTA banner. Thus, although research may be the exception rather than the rule for most health communication campaigns (Atkin & Freimuth, 1989), the following NAIEP examples illustrate how health communicators and social marketers can benefit by making formative evaluation an integral component in their education and prevention efforts.

PRECAMPAIGN RESEARCH

In general, research undertaken before a campaign facilitates campaign planning by identifying potentially relevant issues, campaign themes, target audiences, message concepts, and useful media channels/message vehicles (see Table 9.1). The idea is to learn as much as possible about the intended audience(s) before specifying campaign objectives or devising message strategies (Atkin & Freimuth, 1989; Palmer, 1981). For NAIEP (as well as for the ARTA campaign), this typically involves describing health problems in terms of: who is affected (i.e., potential targets), where they live (i.e., location), how they are affected (i.e., susceptibility and severity), how common the problem(s) is/are (i.e., prevalence), what host and environmental factors contribute to or cause the problem(s) (i.e., determinants), and the known or suspected barriers to solving the problem(s) (Cole, Pogostin, Holtgrave, Rios, & Collier, in press).

Operationally, literature and survey data reviews (e.g., empirical findings reported in the health communication or scientific literature, National Health Interview Survey results) are the most commonly used research methods, but NAIEP also extensively employs two qualitative research methods: expert

TABLE 9.1 Research Used to Inform the "America Responds to AIDS" Campaign

| Campaign Phase | Research Undertaken | Definition |
|---|---|---|
| Precampaign | STRATEGIC PLANNING RESEARCH | Research that informs campaign or message design by identifying potential problems, target audiences, campaign concept or themes, and useful media channels or message vehicles. |
| | NEEDS ASSESSMENTS | Research that collects information to estimate what is "needed" (e.g., money, information, skills, social support) to solve defined problems of a target audience. |
| Campaign/ Message development | TARGET AUDIENCE ANALYSIS | Research that selects, segments, and/or describes the target population(s) that the campaign is intended to address. |
| | FORMATIVE EVALUATION | Research undertaken to compare alternative campaign strategies or alternative campaign messages and/or improve the implementation operation, effects, or efficiency of a chosen strategy. Includes idea generation concept testing, positioning statement, copy or message testing, and test market research. |
| | MESSAGE EFFICACY/ RESPONSE RESEARCH | Research designed to determine if under optimal conditions a campaign, messages, and/or produced materials will have the desired effect(s). |
| Postcampaign | PROCESS EVALUATION | Research that attempts to determine when, where, how often, and to whom, campaign materials are being disseminated, shown, or aired. |
| | OUTCOME/ EFFECTIVENESS EVALUATION | Research designed to answer questions about the effects of a campaign or campaign materials and that compares this information with previously stated communication and/or behavioral objectives to determine the extent of discrepancy or congruence that exists. |
| Ongoing/Ad hoc | EXPLORATORY RESEARCH | Investigations designed to addressed communication issues as they arise including (a) recurring communication issues that have relevance beyond a single campaign or PSA, (b) assessing or developing research methods, or (c) evaluating the need for a mass media-based intervention. |

interviews and focus groups. In the case of the ARTA campaign, this pre-campaign research process often began with "issue identification" meetings with a wide range of HIV/AIDS opinion leaders. For example, the issue identification process for Phase VI of the ARTA campaign (launched in 1993) included interviews with officials from the American Medical Association, the National Association of Broadcasters, Americans for a Sound AIDS Policy, the National Leadership Coalition on AIDS, and the U.S. Chambers of Commerce, along with representatives from state health departments, community-based public health organizations, and NAIEP's national partner organizations (e.g., the American Red Cross).

Both formal (e.g., conferences or structured questionnaires) and informal (e.g., relatively unstructured telephone interviews) data collection methods were used to identify and compile a list of "expert-suggested," audience-specific problems related to HIV and AIDS education and prevention. Once this series of discussions identified a list of issues or audience-specific problems (e.g., persuading 18- to 24-year-old males to use condoms consistently) that could be addressed within the context of the ARTA campaign, literature/data reviews and focus group discussions were used to further describe health-relevant problems and their determinants. Literature reviews assisted in defining the scope, size, and seriousness of issues, and the focus group discussions provided a way to gauge public knowledge and understanding of the issues, to assess the merits of developing new messages and materials, and to generate message concepts (i.e., partially formulated message ideas).

At this point in the precampaign stage, health communicators face some of their most difficult decisions—prioritizing and deciding which audience(s) will be the target(s) of the intervention. In other words, where can limited resources and campaigns be most effectively and efficiently directed? The answer to this question, as both the ARTA experiences and the advice of many health communication experts attest (Cole et al., in press; Frankle & Owen, 1978), is a judgment that takes into consideration a number of factors, including (a) how many people are affected; (b) the seriousness of the problem (i.e., diseases that kill or disable should take precedence over those that do not); (c) the availability of scientific knowledge concerning how to address the problem; (d) the availability of human and technical resources required to address the problem; (e) the desires of community leaders; (f) the costs/benefits associated with attempting to solve the problem; and (g) the desires of the community at large.

Once a target audience has been selected, focus group discussions and depth interviews are often invaluable tools for assessing the needs of people in that group (see Table 9.1). By obtaining information on target audience members' knowledge, beliefs, and/or behaviors, a health communicator is better able to determine what is needed to correct the problem (e.g., more information, better information distribution, or information that addresses misconceptions). Most recently, NAIEP is attempting to integrate qualitative research methods in a dynamic fashion as part of a broader Prevention Marketing Program. Unlike the ARTA campaign where qualitative research was primarily conducted prior to launching a new phase, the Prevention Marketing Program hopes to use focus group discussions and depth interviews as a way of doing "ongoing" target audience needs assessments.

In 1993, for example, NAIEP proposed to develop materials and messages directed at preventing sexual transmission of HIV and other sexually transmitted diseases among three distinct groups of people 25 years of age and under: (a) those who are sexually active and at sexual risk (e.g., have unprotected sex); (b) those who are sexually active and have relatively low sexual risk (i.e., use condoms consistently and correctly); and (c) those who are not sexually active. Under the Prevention Marketing Program approach, focus group discussions would be employed throughout the health communication intervention process to stay abreast of the knowledge, motives, and beliefs underlying each group's sexual behaviors as well as to identify the institutions, people, messages, and message channels that are currently most influential. This continual feedback will be used to update and refine message and media strategies or tactics, with the end result being more effective prevention and education materials.

## CAMPAIGN CONCEPT AND
## MESSAGE DEVELOPMENT RESEARCH

Once potential target audiences and health communication problems and their determinants have been identified, the next step in the NAIEP campaign and message design process involves reducing the number of campaign concepts, defining a campaign's specific communication and/or behavioral objectives, and developing potential messages. This stage usually begins by going back to the same organizations and individuals consulted in the pre-campaign stage to get their reactions to a narrowed list of campaign themes and message concepts.

In addition to external and internal expert review panels, NAIEP convenes cross-cultural panels (i.e., advisory boards that have representatives from ethnic and minority groups) to ensure themes and concepts are viable and appropriate for specific minority audiences. Precampaign research for Phase VI of the ARTA campaign, for example, indicated that many public health practitioners supported the development of messages that stressed the benefits of early HIV testing and detection for at-risk individuals (e.g., early treatment can potentially prolong their lives). One of the draft TV PSAs depicted this message using a fast-moving train to symbolize the idea that many people, when first diagnosed with HIV, feel like they have no control (i.e., "they can't stop the train"). The PSA then symbolized early treatment slowing the progression of HIV and AIDS by having the train slow to a stop and using an endtag that read, "Early treatment can mean a longer life." Early copy testing showed this creative execution was quite memorable, but that the train imagery was offensive to Native and Asian Americans (e.g., trains and railroads symbolized the westward expansion of the United States and the end of Native American culture). Moreover, HIV-infected people concurred that the fastmoving train induced the sense of being out of control, but this feeling raised their anxiety levels and obscured the benefits of early HIV testing.

In line with the NAS recommendations, traditional formative research methods (see Table 9.1) are also used in the campaign/message development stage to eliminate weaker approaches and to identify promising concepts. Early concept tests (e.g., focus group discussions) are used to identify themes, concepts, or rough messages that should be developed further. Often, focus group discussions conducted at this point directly inform message design by providing the central idea or theme used in a campaign. For example, the taglines for Phase V ("HIV is the virus that causes AIDS") and Phase VI ("One in 250 Americans is infected with HIV") of the ARTA campaign were derived from comments made in focus group sessions.

Formative evaluation at this stage also assists in creating messages that reflect the target audience's vernacular (Atkin & Freimuth, 1989). As such, formative evaluation not only helps identify what messages may be most appropriate for specific audiences, but obtains insights into how members of other affected audiences (e.g., "the general public") currently view a problem or issue (Flay, 1986; Marchman & Jason, 1992; Salmon & Jason, 1991). The development of materials for ARTA Phase V provides a good example. In the concept generation process, many health experts said there was a need for messages that combatted discrimination against HIV-positive people by attacking the misconceptions surrounding HIV infection (e.g., that HIV could be transmitted via casual contact). Testing this concept in focus groups with members of the general public, however, revealed that discrimination was a complex issue, and not particularly tied to myths about HIV-positive people. Many focus group participants were concerned about casual transmission and the burden HIV and AIDS placed on health care systems, but discrimination against HIV-positive people was driven more by prejudice against homosexuals than by transmission misconceptions. Given the extent and depth of this belief, it was decided not to do a campaign that dealt solely with discrimination issues. Rather, the focus group comments suggested that PSAs showing HIV-positive people leading active and productive lives would be the preferable way to combat the stereotypes that fostered discrimination.

Finally, after adjustments are made to creative concepts and draft materials are produced, a second type of formative evaluation, copy testing, is used to ensure that highly regarded concepts are effectively translated into creative executions before the production process goes very far. The ARTA campaign accomplished this by using "early" copy testing; that is, focus group discussions or mall intercept interviews that exposed participants to storyboards (i.e., a series of sketches showing key scenes) or animatics (i.e., films of storyboards with a soundtrack). Reactions to these relatively unfinished materials guided creative development (e.g., assessing the believability or communication effectiveness of different appeals or spokespeople), assisted in copy formulation, and provided a way to compare alternative executions before time and money was spent producing a PSA.

A February 1990 study, for example, used mall intercept interviews and an experimental design (i.e., random assignment of participants to test and control conditions) to assess, among other things, the potential impact of a TV PSA that encouraged individuals engaged in high-risk activities to get tested for HIV infection (Middlestadt, 1990). The PSA (in animatic form) showed an HIV-infected father holding a baby and talking to the infant about HIV infection and the benefits of early detection (i.e., earlier treatment may let him live longer so that he may see his newborn child walk and talk). The creative concept was well received by medical and public health officials as well as a cross-cultural review panel, but the animatic produced unintended negative reactions among less educated viewers (i.e., less than a high school education). Exposure to the PSA caused these viewers to become concerned with how the father got infected and fearful that HIV could be transmitted to the infant and other family members via casual contact and thus failed to convey the benefits of early testing and detection. The PSA was dropped from further consideration.

## MESSAGE EFFICACY
## AND RESPONSE RESEARCH

The third type of research used by NAIEP to inform message design evolved from the NAS recommendations to determine if, under optimal conditions, a campaign or message will have the desired effect(s). In general, the question of efficacy is best answered with randomized experimental or quasi-experimental designs in which the proposed media campaign is implemented in a number of test markets and compared to data gathered in a number of other, randomly assigned or matched control markets (Evaluating AIDS Prevention Programs, 1989). To judge a campaign's effects and effectiveness adequately, NAS suggested a 6- to 12-month test period and testing alternative campaigns before rolling out a national HIV/AIDS prevention or education campaign.

Budget limitations, time constraints, inability to control the implementation of a PSA campaign, and ethical concerns over providing materials to some communities but not others, have necessitated modifications in both the emphasis and methods of efficacy testing (Donovan, Jason, Gibbs, & Kroger, 1991). The focus of NAIEP's efficacy research has shifted from determining how well an entire campaign works when implemented optimally, to assessing the communication effects and effectiveness of individual messages (e.g., PSAs) that may be used in a campaign. Much of this evaluation still takes place before materials are nationally distributed, but the emphasis is on studies that directly inform message design or facilitate message dissemination (e.g., provide media outlets with information regarding likely viewer reactions to a TV PSA). Often, these efforts use "late copy testing" methods that expose recruited samples to relatively finished materials or PSAs.

The results of a 1990 efficacy study, for example, supported the use of a TV PSA that some public health officials had speculated would be deemed offensive by TV viewers. The PSA, "Sofa," and another PSA entitled "Wonderful World" were tested in two communities (the former in Memphis, TN, the latter in Springfield, IL) using an in-home viewing method (Siska, Jason, Murdoch, Yang, & Donovan, 1992). Participants were recruited by telephone to watch a 10 p.m. newscast in their own homes, during which they saw one of the two PSAs. "Wonderful World" depicted children in a field and a little girl talking about wanting to grow up in a better world. "Sofa" showed a young couple on a sofa kissing while an announcer on the television in front of them talks about AIDS.

The study provided two pieces of important information. First, the findings disproved the concerns of public health officials about "Sofa" by providing evidence that the PSA did not generate strong negative reactions. Of the 211 people in the test exposed to the "Sofa" PSA, only 1 person described it as "offensive" and another said it was "too passionate to be shown on TV." Further, the Tennessee TV station that aired the PSA received only 5 complaints; far fewer than the 25 or more calls/letters that served as that station's benchmark for a "strong reaction." Second, "Sofa" not only attained higher recall levels than "Wonderful World" (73% vs. 45%), it also increased the number of respondents mentioning AIDS as an important issue (from 20.8% to 32.2%). This information not only provided direction for subsequent national distribution of these PSAs, but also provided evidence for future PSA development that direct and relatively explicit approaches to message execution are more effective than indirect or subtle approaches.

POSTCAMPAIGN
RESEARCH AND EVALUATION

Formative and efficacy evaluations conducted during the process of developing a campaign most directly ensure that only those materials that are potentially the most effective are produced for the media (Salmon & Jason, 1991), but the ARTA experiences suggest postcampaign evaluations play a valuable role in influencing and shaping the messages of ongoing campaigns. As such, the two primary types of postcampaign research used in the ARTA campaign, process evaluation and outcome/effectiveness evaluation, served a dual role. First, in accordance with the NAS recommendations, the research either attempted to determine when, where, and how often campaign materials were being shown or used (i.e., process evaluation), or whether the campaign phases were making a difference (i.e., outcome/effectiveness evaluation). Second, the research made a formative contribution by influencing the topics, messages, and media used in subsequent phases.

As Salmon and Jason (1991) point out, the most basic process evaluation question is: "Is the campaign being implemented at the intended levels?" (p. 643). As such, it is primarily concerned with identifying exactly what materials were disseminated to and successfully placed in the media and who was potentially or actually exposed to those messages. From a formative (i.e., "informing") perspective, NAIEP obtains such information in order to facilitate the use and airing of prevention/education materials—with increased distribution assumed to increase the likelihood of influencing target audiences' HIV and AIDS-related knowledge, attitudes, and beliefs. Most of the ARTA campaign's initial process evaluation involved using the Broadcast Advertisers Reports (BAR) to gauge the level of audience exposure to the broadcast materials, particularly television. BAR, a service purchased from the Arbitron Corporation, monitors commercial advertising on television and radio stations.

For the ARTA campaign, BAR data not only helped assess when and how often PSAs were being aired (see Gentry & Jorgensen [1991] for a more detailed description), the reports provided considerable evidence that TV and radio PSAs were highly visible and cost-effective communication tools. Between 1987 and 1990, for example, the ARTA campaign received an estimated $65 million in donated air time and accounted for 47% of all HIV/ AIDS PSA donations (Gentry & Jorgensen, 1991). Further, as of January 1992, each adult American aged 18 to 54 had been exposed to ARTA PSAs an average of 56 times at a cost of about 1 cent per exposure (CDC HIV/AIDS Prevention Factbook, 1992).

In 1993, NAIEP began using radio and TV airing data from Broadcast Data Systems (BDS), another company that monitors commercial and PSA airplay. BDS not only provides aggregate airplay data, it also can monitor the airing of individual PSAs. This capability should enhance the "formative" value of NAIEP's process evaluation by providing answers to three questions that repeatedly arise in the campaign development and message design process: What campaign themes do broadcast station and network managers deem most useful or appropriate for their audiences? What specific PSAs in a campaign attain the most airplay? And what types of messages (e.g., HIV/AIDS awareness, safer sex, or condom-use) and creative executions (e.g., spokespeople, fear appeals) receive the most airplay?

The second type of postcampaign research, outcome or effectiveness evaluation, ideally focuses on determining whether campaigns or messages successfully achieve the desired outcomes. Unlike the large-scale community-based health education programs where matched pairs of treatment and comparison communities provide a means to evaluate media campaigns (e.g., the Stanford Five City Project or Minnesota Heart Health Program), NAIEP's ARTA campaign precluded quasi-experimental designs. Nationwide implementation and ethical concerns over withholding materials made it impossible to develop reasonable comparison groups, and financial and logistical costs of lagged or regionally segregated "roll-outs" of materials were prohibitive (Salmon & Jason, 1991). As a result, ARTA outcome evaluations have involved analyzing national probability sample survey data (e.g., National Health Information Survey) in order to identify segments of the general public that lack basic or essential knowledge (such as how HIV is transmitted).

Still, as many evaluation researchers have suggested (e.g., Maccoby & Solomon, 1981; Salmon & Jason, 1991), the primary value of such methods lies not in their ability to isolate cause-effect relationships, but in the contribution they make to planning the next campaign. In the case of the ARTA campaign, national probability surveys provided information about where audiences learned about HIV and AIDS, as well as the current HIV- and AIDS-related knowledge, attitudes, beliefs, and behaviors (KABB) of key target groups (e.g., the general public as well as such specific segments as 18- to 39-year-olds). Surveys, for instance, have indirectly documented the impact of broadcast PSAs, but more directly have highlighted TV's impact as a source of HIV and AIDS information. The 1991 National Health Interview Survey, for instance, found that TV ads were the primary source of recent AIDS information for 72% of Americans (Hardy, 1992), and another study found 48% of injecting drug users first learned about HIV and AIDS from television sources (*Morbidity and Mortality Weekly Report,* 1991).

Similarly, results from the 1991 National Planning Survey (NPS) will likely influence the development and design of materials directed at 18- to 39-year-olds. The NPS survey, which involved interviews with 1,622 randomly selected 18- to 64-year-olds, suggested that many 18- to 39-year-olds would be receptive to messages and materials regarding HIV and AIDS prevention (e.g., 67% supported the use of TV commercials about how to use a condom as an HIV and AIDS prevention method) (Wooten, Jason, & Gentry, 1992). The results indicated that most young adults who reported putting themselves at risk had taken steps to reduce their risk, but suggested that education and prevention materials likely need to stress and support correct and consistent condom use, and address some widely held misconceptions. For example, of those who reported taking steps to reduce the likelihood of contracting HIV, the favored methods appeared to be occasional condom use (71%), talking with a sexual partner (68%), and/or changing sexual behaviors or lifestyles (59%). Only 19% of those respondents who reported having more than one sexual partner in the past year said they were "always" using a condom. Further, 36% incorrectly believed that natural lambskin condoms were at least as effective as latex condoms for preventing HIV infection, and 20% did not know which type was most effective.

EXPLORATORY RESEARCH

Exploratory, or "ad hoc," investigations designed to address communication issues as they arise are a final category of research that has proven valuable for campaign development and message design. Typically, these studies are undertaken to (a) address recurring communication issues that have relevance beyond a single campaign or PSA, (b) assess or develop communication research methods (e.g., Baggeley et al., 1992), or (c) evaluate the need for a mass media-based information or education intervention (e.g., TV PSAs or brochures/pamphlets). Experimental and quasi-experimental designs and focus group discussions are the most commonly used methods.

A recent exploratory study (Nowak, Jorgensen, Salmon, & Jason, 1993), for example, addressed two questions that often arise when TV PSAs are used to promote a hot line or information service phone number: (a) Does increasing the length of time the number appears on the TV screen increase viewer recall of the number? and (b) Does an all-mnemonic phone "number" result in a substantial increase in phone number recall? An experiment using a 2 × 3 factorial design, with a control group, was conducted. One hundred ninety seven college students were exposed to a highly targeted ARTA TV PSA ("Campus") that modeled a female college student discounting her susceptibility to contracting HIV. The phone number (1-800-342-AIDS vs. 1-800-HIV-AIDS) and the length of time the number was shown (the last 3 seconds, the last 6 seconds, and continual 30-second display) varied among treatment groups.

Although this study focused on relatively short-term message effects, the results indicated the telephone number used and the length of time it was displayed affected viewers' subsequent recall. The all-mnemonic "number" more than tripled the number of students who could recall the National AIDS Hotline number (76% vs. 21%), and had a far greater impact on memory than display time. Time, by itself, increased recall only when there was a considerable display disparity (i.e., 30 seconds produced greater recall than 3 seconds). Phone number display time also was related to sponsor recall. Here, a 6-second endtag doubled the number of students who were able to recall that the CDC sponsored the PSA, whereas both extremely short and long exposures to the number reduced sponsor recall. Still untested, however, is whether all-mnemonic phone "numbers," such as 1-800-HIV-AIDS, create or foster an undesired perception that the service being promoted is primarily for people already infected, rather than for everyone who desires more information regarding the topic.

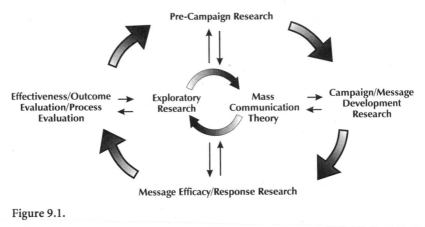

Figure 9.1.

## Conclusion

The NAIEP experiences outlined above hopefully have shown that health communication campaigns should not rely exclusively on formative evaluation to inform campaign and message design. Rather, at least seven other major types of research, encompassing a variety of research methods, can be effectively incorporated into ongoing health communication education and prevention campaigns. Thus, as the framework outlined in Figure 9.1 shows, research undertaken at each of the major stages in the ARTA campaign process, including needs assessments, message efficacy, and process evaluation, was able to make "formative" contributions by providing data that influenced and shaped message design. By using a variety of methods and sources, including secondary data, focus group discussions, expert interviews, central location interviewing, experiments, and survey research, NAIEP has attempted to create a "cycle of research" that identifies deficiencies in the public's HIV- and AIDS-related knowledge, attitudes, or behaviors; provides a basis for formulating new campaign strategies and directions; and helps in the creation and refinement of HIV/AIDS prevention and education materials and messages. Thus, along with directly assisting in the message or PSA creation process, NAIEP's research efforts increase the communication effectiveness of education and prevention materials by (a) improving problem and target audience definition; (b) facilitating the use NAIEP materials by media outlets; and (c) effectively integrating appropriate social scientific theories and previous research (Wallack 1990).

Further, as Figure 9.1 also shows, the research process, like the campaign, is best viewed as dynamic and interactive. Not only does the endpoint of one campaign or campaign phase signal the beginning of the next, but the four phases of evaluation, as well as exploratory research and mass communication theories, are intertwined in an ongoing quest to design maximally effective education and prevention materials (Salmon & Jason, 1991). Not surprisingly, as the ARTA program often found, research undertaken at one stage of the campaign or message development process will have implications and/or value in other stages or future studies. Focus group findings from the precampaign formulation stage, for example, often shape campaign and message development studies, and efficacy, process, and outcome evaluations frequently suggest topics in need of exploratory research and/or further theoretical development.

The ARTA research experiences described here also have been dynamic and interactive in that they have necessitated drawing on the knowledge and experience of a number of scientific and social scientific disciplines. Depending on the topic and issue at hand, NAIEP's research efforts have used mass communication, marketing and advertising, and health communication theories, frameworks, and methods to define research problems, formulate research designs, and operationalize research constructs. Rather than relying exclusively or extensively on one theoretical framework or model, a transtheoretical approach has been employed. Under this approach, the salient factors or features from the mass communication, social marketing, or behavior change theories most applicable to a given research situation are used (Cole, Holtgrave, & Rios, 1993). This necessitates giving up the structure that a singular framework offers, but provides needed flexibility, as well as a way to incorporate advances in behavioral and communication science thinking and methods. To date, ARTA's formative and "informing" evaluation studies have used Ajzen and Fishbein's (1980) theory of reasoned action to identify the determinants of attitudes toward early HIV testing and treatment, Bandura's (1977) social learning theory to understand viewers' reactions to TV PSAs, and Prochaska and DiClemente's (1984) stages of change model to identify and define potential target audiences.

Overall, NAIEP's research undertakings have assisted in campaign development and message design by furthering our understanding of how audience members respond to HIV and AIDS education and prevention materials. Just as important, though, the efforts to date also are a reminder that much remains to be learned about developing and placing media messages that can foster the behavioral changes necessary to markedly reduce HIV transmission and infection (Kroger, 1991).

# References

Atkin, C. K., & Freimuth, V. (1989). Formative evaluation research in campaign design. In R. E. Rice & C. K. Atkin (Eds.), *Public communication campaigns* (2nd ed.) (pp. 131-150). Newbury Park, CA: Sage.

Baggeley, J., Salmon, C. T., Siska, M., Lewis-Hardy, R., Tambe, P. B., Jorgensen, C., Harris, R., & Jason, J. (1992). Automated evaluation of AIDS messages with high-risk, low-literacy audiences. *Journal of Educational Television, 18,* 83-95.

Bandura, A. (1977). *Social learning theory.* Englewood Cliffs, NJ: Prentice Hall.

Centers for Disease Control and Prevention. (1992). *HIV/AIDS prevention factbook.* Washington, DC: U.S. Department of Health and Human Services, Public Health Service.

Cole, G. E., Holtgrave, D. R., & Rios, N. M. (1993). Systematic development of trans-theoretically based behavioral risk management programs. *Issues in Health & Safety, 67,* 67-93.

Cole, G. E., Pogostin, C. L., Holtgrave, D. R., Rios, N. M., & Collier, C. B. (in press). Public health program evaluation: Problems and solutions. *Risk: Health, Safety, and Environment.*

Donovan, R. J., Jason, J., Gibbs, D. A., & Kroger, F. (1991). Paid advertising for AIDS prevention—Would the ends justify the means? *Public Health Reports, 106,* 645-651.

Evaluating AIDS Prevention Programs. (1989). S. L. Coyle, R. F. Boruch, & C. F. Turner (Eds.), *Panel on the Evaluation of AIDS Interventions, Committee on AIDS Research and the Behavioral, Social and Statistical Sciences.* Washington, DC: American Association for the Advancement of Science.

Flay, B. R. (1986). Efficacy and effectiveness trials (and other phases of research) in the development of health promotion programs. *Preventive Medicine, 15,* 451-474.

Frankle, R. T., & Owen, A. Y. (1978). *Nutrition in the community: The art of delivering services.* St. Louis: C. V. Mosby.

Gentry, E., & Jorgensen, C. (1991). Monitoring the exposure of "America Responds to AIDS" PSA campaign. *Public Health Reports, 106,* 651-655.

Hardy, A. M. (1992). AIDS knowledge and attitudes for January-March 1991 (Advance data from *Vital and Health Statistics,* No. 216). Hyattsville, MD: National Center for Health Statistics.

Keiser, N. H. (1991). Strategies of media marketing for "America Responds to AIDS" and applying lessons learned. *Public Health Reports, 106,* 623-627.

Kroger, F. (1991). Preventing HIV infection: Educating the general public. *Journal of Primary Prevention, 12,* 7-17.

Maccoby, N., & Solomon, D. S. (1981). Heart disease prevention: Community studies. In R. E. Rice & W. J. Paisley (Eds.), *Public communication campaigns* (pp. 105-126). Beverly Hills, CA: Sage.

Marchman, K. L., & Jason, J. (1992). Evaluating the "America Responds to AIDS" campaign. In B. V. Lewenstein (Ed.), *When science meets the public* (pp. 69-82). Washington, DC: American Association for the Advancement of Science.

Middlestadt, S. E. (1990). Limitations of the social marketing approach: An illustration from the National AIDS Information and Education Program. In P. A. Stout (Ed.), *Proceedings of the Annual American Academy of Advertising Conference* (pp. 183-184). Richmond, VA: University of Richmond Press.

*Morbidity and Mortality Weekly Report.* (1991, July 19). HIV-infection prevention messages for injecting drug users: Sources of information and use of mass media—Baltimore 1989 (pp. 465-471). Washington, DC: U.S. Department of Health and Human Services.

Nowak, G. J., Jorgensen, C., Salmon, C., & Jason, J. (1993). Educating young adults about HIV and AIDS. *Journal of Direct Marketing, 7,* 31-41.

O'Keefe, G. (1985). "Taking a Bite Out of Crime": The impact of a public information campaign. *Communication Research, 12,* 147-178.

Palmer, E. (1981). Shaping persuasive messages with formative research. In R. E. Rice & W. J. Paisley (Eds.), *Public communication campaigns* (pp. 227-238). Beverly Hills, CA: Sage.

Prochaska, J. O., & DiClemente, C. C. (1984). *The trans-theoretical approach: Crossing traditional boundaries of theory.* Homewood, IL: Dow Jones/Irwin.

Salmon, C. T., & Jason, J. (1991). A system for evaluating the use of media in CDC's National AIDS Information and Education Program. *Public Health Reports, 106,* 639-645.

Salmon, C. T., & Kroger, F. (1992). A systems approach to AIDS communication: The example of the National AIDS Information and Education Program. In T. Edgar, M. Fitzpatrick, & V. S. Freimuth (Eds.), *AIDS: A communication perspective* (pp. 152-161). Hillsdale, NJ: Lawrence Erlbaum.

Sinnock, P., Murphy, P. E., Baker, T. G., & Bates, R. (1991). First 3 years of the National AIDS Clearinghouse. *Public Health Reports, 106,* 634-638.

Siska, M., Jason, J., Murdoch, P., Yang, W. S., & Donovan, R. (1992). Recall of AIDS public service announcements and their impact on the ranking of AIDS as a national problem. *American Journal of Public Health, 82,* 1029-1032.

Wallack, L. (1990). Mass media and health promotion: Promise, problem, and challenge. In C. Atkin & L. Wallack (Eds.), *Mass communication and public health* (pp. 147-163). Newbury Park, CA: Sage.

Wallack, L. (1981). Mass media campaigns: The odds against finding behavior change. *Health Education Quarterly, 8,* 209-260.

Waller, R. R., & Lisella, L. W. (1991). National AIDS hotline: HIV and AIDS information service through a toll-free telephone system. *Public Health Reports, 106,* 628-634.

Woods, D. R., Davis, D., & Westover, B. J. (1991). "America Responds to AIDS": Its content, development process, and outcome. *Public Health Reports, 106,* 616-622.

Wooten, K., Jason, J., & Gentry, E. (1992, July). *Determinants of condom use among 18- to 39-year-old adults.* Paper presented to 8th International AIDS Conference, Amsterdam, The Netherlands.

# 10 Choosing Audience Segmentation Strategies and Methods for Health Communication

## MICHAEL D. SLATER

## Introduction and
## Definition of Audience Segmentation

Audience segmentation is the foundation upon which the success or failure of a public communication effort is built (Atkin & Freimuth, 1989; Grunig, 1989; Rogers & Storey, 1987). Success might not be assured by intelligent segmentation—there are too many other contingencies regarding resources, quality of implementation, and the inherent difficulty of the task. Poor or nonexistent segmentation of audiences, on the other hand, is likely to doom public communication or education programs.

What, then, is audience segmentation, and why does it matter so much? Before proposing a formal definition, it is useful to approach the question intuitively. Each of us is often engaged in persuasive or educational communication efforts directed at colleagues, family, friends, acquaintances. In each case, it is second nature to adapt the style and content of our communication to the idiosyncrasies of our audience. We may threaten, cajole, or plead with our children; temper our requests with terms of endearment in conversation with our spouse or significant other; modestly allude to our achievements when meeting with our supervisors. What is appropriate in one case will not, normally, be appropriate in another. The contexts, the expectations, the needs, the frames of reference of our audience in each case differ obviously and dramatically.

By the same token, the expectations, needs, and frames of reference of audiences for health information differ as well. Unfortunately, the nature of these differences is not as obvious. Ideally, we would have intimate knowledge of each audience member's concerns, fears, interests, and desires, and adjust our communication accordingly. Instead, we are confronted with the necessity of communicating to a public or community that is largely faceless with the exception of those unrepresentative individuals from that community with whom we happen to be acquainted. Moreover, our communication tools—the media, community organizations, and others—permit only limited variation in content, tone, and theme. We, as health communicators, must make a limited number of distinctions among our audience and make them in a way that permits us to tailor our messages to persons with widely varying concerns, needs, and levels of knowledge.

Audience segmentation, then, is easiest to define in functional or operational terms. Grunig (1989) summarizes the criteria for segmentation found in the marketing literature: "In general, segments must be definable, mutually exclusive, measurable, accessible, pertinent to an organization's mission, reachable with communication in an affordable way, and large enough to be substantial and to service economically" (p. 203).

The crucial point here is that it is more efficient, in term of maximizing impact with given resources, to identify people who are similar in important respects and tailor one's communication content and delivery to them. To rephrase this in operational terms, audience segments have the following qualities: (a) members of a segment share similar antecedent qualities—knowledge, concerns, motivations—that determine the health behavior in question and that permit tailoring of messages or interventions to those members; and (b) members of a segment can be reached through similar media, organizational, or interpersonal channels.

The rationale for segmentation, then, is straightforward and intuitive. How best to proceed in segmenting audiences for health campaigns is a good deal less apparent. The health communication planner must: (a) identify which antecedents are most crucial in influencing whether or not people will change a health behavior; (b) identify which groups of people in a larger community—perhaps as large as an entire nation—share similar patterns of those antecedent concerns, needs, and motivations; (c) profile these groups or segments with respect to those antecedents; (d) identify information channels commonly used—and trusted—by these groups or segments; (e) develop messages or interventions that are responsive to the group's identified perspectives, needs, and concerns, and that are appropriate to the communication channels selected for use; and (f) test the message or intervention with representative members of each targeted segment (see Atkin & Freimuth, 1989).

Clearly, as asserted earlier, the whole process is founded on the identification of those antecedents used to create the audience segments. Unfortunately, there is no simple formula or "cookbook recipe" for identifying antecedents or creating segments. As a result, the process of audience segmentation has developed a reputation for being more art than science, a matter of informed and intelligent guesswork. In fact, as will be explained later in this chapter, there is some excellent social scientific methodology that can be brought to bear on the problem. As will be seen, however, the problem of intelligently grouping or classifying people based on a complex variety of motivational, behavioral, situational, and knowledge variables is one of the more challenging problems in social science and can demand more resources than may be available in many campaign efforts (see Slater, 1994; Slater & Flora, 1993). In such cases, the art in audience segmentation is a matter of choosing the right shortcuts, of finding segmentation criteria that might not be exhaustive but that explain enough variance in the health behavior outcome to be useful.

In fact, most existing approaches to segmentation are in one fashion or another shortcuts. It may be useful, then, to examine the pros and cons of these shortcuts, establish some criteria for when shortcuts are in fact justified, and explore more systematic approaches to the segmentation problem (see Grunig [1989] and Slater [1994] for extensive discussions of these alternative approaches to audience segmentation).

## COMMON APPROACHES
## TO AUDIENCE SEGMENTATION

Many of the segmentation shortcuts are well known. The most common approach to segmenting audiences is demographic—distinguishing audience members by, among other things, race, gender, ethnicity, income, or age. Such an approach is valid insofar and only insofar as the demographic variables are correlated with the antecedent variables—knowledge, constraints, motivations—that in fact influence enactment of the health behavior. Using demographics as a primary basis for segmentation is error-ridden to the degree that the correlations between demographics and the actual determinants of the behavior are imperfect. After all, the argument for using demographics is fundamentally based on complex causal relationships: that shared education, race, and cultural factors equate to common life experiences that will tend to engender similar motivations and situational constraints. Moreover, the argument states that these shared motivations and constraints, in turn, influence health behavior. Obviously, there is less error in grouping individuals on the more proximate variables (motivations and constraints) rather than the more distal ones (the demographic variables), so long as the proximate variables are reasonably well measured.

The causal assumptions in demographic segmentation have an even more serious potential flaw. Will shared demographic characteristics, in fact, reliably influence the intervening motivations and constraints? Consider two 17-year-old African Americans, both in single-parent households under the poverty line, living in urban areas. One may have a history of physical abuse from a series of males in the household, a long arrest record, and be a substance abuser at high risk of AIDS; the other may be well integrated into voluntary associations in and out of school and be in almost every important sense a very different type of person. Another example: Consider the dietary patterns of two 30-year-old college-educated Euro-American women living in the same city with incomes near the national median; one is overweight, never exercises, and considers ice cream and recreation synonymous; the other is a slender, jogging vegetarian. Clearly, demographics alone provide us with precious little help here.

Certain approaches to demographic segmentation can increase its utility. Geo-demographic approaches, such as PRIZM (Claritas, 1985), use census data to provide detailed demographic profiles of small, geographically defined areas. Such detailed data can reduce some of the error associated with demographic approaches, and can represent an efficient way to segment audiences when: (a) dealing with very large, diverse audiences; (b) the resulting segments are easy to target using the residents census data (e.g. a direct mail campaign); and (c) more rigorous approaches to segmentation are not available or convenient (see Chapter 12 in this volume).

A more sophisticated approach is to segment audiences using one or more of the motivation or constraint variables that influence behavior. A wide variety of variables have been linked to the enactment of behaviors in general and health behaviors in particular. These include attitudinal beliefs and perceptions of relevant social norms (Ajzen & Fishbein, 1980); self-efficacy and presence of behavioral models (Bandura, 1986; Strecher, DeVellis, Becker, & Rosenstock, 1986); salience of, and involvement with, the health behavior (Chaffee & Roser, 1986; Grunig & Hunt, 1984); perceived preventability and costs of alternatives (Maiman & Becker, 1974); and constraints regarding the behavior (see Slater & Flora [1993] for a more detailed discussion of antecedents or behavioral determinants of health behaviors and their role in health audience segmentation).

If one, two, or even three such variables can convincingly be documented as having a dominant influence on the health behavior in question, a variety of segmentation opportunities become available. For example, if the segmentation variables are distributed more bimodally than normally, one can dichotomize the variable or variables. If there is more than one, these dichotomized variables can then be matrixed, generating an instant typology. Or, more commonplace, one can begin with demographic segments, then segment them further using one or two of the motivational or constraint variables. For example, one can compare more or less self-efficacious middle-aged, middle-income Latin American women with respect to diet or mammography intent, or segment Euro-American adolescent males into those with peer norms supportive of and not supportive of drug use.

These are not bad approaches, with several important qualifications. First, one must be successful in finding the right key variable(s) as the basis for one's typology. If one does so successfully, the segments that result can be quite useful. If the variable turns out not to discriminate between distinctive and functionally significant reasons for enacting or not enacting the health behavior, then the approach fails. There is also considerable error even if the variable is a valuable one, if there are other important variables that are not used in the segmentation analysis (and most health behaviors are in fact complex social behaviors with multiple determinants). Also, if the variable is normally distributed, then dichotomizing the variable represents an artificial and error-ridden way of assigning group membership.

## Qualitative and Quantitative Methods:
## Some Issues in Audience Segmentation

Quantitative research methods such as surveys, and qualitative methods such as focus groups and in-depth interviewing, may be adapted to each of the above segmentation approaches. Random-sample surveys offer the obvious advantage of representativeness. Representativeness is a crucial issue in audience segmentation. If the sources of information about one's audience are not, in fact, representative of that audience and its segments, the results of the audience research will be misleading. On the other hand, surveys have two significant limitations for audience segmentation research. The first limitation concerns the selection of behavioral antecedent variables to measure. A survey can be fielded to measure demographics and the various antecedents suggested by existing research. These antecedent variables, however, are typically the outgrowth of sociological or psychological theory and do not necessarily reflect the cultural and normative specifics of social life in diverse communities. Key determinants can be missed altogether without qualitative research efforts intended to identify them. For example, some recent focus group research supervised by the author found that a significant obstacle to AIDS prevention behavior among certain African American female university students was the perceived shortage of available African American men (Laws, 1993). Assessments of this perception would not have been included in a survey had one been fielded before those focus groups were conducted.

The problems inherent in qualitative approaches to audience segmentation are even more troubling. The most obvious problem is that of representativeness. Many campaign planners seem to acknowledge and then ignore the lack of representativeness and the resulting questionable generalizability of information obtained in most approaches to qualitative data collection. The implicit assumption seems to be that people recruited to focus groups are at least approximately representative of some population segment. The loss of some accuracy in generalizability is typically deemed justifiable in exchange for the rich information gained and the relative ease, from a technical point of view, of collecting the data.

There are two serious drawbacks to using qualitative data for the purposes of audience segmentation. The first regards the representativeness of the focus group participants. If the problem was simply one of error, of less representativeness, the trade-off would be straightforward. The people who agree to participate in focus groups are generally atypical, however: Agreeing to give up a large part of one's day to discuss matters with strangers under the auspices of an outside institution is not something everyone will do. In other words, relying primarily on data from focus group participants introduces *systematic*, not random, bias into the sample. Systematic sampling bias does not just introduce error; it distorts one's understanding of underlying realities. This is particularly problematic when targeting hard-to-reach audiences; the likelihood that participants are atypical will increase as harder-to-reach target audiences are selected. The information obtained is often useful and sometimes essential, but should be handled far more cautiously than seems to be the general practice.

A more subtle but equally troublesome problem concerns the assumptions behind the development and recruitment of focus groups or of candidates for in-depth interviews. In order to recruit a focus group, one must define who the focus group is to represent. In other words, one begins by defining a priori what the audience segments are, rather than using information learned from the audience to create the segments. More often than not, the a priori definition of the segments is demographic.[1] At best then, this approach can provide a general sense that there appear to be several types within the group—though one does not know how representative those groups are, or if the systematic bias inherent in focus group recruitment has excluded or given disproportionate representation to one type.[2] It is a classic Catch-22 dilemma: focus groups are run to help understand and identify audiences, but one must have audience segments in mind in order to recruit focus groups.

This trap can be avoided to a limited extent by collecting quantitative data in the focus group context, if enough groups are run to make this viable. For example, the author collaborated on an audience research study in which focus group participants were recruited based on region of the country and urban versus rural origin. Questionnaire data were also collected. It turned out in analyzing both focus group and quantitative data that the distinction between urban and rural participants was almost meaningless; a more meaningful distinction was to distinguish between high and low concern with the issue (Kendall, Auld, Slater, Keefe, & Chipman, 1991). This approach, however, is palliative, and not a solution to the inherent problem.

What, then, from both a conceptual and methodological point of view, is a better approach to audience segmentation?

## AUDIENCE SEGMENTATION AND THE PROBLEM OF MULTIVARIATE CLASSIFICATION

The audience segmentation problem is, conceptually and methodologically, a challenging one. The central difficulty is that the audience segmentation task is largely at odds with the elegant, theory-building approaches upon which social scientists are trained and that they favor. Social science theories are built one variable at a time and rarely seek to incorporate more than four or five variables in toto (Stinchcombe, 1968). The theories are intended to apply to virtually all persons in a population; if a theory operates differently for different types of people, a contingency variable is incorporated into the model.

In contrast, health audience segmentation is based upon the variables that determine a given health behavior. Many such variables can be identified from many competing (or, more accurately, complementary) theoretical models. It is likely that some models will describe the behavior of some types of people; other models, or variables from those models, may better describe others. It is, in fact, the distinctive pattern of variables, and the characteristic value on those variables, that should distinguish audience segments.

This problem, though unusual in the social sciences, is a familiar one in biology. In fact, the problem on which biology was founded is almost precisely comparable—the problem of taxonomy. Taxonomy, like audience segmentation, is a problem in multivariate classification. One has a great deal of data about individuals (or, in biology, about specimens). The data are gathered on many different variables. The taxonomist, or the person doing audience segmentation, must identify which combination of similarities best distinguishes various groups; and the variables on which similarities are noted may vary from group to group (Abbott, Bisby, & Rogers, 1985).[3]

Audience researchers, unlike the taxonomists of old, do not have years to evolve and refine classification strategies. Fortunately, the problem of multivariate classification is amenable to mathematical analysis and has resulted in the development of algorithms for grouping or clustering individuals (or specimens) based on shared characteristics across many variables. This process is called *numerical taxonomy* in the biological sciences (Sneath & Sokal, 1973). The mathematical approaches to these methods are known as *cluster analyses* in the statistical packages commonly in use in the social sciences (see Aldenderfer & Blashfield, 1984).

Cluster analyses are well known from their use in lifestyle or psychographic analyses in the marketing field (Weinstein, 1987; Wells, 1974). In some respects, their use in marketing has given the technique a problematic reputation. The principal problem has been the highly visible VALS typology (Mitchell, 1983), which attempted to explain a wide range of behaviors through a single typological structure. Not surprisingly, a general approach of this type lacks utility for public health applications. Use of these multivariate techniques is more promising when the selection of variables to be included is specific to the behavior—in this case the health behavior—of interest (Morris, Tabak, & Olins, 1992; Slater, 1994; Slater & Flora, 1991, 1993).

An example should clarify the utility of the approach. The author and a colleague conducted a cluster analytic segmentation study with respect to cardiovascular disease risk and found seven principal audience segments. Two of them were very similar demographically: white, middle aged, middle income. One of these was the lowest risk segment in the population: Its members tended to have among the healthiest diets, engaged in moderate exercise, were willing and believed themselves able to change health behaviors, and were attentive to health information. The other proved to be the highest risk segment: They accounted for most of the cigarette smoking and alcohol use, had unhealthy diets, had little interest in changing their behavior, and despite being avid users of the media they avoided information on health (Slater & Flora, 1991).

Clearly, demographic analyses would have been likely to confound these two groups. Equally clearly, this segmentation analysis cautions the planner that, at least in this population, media-based efforts will support the behavior change activities of lower risk populations, but alternative interventions are required to best reach the higher risk segment.[4]

Although cluster analytic approaches are especially appropriate conceptually and methodologically to the task of audience segmentation, they do have one major drawback: They require considerable effort to prepare and field. The time and care needed to research the appropriate variables for inclusion in what usually proves to be a lengthy survey instrument, the cost of fielding such a survey, and then the subsequent analyses add up to a significant resource demand.

The VALS typology does provide an ingenious model for reducing these costs—by developing the typology and then amortizing the development cost by making it available for many different campaigns. Once a cluster analytic typology is developed, it is possible to identify the instrument items that best define cluster membership and to produce a short scale that can be used in the field, either for low-cost surveys or to identify segment members for focus group research. This would permit health planners in the field to use powerful segmentation schemes to inform their efforts at a very low cost. However, though it is quite feasible to conduct such segmentation studies concerning various health behaviors, such efforts have not yet been conducted. Failing the availability of such tools, what are some alternative ways of deciding how to allocate scarce research and planning resources?

AUDIENCE RESEARCH:
MATCHING APPROACHES AND
RESOURCES TO THE SCOPE OF THE TASK

Health communication planners, when preparing a campaign or intervention program, are confronted with some hard decisions regarding audience research. What is feasible given budget and time constraints? What is necessary, what merely desirable? Which efforts will yield the greatest return in improving the probability of campaign success?

Audience segmentation is one of several components of the audience research process—sometimes the most challenging component. Obviously, if existing research already provides a sound basis for segmentation, considerable resources may be directed instead to other phases of audience research,

TABLE 10.1 Adapting Segmentation Strategies to Resources and Existing Knowledge Concerning Segmentation for the Given Health Behavior and Community Type

|  | *Low Resources* | *High Resources* |
|---|---|---|
| Segments not known | Literature searches | Literature searches |
|  | Key informant interviews to establish a range of perspectives | Key informant interviews |
|  | Key focus groups if possible | Preliminary focus groups to identify additional variables of concern |
|  |  | Survey of population followed by a cluster or other type of segmentation analysis |
|  |  | Focus groups with segment members |
| Segments known | Key informant interviews to validate segments | Focus groups with segment members |
|  | Save resources for message testing | Intensive message testing with members of each segment selected for targeting |

such as message or intervention pilot testing. As suggested earlier, national-sample-based cluster analyses could provide such segmentation schemes with the short instruments needed to identify segment members and recruit participants for in-depth interviews and focus groups, especially for message-testing purposes. Unfortunately, such schemes are not currently available. If, however, campaigns addressing a similar health problem have been carried out with similar audiences, and have been preceded by a sound and systematic audience segmentation research effort, it makes sense to borrow from the earlier efforts. In that case, resources can be concentrated, if they are limited, on message testing. If resources are greater, one can expand on one's knowledge of the segments by identifying members and carrying out focus group discussions of the health issue, as well as doing more intensive message testing with each targeted segment (see Table 10.1).

Conversely, one has several choices if there is not a truly satisfactory audience segmentation scheme to tap (and this, of course, is the more likely scenario at present). If resources are adequate, one should conduct a thorough literature review to identify relevant antecedent variables that are likely to determine the health behavior of interest; and carry out some preliminary focus groups with demographic or at-risk groups of interest and/or in-depth interviews with persons with substantial experience with similar populations, to further develop the survey instruments. At that point, a survey can be fielded. Typically, as suggested above, a cluster analytic approach will yield the most useful segmentation model. If, however, the health behavior is in fact strongly determined by just one or two risk factors, perhaps these factors can drive the segmentation model.

If segments are unknown, good schemes are unavailable, and resources are limited, the problem is both more difficult and all too common. Audience segmentation is one case where almost any research, if done intelligently, is better than no research. Any data, quantitative or qualitative, that sensitizes the communicator or intervention planner to the concerns, needs, or constraints of the intended audience should only serve to improve the communication effort, even if that information is limited and partial. No matter how few the resources are, it should be possible to conduct a literature search to identify likely variables that would distinguish one's audience members with respect to the health behavior of concern. It should be possible regardless of resources to interview, even informally, a range of persons knowledgeable about the populations one is trying to reach, to get insights or be alerted to potential pitfalls. A reasonable minimum standard would be to identify relevant demographic variables and subgroups based on key motivation or constraint variables. If resources are slightly greater, it should be possible to do a few focus groups with key at-risk populations, using criteria suggested by the literature search to qualify participants for focus group participation.

The optimal approach to audience segmentation, then, is clearly indicated by the High Resources column in Table 10.1. Ideally, one would begin with a literature search to identify the relevant segmentation variables; enhance the search with qualitative research to identify culturally based variables to incorporate in a survey instrument; conduct a random-sample survey; develop a segmentation scheme based on a cluster analysis; validate that scheme using the survey data; recruit focus group participants from each identified segment of interest, for the purpose of getting additional insights; and develop and test messages or interventions with focus groups or intervention participants also recruited from the identified target segments. Almost as optimal would be to access existing appropriate segmentation schemes with instruments for identifying segment members and carry out only the last activities.

Given resource realities, such efforts are likely to remain the exception rather than the rule. If one understands the principles of audience segmentation and the pros and cons of the available alternatives, however, it is far more likely that one's efforts at segmentation will be intelligent, sensible, and useful.

## Notes

1. It should be noted that demographic criteria are the most common way to qualify focus group participants, but are not the only way. A simple, brief questionnaire—typically a single page—can be used to qualify prospective participants with respect to both motivational and constraint variables.

2. In a sense, then, demographic criteria for defining focus group membership—especially racial/ethnic criteria—involves stereotypic assumptions: that persons of a given race are largely homogeneous with respect to given attitudes and behaviors, at least in comparison with those of another race or ethnicity. A more valid rationale for ethnically based focus groups is to identify issues or responses that are culturally characteristic and must be taken into account in segmentation survey instrument development or in message design.

3. This comparison of taxonomy and audience segmentation, and the problem of multivariate classification, is developed in greater and more technical detail in Slater (1994).

4. For another example of a recent cluster analytic approach to health audience segmentation, see Morris et al. (1992).

## References

Abbott, L. A., Bisby, F. A., & Rogers, D. J. (1985). *Taxonomic analysis in biology.* New York: Columbia University Press.

Aldenderfer, M. S., & Blashfield, R. K. (1984). *Cluster analysis.* Beverly Hills, CA: Sage.

Ajzen, I., & Fishbein, M. (1980). *Understanding attitudes and predicting social behavior.* Englewood Cliffs, NJ: Prentice Hall.

Atkin, C. K., & Freimuth, V. (1989). Formative evaluation research in campaign design. In R. E. Rice & C. K. Atkin (Eds.), *Public communication campaigns* (2nd ed.) (pp. 131-150). Newbury Park, CA: Sage.

Bandura, A. (1986). *Social foundations of thought and action.* Englewood Cliffs, NJ: Prentice Hall.

Chaffee, S. H., & Roser, C. (1986). Involvement and the consistency of knowledge, attitudes, and behaviors. *Communication Research, 13,* 373-399.

Claritas. (1985). *PRIZM: The integrated marketing solution.* Alexandria, VA: Claritas, Inc.

Grunig, J. E. (1989). Publics, audiences, and market segments: Segmentation principles for campaigns. In C. T. Salmon (Ed.), *Information campaigns* (pp. 199-228). Newbury Park, CA: Sage.

Grunig, J. E., & Hunt, T. (1984). *Managing public relations.* New York: Holt, Rinehart & Winston.

Kendall, P. A., Auld, G., Slater, M. D., Keefe, T., & Chipman, H. (1991). *Communicating about agricultural chemicals in the food supply: A risk/benefit approach* (Technical Report to the U.S. Department of Agriculture, Project No. 89-EXCA-3-0989). Ft. Collins: Colorado State University, Department of Food Sciences and Human Nutrition.

Laws, S. (1993). *African-American women on a predominantly white university campus: Attitudes and beliefs about HIV/AIDS and testing* (Master's thesis, Department of Technical Journalism). Fort Collins: Colorado State University.

Maiman, L. A., & Becker, M. H. (1974). The health belief model: Origins and correlates in psychological theory. *Health Education Monographs, 2,* 384-408.

Mitchell, A. (1983). *The nine American lifestyles.* New York: Warner Books.

Morris, L. A., Tabak, E. R., & Olins, N. J. (1992). A segmentation analysis of prescription drug information-seeking motives among the elderly. *Journal of Public Policy and Marketing, 11,* 115-125.

Rogers, E. M., & Storey, J. D. (1987). Communication campaigns. In C. R. Berger & S. H. Chaffee (Eds.), *Handbook of communication science* (pp. 817-846). Newbury Park, CA: Sage.

Slater, M. D. (1994). *Taxonomy, classification, and behavioral determinants: Reconceptualizing audience segmentation.* Manuscript submitted for publication.

Slater, M. D., & Flora, J. A. (1991). Health lifestyles: Audience segmentation analysis for public health interventions. *Health Education Quarterly, 18,* 221-232.

Slater, M. D., & Flora, J. A. (1993). Is health behavior consumer behavior? Health behavior determinants, audience segmentation, and designing media health campaigns. In E. Clark, T. Brock, & D. Stewart, (Eds.), *Attention, attitude and affect in response to advertising.* Hillsdale, NJ: Lawrence Erlbaum.

Sneath, P.H.A., & Sokal, R. R. (1973). *Numerical taxonomy: The principles and practice of numerical classification.* San Francisco: Freeman.

Stinchcombe, A. (1968). *Constructing social theories.* New York: Harcourt Brace.

Strecher, V. S., DeVellis, B. M., Becker, M. H., & Rosenstock, I. M. (1986). The role of self-efficacy in achieving health behavior change. *Health Education Quarterly, 13,* 73-91.

Weinstein, A. (1987). *Market segmentation.* Chicago: Probus.

Wells, W. G. (1974). Lifestyle and psychographics: Definitions, uses, problems. In W. G. Wells (Ed.), *Lifestyle and psychographics* (pp. 325-363). Chicago: American Marketing Association.

# 11 The Gatekeeping Process

## THE RIGHT COMBINATIONS
## TO UNLOCK THE GATES

### JOHN McGRATH

*The media gatekeeper* is a deceptively simple metaphor for a decidedly complex process. At the most rudimentary level, the gatekeeping metaphor suggests a keeper with absolute authority who stands at the media gate and decides which messages will pass through the gate to reach the media audience. At a more complex level, the metaphor can signify a series of keepers with various degrees of authority who may create, reshape, or advance information through their gate to the next gatekeeper, or withhold information altogether. Insights into how information and messages are advanced, reshaped, or withheld at each gate can help health communicators create and package messages that are more likely to reach their target audiences.

This chapter will examine some of the key themes in gatekeeping research over the past 40 years. The gatekeeping function will then be discussed in terms of health communication campaigns. Six specific stages of health communication campaigns will be examined, and a variety of gatekeepers who can influence a campaign at each of these stages will be identified. The media gatekeeper will be examined in detail. The chapter will then present a framework to involve media gatekeepers in a specific health issue and increase the exposure of that issue in the media.

## Background

Perhaps the most useful definition of gatekeeping was provided by Shoemaker (1991) in the introduction to her monograph on gatekeeping: "Simply put, gatekeeping is the process by which the billions of messages that are available in the world get cut down and transformed into the hundreds of messages that reach a given person on a given day." Over the past several decades the gatekeeping process has received considerable attention from communication researchers.

Lewin (1947) was one of the first researchers to call attention to the function of gatekeeping. He developed a theory of channels and gatekeepers to explain how large social changes such as modifying the eating habits of a population could be introduced into a community. In illustrating his theory, he described two channels through which food travels to reach the table: the grocery channel and the garden channel. Lewin held that at various stages along each channel a gatekeeper decides to advance or withhold a food item from the channel. The decisions of each gatekeeper in the channel determine what foods are eventually served at the dinner table.

Lewin contended that forces in front of and behind each gate helped or hindered passage through the gate. For instance, in the grocery store channel, the force of pleasing the family with ice cream on a hot summer night may encourage a shopper (gatekeeper) to buy a gallon. The force trying to cut down on the family's fat consumption, however, may discourage the gatekeeper from purchasing the ice cream.

A key aspect of Lewin's theory holds that the act of passage through the gate can change the polarity of the forces. For instance, a negative force (e.g., "too high in fat") might apply before the gatekeeper bought the ice cream. But once the keeper allowed the ice cream to pass through the gate, the positive forces (e.g., "this will please the family") may take over, thereby allowing and even encouraging the consumption of the ice cream.

Lewin noted that this theory could apply to a variety of situations beyond the selection of food items, including news traveling through the communication channels. But one of the questions his theory raised was how media gatekeepers decide to advance or withhold information. In an early attempt to answer this question, White (1950), a student of Lewin's, designed a study he hoped would give an answer. White persuaded a newspaper editor in a small-city newspaper, whom he called Mr. Gates, to write down why he selected certain wire stories for inclusion in the paper and why he rejected others, for a one-week period. After reviewing the reasons Mr. Gates gave for selecting certain stories, and comparing the stories selected to the stories rejected, White concluded that personal bias was the main determinant of news decisions. White believed that Mr. Gates's decisions were highly subjective and often based on whether or not he believed the story to be true. A few years later, however, another investigator reached a different conclusion.

Gieber (1956) studied the way that 16 newspaper editors select stories from wire services. He contended that newspaper editors were caught up in the details and mechanics of getting a newspaper out and had little time to apply personal bias to decision making. The routines of the production influenced selection more than personal bias, according to Gieber.

Several years after the first "Mr. Gates" study, Snider (1967) sought to replicate White's study with the original Mr. Gates. Snider spent time with Mr. Gates, noting how and why he made decisions, and reached conclusions similar to White's. Mr. Gates reported that he continued to select stories based on what he liked and what he thought his readers wanted.

In addition to personal choice and organizational routines, Donohew (1967) argued that the attitude of the publisher or the media owners played a significant role in the gatekeeper's decisions. In fact, he concluded that the publishers attitude appeared to be the strongest force in determining what items enter the news channel.

The gatekeeping discussion was broadened by Donohue, Tichenor, and Olien (1972) when they argued that gatekeeping went beyond a single decision by a single individual to accept or reject information. They contended that through timing, positioning, repetition, and shaping of messages, gatekeepers influence not only passage through a gate but treatment once a news item passes the gate. A two-column story with picture on the upper fold of page 1 is a vastly different story from a single column toward the back of the paper with no picture. Yet both stories passed through the original gatekeeper.

In the mid-1970s two separate studies reanalyzed the original "Mr. Gates" study. McCombs and Shaw (1976) and Hirsch (1977) challenged White's conclusions that the gatekeeper's personal bias determined news selection. Both studies argued that wire service priorities (i.e., how these services are staffed, how they are organized, how their budget is organized, etc.) were a greater determinant of news content than the personal choice of an editor.

The major themes in the gatekeeping literature have attributed the selection of information to personal bias and to organizational routines. Windahl, Signitzer, and Olsen (1992) summarized this literature by noting that the media gatekeeper's decisions may be based on a rich mixture of general principles of news values, organizational routines, input structure, and plain idiosyncrasy.

Shoemaker (1991) proposed an important advancement to the gatekeeping concept. She suggested that wire services develop stories congruent with what newspapers want to receive. In this manner, the information producer (the wire service) produces information that meets a need of the information distributor (the gatekeeper), and in doing so facilitates passage of the information through the gate. The purposive creation of media content to meet the need of the gatekeeper is an important concept that will be elaborated throughout this chapter.

The majority of gatekeeping studies in the media have examined the role and decision-making processes of one particular media function: the news worker as gatekeeper. News workers do play an important role in health communication campaigns. News is one of several channels through which health information reaches target audiences. Yet health campaigns typically invest a substantial effort in radio and/or TV public service announcements (PSAs) to reach target audiences with specific messages. And the gatekeepers in this role, most often the community affairs directors,[1] have not been studied to the same extent as news workers. It seems reasonable to assume, however, that the decisions of community affairs directors, like those of their colleagues in the newsroom, are based on a mixture of general principles, organizational routines, inputs (what they receive), and personal choice. The context in which the decisions of community affairs directors are made will be discussed in detail below. First, it will be helpful to examine how a variety of gatekeepers can influence a health communication campaign at every stage in its development.

## Identifying the Gatekeepers
## in a Health Communication Campaign

When a significant health concern is identified by public health officials, advocacy groups, or political forces, health communicators are frequently called upon to develop communication programs that raise awareness and contribute to the reduction or elimination of the health concern. A communication campaign, as one element of an overall education program, can be an effective way to achieve this goal. Rogers and Storey (1987) identified four features that characterize a communication campaign. They observed that a campaign (a) is purposive, (b) is aimed at a large audience, (c) has a more or less specifically defined time frame, and (d) involves an organized set of communication activities.

The success of a health communication campaign depends to a large extent on how well the "organized set of communication activities" is developed, distributed, and evaluated. One useful model for planning and conducting a health communication campaign, developed by the U.S. Department of Health and Human Services (1989), is often referred to as the health communication wheel. It is based on the practice of social marketing that takes as its starting point the needs and perceptions of a target audience.

TABLE 11.1 Potential Gatekeepers at Each Stage of a Health Communication
Campaign

| Campaign Stage | Potential Gatekeepers |
|---|---|
| Planning and strategy | Administrators, political officials, stakeholders, health communicators |
| Selecting channels and materials | Health communicators, consultants |
| Developing materials and pretesting | Health communicators, stakeholders, creative team, research team |
| Implementation | Community service directors |
| Assessing effectiveness | Health communicators, evaluation team |
| Feedback to refine program | Health communicators, evaluation team, administrators, political officials |

The model identifies six distinct stages in a health communication campaign: (a) planning and strategy selection, (b) selection of channels and material, (c) development of materials and pretesting, (d) implementation, (e)
assessment of effectiveness, and (f) feedback to refine the program. Although the community affairs director is traditionally viewed as the gatekeeper in this scheme, a broader review of gatekeeping reveals numerous
potential gatekeepers at each stage of the campaign development process. A
list of potential gatekeepers who can shape and reshape health communication messages is presented in Table 11.1.

Complex organizations may have additional gatekeepers, yet Table 11.1
demonstrates that gatekeeping is a ubiquitous activity. At every stage in a
health communication campaign, different individuals or groups can exert
their influence or exercise their legitimate authority to design, reshape,
advance, or withhold information. Rogers (1983) noted that gatekeeping is
the communication behavior of an individual or individuals who can withhold information that they control as it flows through their system. From a
health communicator's perspective, this suggests that a campaign needs to
build and maintain a broad base of support for mass media messages to
reach a target audience.

The gatekeeper for PSAs has traditionally been the community affairs
director at television and radio stations. When a PSA arrives at a broadcast
facility, the community affairs director determines if, when, and how often
the PSA will be aired. Hammond, Freimuth, and Morrison (1987) developed a model of the gatekeeping funnel that tracked a PSA campaign from
distribution through gatekeepers to a target audience. They noted that only

an extremely small percentage of a target audience is usually reached by a public service message. Their model depicts a funnel with five stages: distribution of a PSA, gatekeepers' intention to air the PSA, actual airing of the PSA, selective exposure to the PSA, and finally audience response to the PSA: "Gatekeepers play a critical role in this exposure process. Because a PSA must first make it through the media gatekeepers' initial screening before it has any impact on a target audience, it is critical to learn more about the gatekeepers' selection criteria" (Hammond et al., 1987, p. 164).

The gatekeepers and the people at the gate (the community affairs directors and the health communicators) have a symbiotic relationship. Without the community affairs director, the health communicator would find points of access to a broadcast organization limited. Without health communicators and other people in similar functions, the community affairs director would have a more difficult job identifying, collecting, and structuring information about significant community issues. Insights into the real-world environments of the health communicator and the community affairs director can be an important step toward learning more about these gatekeepers and their selection criteria.

## The Communicator's Environment

The development of a health communication campaign can be a complex and expensive process. A communication campaign is often one aspect of a larger educational program that may include professional education, patient education, and community activities. If the effort is national in scope, just the communication aspect of the campaign can cost $50,000 to $150,000 when research, production, duplication, distribution, and all salaries are included in the cost. Product development time can range from 6 to 18 months, depending on the complexity of the issue, the cohesion of the stakeholders, and the type and amount of formative research and message testing required to produce a campaign. The resources needed to develop a credible health communication campaign almost guarantee that the process will be scrutinized carefully.

Within this environment, health communicators have to navigate through an obstacle course that can include obtaining resources, allocating the resources judiciously, forming alliances, guiding a creative team, keeping key constituents informed, and an array of other activities. One way to obtain an insight into the environment of health communicators is to focus on some of the real issues, problems, and constraints they face in the course of their work. The following situations represent some, but by no means all, of the typical "realities" a health communicator typically contends with in developing a health communication campaign.

## REALITY 1: STAKEHOLDERS CAN ASSIST OR OBSTRUCT THE GOALS OF A CAMPAIGN—THEY ARE SELDOM NEUTRAL

Freeman (1983) defines *stakeholder* as any group or individual who can affect or is affected by the achievement of the organization's objectives. A health issue significant enough to warrant a communication campaign frequently has several stakeholders with a keen interest in the process. Patient groups, professional associations, and voluntary associations are some of the typical stakeholders in health communication campaigns. A health communicator should identify the stakeholders and involve them at key stages in the campaign process (see Chapter 9 in this volume). Their support at later stages of the campaign can be crucial. A media gatekeeper may give more time and attention to a campaign endorsed by a coalition of community groups than to one developed by a single organization. Moreover, a stakeholder group that opposes the direction of a health communication campaign can at a minimum divert time and resources away from the goals of the campaign, and, in a worst-case scenario, stop the entire campaign.

## REALITY 2: A VARIETY OF EXPERTS CONTRIBUTE TO THE CAMPAIGN AT DIFFERENT STAGES

Health communication campaigns require different types of expertise at different stages of development. People with expertise in research, creative development, production, and even distribution enter and leave the process at different stages. For instance, different expertise is needed in each of the six stages of the health communication wheel. The players who develop the planning and strategy document may be different from the players who develop and pretest the material; and those players may be different from the ones who produce and distribute the material. At each stage in this process, highly skilled individuals or groups may make recommendations about the direction of the campaign. Yet at all times the overall direction of the campaign should remain with the health communicator. The health communicator is usually the one individual (or team) who provides continuity through each stage of the project. The health communicator must continuously negotiate with the other players (e.g., creative team, research team, production team, etc.), whose advice may at times be helpful and at other times off strategy, and with legitimate gatekeepers who have the authority to advance or withhold a product.

Unfortunately, there are no rules in this part of the game. As other players and gatekeepers enter and leave the process, the health communicator should apply a strong sense of direction and continuity to the campaign and at the same time exercise skill in negotiating changes to the campaign. Change in the campaign from its inception to its launch is inevitable. The health communicator should ensure that the changes suggested by the other players and gatekeepers strengthen and advance the campaign rather than dilute it.

## REALITY 3: A HEALTH
## COMMUNICATION CAMPAIGN IS OFTEN
## THE FIRST TARGET OF "BELT TIGHTENING"

One important role of the health communicator is to harness the resources of an organization in order to develop programs and products that contribute to the health of individuals and communities. Ironically, success in this aspect of a campaign can be a mixed blessing. In some organizations, the larger a communication budget becomes, the more vulnerable it becomes.

Change in political or administrative leadership can also threaten a budget and a campaign. New administrations often scrutinize a department's budget to identify funds for favored projects or programs. The budget of a health communication campaign can be particularly vulnerable, especially if the campaign was closely associated with previous administrators.

Legitimate public health emergencies can also require a "reprogramming" of communication campaigns funds. Occurrences such as floods, hurricanes, other natural disasters, and rapidly spreading contagious diseases all have public health implications. The budget of a health communication campaign can be a tempting target when a rapid response is needed.

One of the best ways to assure the continuation of a funded health communication campaign is to communicate continuously with the funders. The communication activities of a campaign take time to develop. Program planning, research, testing, product development, and distribution may take between 4 and 12 months. During this time health communicators should keep administrators, stakeholders, and interested publics informed of the campaign progress. This can be done through meetings, letters, newsletters, articles, presentations, and phone calls. When administrators and stakeholders understand the process and goals of a campaign and can observe campaign progress they are less likely to encroach on the campaign and more likely to support its objectives.

## REALITY 4: ADMINISTRATORS USUALLY EXPECT EVALUATION

The pressure and urgency to develop a campaign on time and on budget often results in ignoring evaluation as a critical component of the campaign. This can be a serious mistake for two reasons. First, evaluation as an ongoing component of a campaign can help the health communicator achieve campaign goals, avoid major pitfalls, and refine future campaigns (see Chapter 9 in this volume). Second, administrators expect evaluation results, particularly when large sums of money are involved and continued funding may be contingent on demonstrating the effectiveness of a campaign. Program evaluation embraces a wide range of activities that can include formative, process, and summative evaluation. Each type of evaluation is associated with a different set of goals and uses particular techniques. For example, summative evaluation examines the direct, indirect, or unintended impact of an intervention and can help determine whether program goals have been achieved (Flora, 1991). Rigorous summative evaluation requires a design that can attribute the desired change in behavior or health status to the intervention of the communication campaign. Outside of a controlled experiment, it is methodologically challenging to isolate the messages of a communication campaign from other messages and forces in the environment. Yet secondary research such as regional or national surveys, reports of physician visits, and hospital discharge records can provide indicators of trends. Although it may not be possible to identify the communication campaign as the primary cause of change, if these trends show improvement in the health condition being promoted by the communication campaign, a reasonable inference can be made that the communication campaign played a role in moving those trends in the right direction.

## REALITY 5: MANY PEOPLE HAVE UNREALISTIC EXPECTATIONS FOR A HEALTH COMMUNICATION CAMPAIGN

Health communication campaigns have been shown to be effective in specific situations. Rogers and Storey (1987) point out that the mass media campaigns can be very effective in creating awareness and knowledge about health issues. They note, however, that more ambitious effects such as behavioral changes are less certain. Backer, Rogers, and Sopory (1992) suggest that the more effective campaigns set fairly modest but attainable goals in terms of behavior change. It is a mistake to assume that a communication campaign can solve a problem that the health care community or the larger community could not solve.

Health communicators should take or create opportunities to inform administrators, politicians, stakeholders, and others of two important realities. First, not all health problems can be addressed effectively through a communication campaign. For example, if only a small number of people are affected, if there is no consensus within the medical/scientific establishment on treatment, or if members of the target audience are not media users, a mass communication campaign will have little effect on the condition. Second, health communication campaigns that establish ambitious behavioral objectives are unlikely to achieve those objectives through the communication campaign alone. Health communication campaigns play a significant role in improving health, but campaigns are one element in a larger health care context.

## The Gatekeepers' Environment

For most health communication campaigns, community affairs directors are the principal media gatekeepers, and they are gatekeepers in every sense of the word. When it comes to health communication messages, they can design, reshape, withhold, or advance (in this case broadcast) a message. It's difficult to generalize about the community affairs directors in the 900 or so TV stations and 10,000 or so radio stations in the United States. In the larger stations and in the largest markets, they head a complex department and may have several staff reporting to them. In the smaller stations and in the smaller markets, they may be in charge of community affairs as well as several other functions at the station.

The issues, problems, and constraints discussed below are based on a composite of panel presentations and discussions held over the past 4 years at the annual meeting of the National Broadcast Association for Community Affairs (NBACA), the professional association of community affairs directors. At the fall 1992 meeting, the National Heart, Lung, and Blood Institute, in conjunction with the American Heart Association, conducted a series of in-depth interviews with 14 community affairs directors, exploring issues such as factors that determine the selection and frequency of air time for a particular topic or the relative importance of various public service issues. Although a variety of issues, problems, and constraints emerged from these interviews, the issues below capture some of the main themes that community affairs directors are discussing among themselves.

REALITY 1: GATEKEEPERS' ACTIVITIES
ARE EXPECTED TO GENERATE OR ENHANCE
REVENUES FOR THE STATION

The world of the community affairs director is different than it was 10 or even 5 years ago. A television community affairs director at a recent NBACA conference described one aspect of the changing environment:

> My general manager used to think of me as the singing nun who played the guitar for children on Saturday morning. He never fully understood what I did. But now the general manager sees my department as a profit center for the station. We are expected to generate revenue like other departments.

In this new role, rather than just programming PSAs, the community affairs director is looking at ways PSAs can generate revenues for the station or "added value" for an existing advertiser. For instance, the community affairs director might now convince an existing advertiser to expand its advertising and include a health message in its ad in a collaboration with a community health group. The community affairs director might also suggest an existing advertiser support a health promotion event that gives visibility to the advertiser and the station in the community. This added responsibility of community affairs directors does not eliminate the more traditional role for their department. TV and radio stations continue to broadcast prepackaged PSAs submitted by local and national organizations. Yet at most stations, health communicators will get more attention for their health issue if they develop a package that includes a way for the station to generate revenues.

This trend at TV stations can be more of an opportunity than an obstacle. Health communicators can build a coalition of commercial companies and community groups with an interest in their health issue. National or local companies that have a natural fit with the health message (e.g., food stores, equipment manufacturers, companies that market health care products) could become part of a coalition with a health organization, and may be willing to support promotions that bring visibility to the station, the company, and the health issue. But health communicators should be extremely cautious of sending mixed messages. Many product producers would be delighted to associate their essentially unhealthy product with a health message.

## REALITY 2: GATEKEEPERS STRIVE
## TO FIND A UNIQUE POSITION FOR
## THEIR STATION IN THE MARKET

Television stations compete in a market with two, three, or perhaps four other stations in that market. In addition to competing for ratings, stations compete for an image in their market. One station in a community may be the "education station" and another may be "the station that cares about the environment" or "the station that cares about you." Some stations promote such an image over several years (or as long as a particular general manager survives at the station), others have quarterly or semiannual campaigns. Often a station-wide effort may involve several departments such as news, publicity, and sales, as well as community affairs. The community affairs director is often the point person in identifying opportunities for the station to enhance its image in their chosen area. The community affairs director may be responsible for developing and carrying out (usually with no staff) a series of activities within a specific time period that positions the station in relation to the other TV stations in that market.

On a market-by-market basis within a state or region, health communicators may be able to form a useful alliance with individual gatekeepers. For instance, a health communicator could canvass each TV station in different markets and determine if the station is planning a station-organized campaign around a health issue such as education, drugs, child health, and so on. If such a station is identified, the health communicator could offer to join in a partnership and try to invite others into the alliance to bring added visibility and credibility to the station's campaign.

Health communicators should be alert to the latent potential in a station's campaign. For instance, if a station is promoting itself as "The Station 4 Education," the health communicator can package good health in an education wrapper—good nutrition for a good education; education and exercise, a winning team.

## REALITY 3: GATEKEEPERS WORK
## IN A PRESSURE COOKER ENVIRONMENT
## AND ARE ALWAYS IN A TIME CRUNCH

Community affairs directors feel that they are exceptionally busy people. Most report that reviewing and scheduling public service announcements is only one aspect of their job. They are often expected to represent the station at community functions, maintain ties with community organizations, correspond with people or groups unhappy with the station for some reason (a program aired or not aired), and assume administrative responsibilities within the station. Many describe their job as filled with stress and too much for one person to do. The health communicator has to break through this whirlwind of activity and get the gatekeepers' attention long enough, and in a manner adequately compelling, to convince them to let the message pass through their gate.

A concise, well-documented, and visually appealing statement outlining why an issue is important to the community can cut through the paper clutter and get the gatekeeper's attention for a few moments. The statement should describe how the campaign will improve the situation/reduce the problem.

## REALITY 4: GATEKEEPERS ARE MORE
## RECEPTIVE TO PEOPLE AND ORGANIZATIONS
## THEY KNOW ON A PERSONAL BASIS

In panel presentations and in interviews, most community affairs directors agreed that personal contact with community representatives was useful in understanding local and national issues. In addition, almost all expressed the feeling that a positive, ongoing relationship between a station and a sponsoring organization plays a role when deciding what issues to promote and what PSAs to play. Their comments were tempered, however, with the observation that some organizations are too "pushy," "aggressive," or "demanding" when it comes to airing a PSA or promoting an issue.

Like the three basic rules in real estate (location, location, and location) there are three basic rules for dealing with community affairs directors— cultivate, cultivate, cultivate. This does not imply wasting their time with unnecessary calls, visits, or letters. Community affairs directors usually find it helpful, however, to know health communicators and to understand why health issues are important to the community. During the course of a year, an occasional letter, phone call, or even visit will achieve this purpose. Each interaction should have a specific purpose. Leave behind or include in your mailing an updated fact sheet, new statistics, new research findings, or other relevant information. But the above caution holds: Keep it simple, keep it brief.

## REALITY 5: GATEKEEPERS ARE COMMITTED TO THEIR COMMUNITIES AND TO THE ORGANIZATIONS WORKING TO MAKE THESE COMMUNITIES A BETTER PLACE TO LIVE

Community affairs directors demonstrated a genuine interest in and commitment to activities that enhance the quality of life in their communities. They said they were part of an organization that must be commercially viable to survive, but survival did not exclude service to the community. In fact, many felt that the station without strong ties to the community might find itself isolated, with no "position" in the community. Most felt it was in the station's interest to work with community organizations to address community problems. Community affairs directors felt that they, perhaps more than anyone in the station organization, know the pulse of the community and the issues, problems, and people that are important to the community. Although they may now have some responsibility for generating revenues for the station, they expressed an equally strong responsibility for using the station's resources to address community issues.

Health communicators can strengthen their relationship with community affairs director by providing feedback on how past station contributions have helped draw attention to or helped alleviate a health problem. Letters, plaques, certificates, or awards at regional or national conferences remind the gatekeepers, and their general managers, that the efforts of the station are making a difference.

## A Framework for Approaching the Gatekeeper

The comparisons between the environment of the health communicator and that of the community service director suggest points of difference and points of similarity. Improving public health and developing effective communication products are important to the health communicator. Improving conditions in the community and generating revenues for the station are important to the community affairs director. There are enough common interests among both groups that each could help the other reach some aspect of their goals.

Community affairs directors are bombarded by hundreds of legitimate "causes," and health communicators often find it difficult to break through the clutter of causes. Yet if community affairs directors feel that an issue is important and that they can actually do something about it, they are more likely to schedule the PSA on that topic.

A theoretical framework that can be adopted by health communicators to approach community affairs directors has been developed by Grunig and Ripper (1992). Grunig's situational theory holds that three variables help explain why people become active in an issue and then take some action (like air a PSA): problem recognition, constraint recognition, and level of involvement. He defined *problem recognition* as an awareness that something is lacking in a situation; that is, that a problem exists. Problem recognition will prompt people to seek information to understand more about the problem and what to do about it. On the other hand, *constraint recognition* discourages people from communicating. People do not communicate about problems or situations over which they feel they have little control or about which they have little self-efficacy to change or affect the situation. *Level of involvement* refers to the degree of importance or significance a situation has to an individual.

Situational theory can be applied to working with the community affairs director as gatekeeper. The first step is to help the gatekeeper recognize your health concern as a problem in the community—how many people does it affect; what are the consequences in terms of individual/family suffering, cost, reduced wages/purchasing power in the community, and so on.

The next step is to identify and resolve the constraints the community affairs director faces. According to situational theory, people do not communicate about a situation that they believe they can do little about. If constraints are removed, however, and people feel they can be effective in resolving a problem, they are more likely to communicate about that problem. In practical terms, a health communicator cannot interview each community service director to identify constraints. Yet for most health communication campaigns, it is reasonable to identify the likely constraints and address them in letters and promotional material directed to community affairs directors. An example is provided in Table 11.2.

Resolving these constraints sounds alarmingly like a segment of a sales training seminar that might be called "Overcoming Objections." Yet there is a very important difference. The presumption of this framework is that the community service director and the health communicator share a common goal of seeking to contribute to the health of their community. Through peeling away each of the likely constraints, the health communicator can lay

TABLE 11.2 Examples of Constraints Faced by Community Affairs Directors and
Their Resolutions

| Constraint | Constraint Resolution |
|---|---|
| Doesn't affect enough people | Though small in number, has a profound effect on individuals and their families |
| Other, more serious issues | Continue to address the more pressing issues, but include this in the mix |
| Station promoting one issue this year | Identify similarities between the issues and/or seek a portion of time for other health issues |

out a clear path for the gatekeeper to recognize how opening the gates to health messages can contribute to the health of people in the community.

The third and final aspect of situational theory is the level of involvement. The more community affairs directors become personally involved with the issue, the more likely they are to schedule the PSAs. This suggests that health communicators develop ways to involve community affairs directors in a health campaign as it is being developed. For instance, gatekeepers can be asked to review a script/text before production, address a local or regional meeting, or respond to a brief questionnaire about their perceptions of conditions in their community.

## Conclusion

The analogy of the gatekeeping funnel proposed by Hammond et al. (1987) pointed out that in many health communication campaigns, a large number of television public service announcements enter the top of the funnel but only a fraction exit the bottom.

This chapter has argued that exiting the funnel is not a random process. Some PSA campaigns are aired more frequently than others, some community affairs directors become more involved in some campaigns than in others, some campaigns create more discussion than others, and some campaigns influence attitudes and behavior in a target population more than others.

Three main ideas were presented in this chapter to help reduce the randomness of success in a health communication campaign and increase the level of gatekeeper interest in a particular health issue. First, a systematic campaign development process will help assure the relevance and appropriateness to the target audience. Second, the environment of the health communicator and that of the community affairs director are quite different, yet their interests overlap. The health communicator is interested in developing effective materials that improve or contribute to public health. The community affairs director is interested in generating or enhancing revenues for a station and helping to solve community issues. The health communicator who can identify some common ground with the community affairs director will have greater success in getting through the gate.

Finally, the three components of situational theory (problem recognition, constraint recognition, and level of involvement) were advanced as a framework to encourage gatekeepers to take some action about an issue. When gatekeepers perceive that a problem is important to their community, and when they sense they can contribute to the solution, they are likely to become involved in the issue. One manifestation of that involvement may be letting information on the issue through their gates.

## Note

1. Television and radio stations use various titles for the function of reviewing and scheduling public service announcements, including Public Service Director, Community Affairs Director, Public Affairs Director, and others. The professional association of the individuals in this role is called the National Broadcast Association for Community Affairs, and it appears that a substantial number of people who carry out this role are called community affairs directors. Throughout this chapter, the title of community affairs director is used to refer to the person within the TV station who can advance, reshape, or withhold and otherwise influence public service announcements.

## References

Backer, T., Rogers, E., & Sopory, P. (1992). *Designing health communication campaigns: What works.* Newbury Park, CA: Sage.

Donohew, L. (1967). Newspaper gatekeepers and forces in the news channel. *Public Opinion Quarterly, 31,* 61-68.

Donohue, G. A., Tichenor, P. J., & Olien, C. N. (1972). Gatekeeping: Mass media systems and information control. In F. G. Klien & P. J. Tichenor (Eds.), *Current perspectives in mass communication research* (pp. 41-69). Beverly Hills, CA: Sage.

Flora, J. (1991). Integrating evaluation into risk communication programs. In A. Fisher, M. Pavlova, & V. Covello (Eds.), *Evaluation and effective risk communications: Workshop proceedings* (EPA/600/9-90/054). Washington, DC: U.S. Environmental Protection Agency.

Freeman, E. R. (1984). *Strategic management: A stakeholder approach.* Marshfield, MA: Pitman.

Gieber, W. (1956). Across the desk: A study of 16 telegraph editors. *Journalism Quarterly, 33,* 423-432.

Grunig, J., & Ripper, F. (1992). Strategic management, publics, and issues. In J. Grunig (Ed.), *Excellence in public relations and communication management* (pp. 117-157). Hillsdale, NJ: Lawrence Erlbaum.

Hammond, S., Freimuth, V., & Morrison, W. (1987). The gatekeeping funnel: Tracking a major PSA campaign from distribution through gatekeepers to target audience. *Health Education Quarterly, 14,* 153-166.

Hirsch, P. M. (1977). Occupational, organizational and institutional models in mass media research: Toward an integrated framework. In P. M. Hirsch (Ed.), *Strategies for communication research* (pp. 13-42). Beverly Hills, CA: Sage.

Lewin, K. (1947). Frontiers in group dynamics: II. Channels of group life; social planning and action research. *Human Relations, 1,* 143-153.

McCombs, M. E., & Shaw, D. L. (1976). Structuring the "unseen environment." *Journal of Communications, 26,* 18-22.

Rogers, E. M., & Storey, J. D. (1987). Communication campaigns. In R. Berger & S. Chaffee (Eds.), *Handbook of communication science* (pp. 817-846). Newbury Park, CA: Sage.

Rogers, E. M. (1983). *Diffusion of innovations* (3rd ed.). New York: Free Press.

Salmon, C. (1989). *Information campaigns.* Newbury Park, CA: Sage.

Shoemaker, P. (1991). *Gatekeeping.* Newbury Park, CA: Sage.

Snider, P. (1967). "Mr. Gates" revisited: A 1966 version of the 1949 case study. *Journalism Quarterly, 44,* 419-427.

U.S. Department of Health and Human Services. (1989). *Making health communication programs work* (NIH Publication No. 89 1493). Washington, DC: National Cancer Institute.

Windahl, S., Signitzer, B., & Olsen, J. (1992). *Using communication theory.* Newbury Park, CA: Sage.

White, D. (1950). The "gate keeper": A case study in the selection of news. *Journalism Quarterly, 27,* 383-390.

# 12 Use of Database Marketing and Consumer-Based Health Communication in Message Design

## AN EXAMPLE FROM THE OFFICE OF CANCER COMMUNICATIONS' "5 A DAY FOR BETTER HEALTH" PROGRAM

R. CRAIG LEFEBVRE

LYNNE DONER

CECILE JOHNSTON

KAY LOUGHREY

GEORGE I. BALCH

SHARYN M. SUTTON

Models for communicating health information to various target audiences draw from a variety of disciplines including mass communication, psychology, consumer research, anthropology, and social marketing (Bunton & Macdonald, 1992: Cafferata & Tybout, 1989; McGuire, 1989). A common theme for researchers and practitioners, regardless of their theoretical

AUTHORS' NOTE: The 5 A Day program is the result of many people's efforts and expertise. We want to acknowledge the contributions of Jerianne Heimendinger and Amy Subar of the Division of Cancer Prevention and Control, NCI; Brian Krieg and Elizabeth Pivonka at the Produce for Better Health Foundation; Ellen Eisner and Ruth Mattingly in the Office of Cancer Communications, NCI; Heidi Lloyd and Debbie Lurie of Prospect Associates; and Stephanie Fu, Dan Snyder, and Nancy Tringali at Porter/Novelli.

framework, is that for messages to be effective among the target populations (i.e., lead to changes in awareness, attitudes, opinions, and/or behavior) they must be crafted in response to the needs and interests of the target groups. In some instances, information about target groups is gathered directly from samples of the target population through either quantitative (e.g., randomized surveys) or qualitative (e.g., focus groups) methods. In other cases, because of a lack of adequate resources or access to the target population directly, information about target populations is gathered through secondary data sources including previously published and unpublished studies, reanalyses of previous surveys, and archival analyses. One of the limitations of these latter approaches is that previous work may be tangential to the primary concerns of communication program designers and may contain significant gaps in information that is necessary to profile the target audience adequately. In such cases, program planners have usually been left with three options:

- Fill in the missing information with their best guesses
- Conduct primary research among the target population to address their questions
- Design the program without tailoring the message (take the "broad brush stroke" approach)

In the past few years, consumer marketers have introduced innovations designed to yield low-cost yet relevant consumer information they can utilize to segment and profile consumers in the product and services marketing field. These include the use of omnibus surveys in which multiple product marketers share the costs of fielding nationally representative surveys through the purchase of space for one or more items; proprietary consumer panels typically conducted by one organization either on behalf of its clients or for direct purchase by any interested parties; the compilation of information about individual consumers of a specific product and/or service through the development of privately owned databases; and geodemographic databases created by information service businesses that link U.S. Census data to existing segmentation schemes and then physically map the location of members of each segment. Such systems can then be linked to a variety of the information tools mentioned above through addresses, segment codes, or other variables to enhance the "core" information contained in the original database and provide specific information about the lifestyles of the target group.

What we present in this chapter is one of the first applications of these new information technologies to the development of a national health promotion program: the Office of Cancer Communications' "5 A Day for Better Health" program. In the development and implementation of the first 2 years of this program, we show how original quantitative and qualitative research was augmented by the selective use of marketing databases to create and refine the target audience for this campaign, as well as the creation of the messages for this campaign. Our discussion will focus on five issues that were critical in this effort:

- the original research that was conducted to begin the planning process
- the theoretical models that framed our approach and strategy
- how databases were identified and used for message design
- implementation of the program
- processes used to track the implementation of the campaign

Before we move into these issues, we first outline the rationale and main elements of the 5 A Day program and present the Consumer-based Health Communication (CHC) model on which we based the development of the campaign.

## The 5 A Day Program

The 5 A Day campaign had its origins in 1988, when the National Cancer Institute (NCI) awarded the California Department of Health Services a grant for a cooperative program between public health groups and private industry. Ultimately, the California program involved 17 major supermarket chains, representing more than 1,800 stores in California. Encouraged by its success, the program became a nationwide collaboration between the NCI and the fruit and vegetable industry in 1991. The 5 A Day program consists of supermarket point-of-purchase interventions, industry promotional support, a national media campaign, and community interventions to address the needs of specific target populations.

Industry involvement is coordinated by the Produce for Better Health Foundation (PBHF), an independent, nonprofit consumer education foundation funded by voluntary contributions from the fruit and vegetable industry (now numbering more than 120 contributing members). Licensing agreements for use of the 5 A Day logo and materials for in-store promotions and advertising have been established with food retailer members located in all 50 states and Puerto Rico. In addition, nine research grants were made by the NCI in 1993 to evaluate approaches to communicating the 5 A Day message to specific target audiences (e.g., low-income women, blue-collar workers, children, and adolescents).

The goal of 5 A Day is to increase fruit and vegetable consumption by Americans by making them more aware of how eating fruits and vegetables can improve their health and how these foods may reduce the risk of cancer. The program not only encourages eating five or more servings of fruits and vegetables a day, but also offers easy, practical ways to include.them in the diet. The scientific foundation for launching this public health program rests on several major reports by federal and scientific organizations that have examined the relationship between diet and a number of chronic diseases (i.e., National Research Council, 1989; U.S. Department of Agriculture and U.S. Department of Health and Human Services, 1985: U.S. Department of Health and Human Services, 1988). After independently reviewing the scientific literature, each report recommended that American adults eat at least five servings of fruits and vegetables a day to reduce the risk of chronic diseases. Other reviews of the literature have found that for most cancer sites, people who eat more fruits and vegetables are at a consistently lower risk for cancer than people who eat less of these foods (Block, Patterson, & Subar, 1992; Steinmetz & Potter, 1991; Ziegler, 1991). Increasing fruit and vegetable consumption to five or more daily servings among adults is also a national health promotion and disease prevention objective for the year 2000 (U.S. Department of Health and Human Services, 1990).

## Developing Program Strategy:
## The Consumer-Based Health Communication Model

Over the past 2 years, we have been applying an advertising model for strategic planning of communication efforts to the health promotion activities of the Office of Cancer Communications (see Sutton, Balch, & Lefebvre, 1994). This model blends the analytic and diagnostic foundations of health promotion (e.g., Green & Kreuter, 1991) with the strategic methods and consumer focus of private sector communication (e.g., Wells, 1989). Consumer-based Health Communications (CHC) poses a series of key strategic questions that must be answered to ensure relevant and meaningful communication to a program's target audiences. The result of this process is a strategy statement that serves as the underpinning for all communication. Because the strategy statement is based on the realities of the consumer, it guides communication efforts to ensure that they are relevant to the target audience, original so as to command their attention, and effective in leading to the desired behavior. In answering each of the questions that follow, the CHC approach depends on solid consumer research and disciplined imagination.

## WHAT IS THE PURPOSE OF THE COMMUNICATION?

CHC begins with the premise that program planners must understand what they want their audience to do as a direct result of the communication. To gain this understanding, we must determine what the target audience is currently doing instead of the desired behavior. CHC breaks down the steps in the behavior process to show what consumers are thinking and doing. For example, what is their "process" for consuming fruits and vegetables? What do members of the target audience think about fruits and vegetables? Where does the target audience come into contact with them—or not? Do target audience members make a shopping list of fruits and vegetables, or just pick some out while in the store? How do they select them? How does the target audience store them at home? How do they add them to meals—or use them as snacks? As we begin to understand the behavior process, the idea is to find those critical places and times that trigger the enactment, or failure to enact, the desired behavior. The issue then becomes which of those critical points is most susceptible to a communication effort. This decision requires a realistic assessment of what can be accomplished with a communication-based intervention.

## WHO IS THE TARGET?

Many readers will already be familiar with the idea that the larger, heterogeneous population must be segmented into smaller, more homogeneous subsamples—target audiences (see Chapter 10 in this volume). The CHC model takes this process to the next step: The identified target audience needs to be thought of as a person—complete with a name, gender, occupation, and lifestyle. What is important to this person? What are the person's feelings, attitudes, and beliefs about the behavior change (including both perceived benefits and barriers)? What are his or her media habits? Creating a vivid mental picture of the target helps us answer these questions.

CHC impresses on program planners that the target should be vivid and personalized for two reasons. First, effective communication is a highly personal process that occurs between two people—a sender and a receiver. Effective communication from the sender to the receiver says,

> I know a lot about you; I understand you, your problems, aspirations and needs. I want to tell you something that I believe in, am enthusiastic about and believe that you will be enthusiastic about too—as soon as I give you the facts and let you make up your own mind. (Whit Hobbs, quoted in Wells, 1989, pp. 6-7)

In effective public health communication, the target audience must be described as a person, not as a compilation of statistics.

The second reason for vivid targeting of the audience is that this allows limited resources to have more impact because they are concentrated on where they will do the most good. This often raises the concern among some public health professionals that by focusing so narrowly on certain segments of the population, others will be missed. The reality, however, is that—depending on how the health message is executed and distributed—certain groups will always be reached and others will not. The only issue is whether the targeting is done based on research and strategic analyses or by happenstance and default.

## WHAT DOES OUR COMMUNICATION PROMISE?

What will the target find most appealing and motivating about the desired behavior change? It must be something that is persuasive to the target, not the program planners. Many public health messages have clear-cut, scientifically based benefits: for example, reduce your risk of cancer. Yet, these public health benefits may not be persuasive to the target audience. CHC requires that we find the answer to this question in terms of benefits that are personally meaningful and relevant to the target audience. Oftentimes, these benefits may exist in the mind of the consumer ("Eating five fruits and vegetables a day will keep me young"), sometimes they are emotional ("Serving more fruits and vegetables will make me a better parent"), and at other times the benefits may not be the ones the planners originally had in mind ("Eating more fruits and vegetables will help me lose weight"). Whether these benefits are subjective or empirical, they refer to some reward in the future that is valued by the target and will be gained through the behavior change. The message should not necessarily directly convey the promise of the communication; rather, the message needs to be constructed so that the target audience can deduce, or infer, the benefit from the total communication product (e.g., see most cigarette advertisements).

## HOW WILL WE SUPPORT THE PROMISE?

Support for the promise encompasses all the elements that make the promise credible to the target and likely to happen. It can include scientific facts about the behavior change as well as literal or dramatic demonstrations of valued benefits of the change. Emotional appeals and support can often be persuasive, as can the presence of role models or opinion leaders. Support for the promise needs to take into account the perceived barriers to adopting the new behavior, points of resistance to making changes (addressing "Yes, but..." responses), and how the new behavior may fit into the target audience's social and physical environment (e.g., trying to eat more fruits and vegetables in the inner city where supply is much more limited). Support statements are by necessity intertwined with the benefit that is promised, so that the benefit of eating more fruits and vegetables is linked in the target audience's mind with a specific support (e.g., "People I know can do it," "It actually cuts down on my grocery bill") that is relevant to them.

## WHAT APERTURES AND COMMUNICATION TOOLS WILL BE USED?

*Apertures* is used here as an overarching term to describe the times, places, and circumstances when the target is most likely to be receptive to the message. These may be those critical points in the behavior process discovered earlier, such as being hungry for an afternoon snack but not thinking of a piece of fruit. Another type of aperture might be the context in which the target finds the reward especially appealing (the reward of losing weight may be more appealing when out shopping for new clothes). Identifying the critical apertures is a necessary step prior to selecting the most appropriate media tools. For instance, if the target audience is unlikely to make a shopping list prior to going to the grocery store, it is more important to focus on point-of-purchase communication tools than rely on store advertisements in the newspaper or on television.

Media tools include traditional media vehicles such as particular television and radio shows, specific places in newspapers and magazines (the food or nutrition sections), billboards, and transit shelters; and nontraditional ones including infomercials and video news releases. Other tools include 1-800 numbers, church fairs, block parties, and many others. It is also clear that interpersonal channels need to be incorporated into the communication mix for increased efficacy of the message through such means as volunteers, church leaders giving sermons, and peers at the worksite delivering the program. It is the crafting of a strategic, consistent, and synergistic communication program that takes full advantage of the target apertures that will break through the competitive clutter with a single, compelling image.

## WHAT IS THE PERSONALITY
## OF THE BEHAVIOR CHANGE?

Any communication effort aimed at changing a behavior will project an overall tone to the target audience. This tonality is created through the combined message, execution, and channels that the target encounters. This tonality or personality of the communication may be hard to describe or capture verbally—but it is there. One example of attention to personality is given by the creators of a series of Nike commercials with the tag line "Just do it." Note that there is no exclamation mark after the statement. More important to the creators of the ad, however, was the decision NOT to use a voice to say the tagline—it is only shown. Their concern was that the wrong voice, the wrong delivery, and the wrong inflection could have doomed the ads for many viewers. So as not to convey a potential "authoritarian" personality, they decided to let viewers add it for themselves. The "Just do it" campaign depicts people being physically active; Nike shoes are a support. The strategic concept is that if more people are physically active, more people will buy Nike—known as expanding the market versus expanding market share. Health campaign planners need to recognize that personality creates the context in which the entire "message" will be processed. If the personality of the behavior change is off-target, the best benefits and supports will be of limited value (just imagine if they had used wrestling stars instead!).

One way communicators try to understand and shape the personality of their message is to pretend that the behavior change is a person. This projective technique often helps identify the hidden nuances of a campaign or program. A standard approach would be to ask the question of the target audience: "If a person engaged in a certain behavior (e.g., If someone ate five fruits and vegetables a day), what traits would characterize him or her?" These attributes should form a vivid personality that is attractive to the target audience. If eating five fruits and vegetables a day had such attributes as "boring, old fashioned, unpleasant, and dull" among the target audience, then we would need to work to transform the personality into one that is more appealing.

## MODELS OF BEHAVIOR

In addition to marketing concepts, the program planners also looked to psychological theories to help conceptualize the behavior change process. The theoretical framework that helped guide the 5 A Day program's strategy and research was the transtheoretical model of Prochaska and DiClemente (1983). Briefly, this model proposes that stages of behavior change can be conceptualized in five phases:

- *Precontemplation,* in which there is no thought or awareness of the need to change a behavior
- *Contemplation,* in which the target seeks out information about possibly changing his or her behavior
- *Action,* where the target attempts to institute the desired behavior change
- *Maintenance* of the behavior change for an extended period of time
- *Recycling,* when the maintenance phase is discontinued and the target reverts back to a precontemplative or contemplative phase

This model has been shown with other health behaviors to be quite powerful in the design of effective interventions (see Chapters 2 and 3 in this volume). The decision was made to incorporate this type of psychological segmentation scheme into the identification of relevant target audiences for the 5 A Day campaign.

## PULLING IT TOGETHER

Because of budget constraints, the need to begin the national campaign quickly, and the pervasiveness of the low awareness of the target behavior among the general public (see the next section), the team concluded that the first year's activities would be a high visibility, general awareness campaign that would not target behavioral messages to any specific audience segments. Further research was planned, however, to address the CHC questions left unanswered by the currently available research and to elaborate a segmentation scheme based on the stages of change model. The objective was to develop the base from which to evolve the first-year broad spectrum approach to one more tightly focused on a target audience. The next sections detail how this latter process unfolded.

## The 5 A Day Baseline Survey

Before the planning of the program began, a baseline survey was jointly fielded by the NCI and PBHF in August 1991. This national telephone survey of 2,837 Americans, 18 years of age and older, helped quantify the extent of the problem that needed to be addressed by the program. The main results of this survey were as follows:

- Two thirds of the respondents believed that two or fewer servings of fruits and vegetables a day are sufficient for good health
- Only 8% believed they should eat five or more servings a day for good health
- The median daily fruit and vegetable intake was 3.5 servings, with women eating slightly more than men (medians 3.7 and 3.0, respectively)
- Fruit and vegetable consumption increases with age, from a median of 3.0 servings a day among 18- to 35-year-olds to 4.1 servings among people 65 years of age and older
- Fruit and vegetable consumption was similar among white and black respondents (median = 3.4), and slightly less among Hispanics (median = 3.0)
- Education level was associated with fruit and vegetable consumption: People with less than a high school education reported eating 3.3 servings a day whereas people with more than a high school education ate 3.7 servings a day
- Similarly, lower daily fruit and vegetable consumption was found among persons with low incomes (median = 3.1) than those with higher incomes (median = 3.7)
- Overall, 4 in 10 Americans believed that eating fruits and vegetables would help prevent cancer, and 6 in 10 believed it would help them lose weight
- Those people who reported eating the fewest servings of fruits and vegetables also tended to use methods of food preparation that added fat to their diet
- More than 80% of respondents agreed that they liked the taste of fruits, compared to 71% who agreed that they liked the taste of vegetables
- Respondents had a weekly median intake of 12 servings of vegetables and 10 servings of fruits (including juices)

These data served as the primary, quantitative resource from which the program planners began to analyze the problem and to develop research strategies for audience segmentation and campaign message development.

## Consumer Research for 5 A Day

From the initial planning of the 5 A Day campaign, consumer research methods were consistently employed to address various aspects of audience segmentation and message design. A first step was to pretest the messages to be conveyed in Year One of the campaign.

### MALL INTERCEPT INTERVIEWS

In December 1991 the proposed 5 A Day themeline—"Did you know that eating five fruits and vegetables is one of the most important choices you can make to help maintain your health?"—was pretested to determine its understandability, believability, and motivational value among adults. Forty respondents were recruited and interviewed at shopping malls in Atlanta, GA; Milwaukee, WI; and Albuquerque, NM. Screening criteria specified an equal number of males and females between the ages of 30 and 60 years. To ensure a representation of people from minority populations, 25% of the respondents were of minority status (black, Hispanic, or Asian). Exclusion criteria included any person with either past or present heart disease, cancer, or diabetes, and any persons currently following a special diet recommended by their physician, as it was believed that such individuals might have been sensitized to nutrition messages because of their condition.

Each participant was shown five 8½" by 11" posters that were identical except for the ending of the themeline (that part of the message constituting the "promise"). These promise statements were:

- "... to maintain your health"
- "... to stay healthy"
- "... to protect your health"
- "... for your health"
- "... to improve your health"

The order of presentation of each poster was preset to vary across participants so that an equal number of individuals saw each poster in the first and last positions. Posters in the middle positions were randomly presented. After seeing all of the posters, the participants were asked to describe the main idea of the posters and indicate how believable that idea was to them. Participants rank-ordered the five posters for clarity and motivational value, and then indicated why they selected a poster as first or last. Finally, participants were asked what effect adding the words *to help* to each themeline would have in making it more believable, understandable, and motivational. Several conclusions were drawn from these interviews. They included:

- The posters communicated clearly that fruits and vegetables are important for good health.
- Nearly two thirds of the participants considered the themeline to be highly believable.
- Although participants believed that eating five fruits and vegetables was relatively easy, they also felt that other behaviors should take priority (exercising, eating less fat, not smoking).
- Fewer than 4 in 10 participants had made any changes in their diet in the past 2 years. Those people who had made changes had done so mainly to lose weight by reducing their fat and cholesterol intake.
- The words *improve* and *maintain* were the preferred alternatives for the themeline promise.
- Adding the words *to help* to the various themelines served to strengthen each message's believability, understandability, and motivational value.

These findings led to modifications of the key message points for the media campaign and also led program planners to address directly the relative ease and importance of consuming five fruits and vegetables a day, to focus on weight loss as a motivational factor, and to position 5 A Day against other behavior changes on its ease of adoption.

## FOCUS GROUPS

Further formative research was conducted in April 1992 as a follow-up to the mall intercept interviews. Six focus groups were held in three markets (Baltimore, MD; Richmond, VA; Chicago, IL) to address the following objectives:

- Understand the ways in which fruits and vegetables fit into (or do not fit into) consumers' daily food and health routines
- Probe likes and dislikes about fruits and vegetables and identify perceived benefits and barriers to increasing consumption of them
- Explore perceptions and reactions to the 5 A Day program concepts

The findings of these focus groups confirmed many of the results of the intercept interviews. Participants in the focus groups suggested that a positive environment exists for the 5 A Day program because of the increasing interest in, and exposure to, nutrition messages. They also believed that they should be eating more fruits and vegetables, but were not certain what the number of servings should be. When "five" was set as a goal, they saw it as a reachable target regardless of what they estimated their current daily intake to be.

It was also clear that consumers face a number of obstacles in their efforts to eat in a more healthful way. Among the more salient obstacles to be addressed by communication programs were: "boring" presentation of fruits and vegetables at meals, "finicky eaters," lack of convenience (preparation time), and the quality of the produce (how to pick ripe ones and store them at home). Other issues that were raised in the focus groups pointed to depicting how large a "serving" actually is (consumers tended to overestimate a serving size); highlighting how produce incorporated into other foods still "counted" (as in stews, fruit juices); and that the 5 A Day goal was a minimum number, not a maximum one.

The concept of such a program being a collaborative effort on the part of NCI and the produce industry was also tested for its credibility. The participants had positive reactions to the program regardless of its sponsorship and perceived in-store promotions and other industry efforts as positive aspects of the effort.

Finally, the participants were asked for their ideas about how one could eat five fruits and vegetables a day. Several of their suggestions were subsequently employed in food demonstrations that occurred at the 5 A Day launch press conference in July with such titles as: "Through the Day With 5 A Day" (fitting fruits and vegetables into meals), "5 A Day on the Go" (getting fruits and vegetables when eating out), and "Who Has the Time to Cook 5 A Day?" (using the microwave to prepare fruits and vegetables).

MARKETING DATABASES

The nature of these first two formative research methods was such that they allowed the planners to develop a series of messages for the general population to launch the program. It was also recognized, however, that the second phase of the program would need to become more targeted; attention was therefore turned to answering the questions of the CHC model. It was recognized that existing data sources, such as the baseline survey, would not be adequate for this task. It was also clear that resources were not available to conduct a large survey designed to answer these questions. Consequently, efforts were directed toward finding other data sources from which information relevant to the CHC model, especially as it related to fruit and vegetable consumption, could be extracted.

The MRCA's[1] Nutritional Marketing Information Services household panel was identified as a potentially rich source of such information. This proprietary panel survey collects data annually from 2,000 households in the United States, selected to be representative of the population. Complete daily food diaries are kept for each member of the household during a 14-day period. In addition to the diaries, respondents indicate for 26 food categories whether their intake of each category has changed in the past year and provide information about their interests, attitudes, media habits, and other lifestyle information through a self-administered questionnaire.

After meeting with MRCA staff, a customized analysis was conducted of their data that compared two segments of the population: those persons currently eating an estimated five fruits and vegetables a day (corresponding to "maintainers") and those in the Contemplation or "early action" stage (eating 2.5-3.5 servings a day but reporting trying to increase fruit and vegetable consumption). The former segment became the reference group and the latter segment became the target group for the campaign. Although many similarities between the two groups were observed, including comparable education levels and male/female representation, notable differences were found that served to distinguish them (see Table 12.1). Key attributes of the proposed target audience focused on by the program planners included:


- To be between the ages of 25 and 55, and younger than "maintainers"
- To have busy, hectic lifestyles
- To "cut corners" in meal preparation
- To value the importance of convenience
- To be concerned about losing weight
- To view cancer as the health problem to be most concerned about


A second database was also employed to profile further the target audience. In this instance, a single question was added to the 1992 DDB Needham Life Style Survey of 4,000 consumers. The question asked consumers to indicate how many servings of fruits and vegetables they ate or drank the previous day. Nearly 50% of the respondents indicated that they were eating two or three servings per day; this group was used to further characterize the program's target audience.

TABLE 12.1  Differences Between 5 A Day Target and Comparison Groups

| Target Group | Reference Group |
| --- | --- |
| Eats 1.5-2.5 servings/day and has increased fruit/vegetable consumption | Eats 3.5-6.0 servings/day |
| Likely to be 25-55 | Likely to be older, 55+ |
| More likely to have kids at home | More likely to be retired |
| Broad range of incomes | Often has fixed income |
| Many are working women | |
| More in South & North Central | More in North East |
| | Many walk for exercise |
| Busy, hectic lifestyles | |
| Less likely to have traditional eating patterns | Has traditional eating patterns including 3 square meals a day, cooking from scratch, eating fruit with breakfast and vegetables with dinner |
| "Cuts corners" in meal preparation | Healthier meal preparation including use of low-fat recipes and high-fiber foods |
| Taste is important | Views diet as healthy |
| Convenience is important | Takes fruits and vegetables from home |
| Anxiety-ridden about nutrition | |
| More concerned with losing weight; perceives self as pudgy | |
| Concerned about cancer | Concerned equally about cancer, heart disease, high blood pressure, & high cholesterol |
| | More likely to be on medical diet |
| | More likely to have health problems |
| Less sense of urgency about the need to eat healthier | Due to medical problems, eating a healthy diet has immediate relevance |

The lifestyle profile of the target audience developed from the Life Style Survey paralleled that of the MRCA cohort. There were few demographic differences between the two groups. Compared to people already eating at least five servings of fruits and vegetables a day, people eating two or three daily servings were found to lead faster paced lives and have little spare time; were more likely to suffer from conditions such as headaches, lack of sleep, and indigestion; and tended to be impulse buyers. Key media habits of the target audience included:

TABLE 12.2 Adjectives Used by the Target Audience to Describe a "5 A Day Eater" and Themselves

| 5 A Day Eater | | Themselves | |
|---|---|---|---|
| Sensible | (89%) | Dependable | (93%) |
| Healthy | (88%) | Capable | (76%) |
| Disciplined | (86%) | Friendly | (75%) |
| Concerned | (82%) | Sensible | (72%) |
| Fit | (82%) | Careful | (71%) |
| Smart | (80%) | Gentle | (71%) |

- Top television programs watched include local news, news interview shows, and prime-time movies
- Top radio formats are soft rock, classic rock, easy listening, and country-western
- They are not as involved in volunteer and community activities

These data allowed the planning team to address most of the CHC questions. Yet, the issue of the "personality" of the program was still unaddressed. Consequently, a recontact survey of the MRCA consumer panel was conducted. Panel members meeting the original segmentation criteria—eating 2.5-3.5 fruits and vegetables daily and reporting trying to eat more—were mailed a short questionnaire asking them to rate how well each of 29 adjectives described themselves and then how well the adjectives described someone "who eats five fruits and vegetables a day." A total of 140 questionnaires (66%) were returned; 59% of the respondents were women. Table 12.2 presents the top 5 adjectives chosen by this group to describe themselves and the "5 A Day" eater. There were a number of striking findings in these data that addressed the personality of eating 5 A Day.

- Responsibility is an extremely important factor for the target audience. They see themselves as dependable, sensible, concerned, and careful. In contrast, the "5 A Day Eater" is seen as less so. Members of the target audience are always on the go and view themselves as constantly meeting the demands of others, with little to no time to meet their own needs.
- Members of the target audience view the "5 A Day Eater" as smarter and more disciplined than they. As expected, "5 A Day Eaters" are also viewed as more healthy and fit; attributes the target audience simply may not have the time (or luxury) to pursue.

These data were then incorporated into the CHC framework to provide a consistent approach to message execution and delivery in Year Two of the

TABLE 12.3   Summary of the Strategy Statement for Year 2 of the 5 A Day Program

---

Target Audience:

People increasing their fruit and vegetable consumption, but eating less than the minimum of 5 or more servings per day.

Purpose:

Add 2 or more servings of fruits and vegetables a day "the easy way" instead of making it hard.

Promise:

"When I add 2 or more fruits and vegetables a day 'the easy way' instead of making it hard, I feel relieved and more in control of my life . . ."

Supports:

- I'm being shown ways that fruits and vegetables can fit easily into busy lives.
- A great number of studies have shown that a diet rich in fruits and vegetables has a positive effect against cancer.
- Fruits and vegetables taste great.
- I keep hearing the phrase "5 A Day for Better Health," and
- This information is coming from NCI, a credible source of health information.

Personality:

5 A Day eaters are responsible, balanced, and warm.

Apertures:

*Times* when people are preparing their shopping lists, shopping, or choosing foods at a restaurant, or are in transition (start or end of the day, or weekend).

*Places* such as the table, by the TV, in stores or restaurants, in the car, train, or bus, and in the kitchen.

*State of mind* when people are hungry and thinking about what to eat, hassled, starting to relax, and reflecting on their day or planning for tomorrow.

---

campaign. The complete strategy statement is shown in Table 12.3. A visual representation of the target has also been developed in order for all members of the campaign team to understand the target (shown in Figure 12.1).

## Implementing the Campaign: Media Outreach Activities

The 5 A Day campaign has employed a number of media interventions designed to reach the target audience with 5 A Day messages. These interventions were developed using the information gained from the baseline survey and marketing research discussed in the previous section, and were designed to be consistent with the communication strategy crafted using the CHC framework.

**Figure 12.1.** Artist's Sketch of the 5 A Day Target Audience
SOURCE: National Cancer Institute

## THE CAMPAIGN LAUNCH:
## NATIONAL PRESS CONFERENCE

On July 1, 1992, NCI launched the 5 A Day campaign with a national media event in Washington, D.C. The event began with a traditional press conference focusing on the need for the 5 A Day program and the science base for the government's involvement with such a program.

Speakers at the press conference included then Department of Health and Human Services Secretary Louis Sullivan, M.D.; then National Institutes of Health Director Bernadine Healy, M.D.; and the director of NCI's Division of Cancer Prevention and Control, Peter Greenwald, M.D., Dr.P.H. Drs. Sullivan and Healy spoke about the importance of eating fruits and vegetables as a way to increase health and decrease cancer risk. To underscore the need for the program, Dr. Greenwald presented the results of the baseline survey discussed earlier in this chapter.

Following the speakers' remarks, reporters had an opportunity to visit the five food demonstration booths staffed by registered dietitians to illustrate a wide variety of easy ways to add fruits and vegetables throughout the day:

1. **5 A Day—Isn't That a Lot of Food?**

   Depictions of actual serving sizes, to illustrate that five servings a day is less than most people think.

2. **Through the Day With 5 A Day:**

   Depictions of fruit and vegetable options throughout the day, with each "day" adding to five servings.

3. **5 A Day the Low-Fat Way:**

   Secretary Sullivan preparing low-fat Danish potato salad with dill, to emphasize the importance of preparing fruits and vegetables in a healthful way.

4. **5 A Day On the Go:**

   Tips for getting 5 A Day when eating out.

5. **Who Has Time to Cook 5 A Day?**

   Quick preparation tips, featuring microwave ovens, to overcome concerns about preparation time.

To support the national launch and provide reporters with additional background on the role of fruits and vegetables in disease prevention as well as consumers' attitudes and knowledge, a resource kit was developed and disseminated to those attending the press conference and 100 other magazines and newspapers countrywide. Included in the resource kit was a summary of the baseline study findings and a summary of findings from other relevant studies of consumers' consumption and attitudes, as well as other traditional press kit materials, including a news release, speakers' remarks, and reproducible copies of infographics conveying key baseline study findings. In addition, a video news release featuring Olympic swimmer Matt Biondi and the key 5 A Day messages was produced and distributed via satellite to news organizations across the country the afternoon of the press conference.

## MEDIA NEWSLETTER

As a major "tool," or channel, for reaching 5 A Day's target audience, more than 1,000 food editors at magazines and newspapers across the country receive a quarterly newsletter from the NCI entitled *5 a Day: A Food & Health Newsmagazine for the Media*. Each edition of the newsletter is four to six pages long and contains a mixture of stories, recipes, illustrations, and infographics, including a nutrient analysis of a particular fruit or vegetable. The newsletter itself is printed in color; additional reproducible copies of all infographics are included in black and white on a separate page and the entire newsletter is available on a Macintosh disk. All elements of the newsletter are designed to reinforce the major 5 A Day messages and provide a variety of easy ways to eat more fruits and vegetables.

The first newsletter, mailed in conjunction with the July 1992 press conference, supported the launch of the media campaign. The front page featured a brief overview of the 5 A Day program and its government/industry partnership, and a longer story detailing the baseline survey findings that illustrated Americans' lower-than-desirable fruit and vegetable consumption and their low awareness of how many fruits and vegetables they should eat. A sample infographic from the story is shown in Figure 12.2.

The first newsletter also contained story ideas that addressed some of the barriers we learned about in the focus groups. For example, one section of the newsletter focused on conveying the size of fruit and vegetables servings, because actual serving sizes are smaller than most people think they are. This section visually conveyed size by using a photograph of a variety of actual servings, including a melon wedge, a grapefruit half, 6 ounces of juice, and a half cup of cooked green beans (in a measuring cup). This particular story idea took a lighthearted approach, as illustrated by its accompanying text:

Five servings a day . . .
How am I gonna do that?

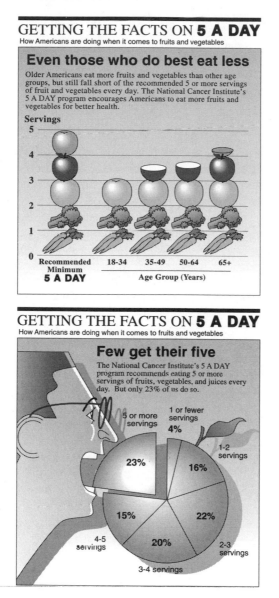

**Figure 12.2.** Sample Infographic From the 5 A Day Newsletter
SOURCE: National Cancer Institute

Relax. It's easier than you think.

You don't have to eat a whole head of cabbage, for goodness sake. Check the serving sizes above. They are normal amounts of food that you can enjoy in many different ways.

Also, keep in mind that five servings is not a limit, but a goal. If you can eat more than five, that's even better. Government health experts recommend five or more servings.

Another section used six vignettes, each focusing on a different person, to illustrate how 5 A Day can be easily integrated into a variety of lifestyles.

Subsequent issues of the newsletter have featured information on topics such as low-fat preparation tips, microwave tips, and "brown bagging" the 5 A Day way. To ensure that consumers understand how 5 A Day fits into their total diet, frequent references to the USDA's Food Guide Pyramid are made. The winter 1993/1994 newsletter included a comparison of the pyramid's recommendations versus the servings in each food group that we actually eat, based on an analysis of the MRCA Nutrition Information Services data on food consumption. This analysis demonstrated that Americans eat much too much fats, oils, and sweets; the right amount of meat, poultry, fish, and eggs; and too little of everything else (including, of course, fruits and vegetables).

## MAGAZINES

National magazines have enormous reach compared to newspapers. For example, *Good Housekeeping* reaches more than 28 million American adults; in contrast, the daily *New York Times,* one of the largest circulation papers in the country, reaches about 3 million. Because of magazines' potential to reach a large proportion of the 5 A Day target audience, distribution of the newsletter is followed up periodically with personal visits by NCI staff to key food editors and writers. These meetings usually involve a briefing on the program and a discussion of long-term story ideas for their publications.

## 5 A DAY WEEK

In 1993, NCI's efforts centered on launching National 5 A Day Week, September 13 through 18. Based on the CHC strategy, NCI's consumer messages for 5 A Day Week focused on easy ways to get an additional one or two servings of fruits and vegetables each day and emphasized the following behaviors:

- Have fruit or juice with breakfast every day
- Snack on fruits and vegetables daily
- Stock up on dried, frozen, and canned fruits and vegetables
- Store fruits and vegetables within sight and easy reach
- Microwave vegetables for dinner

A number of media interventions were used to support 5 A Day Week, including:

- The 5 A Day media newsletter, which highlighted the week and the tips outlined above.
- Print, radio, and transit public service announcements (PSAs). The publications receiving the 5 A Day newsletter also received the PSA, as did all retailers participating in the 5 A Day program. The radio PSA, "The Talking Supermarket," was mailed to 1,000 stations and an alert was faxed to each station urging their use of the PSA during 5 A Day Week. In addition, 200 dioramas were distributed for display in airports across the country, and one print PSA was adapted for use on buses and subway platform displays in the Washington, D.C., metropolitan area.
- NIH Radio News Service made the radio PSA and a one-minute news story interview with Kay Loughrey, director of NCI's 5 A Day media activities, available to radio stations. Both the PSA and news story were accessed by 597 radio stations.
- NCI's Dr. Greenwald was interviewed for CNN Radio's "Healthwatch" segment, which feeds to 600 stations nationwide and reaches an estimated 7.5 million listeners.

In future years, the 5 A Day campaign will continue to include 5 A Day Week and the media newsletter in its repertoire of media interventions. Other interventions will be developed and implemented as well.

## Industry Activities

As noted earlier, the 5 A Day campaign is a cooperative effort of the NCI with the Produce for Better Health Foundation. This foundation was incorporated as a nonprofit 501(c)(3) organization in 1991 to coordinate industry efforts toward 5 A Day. The primary emphasis of the industry partners is to provide advertising and in-store promotional support of 5 A Day messages. Thus, fruit and vegetable growers and related associations (e.g., Tanimura and Antle, California Avocado Commission), food packagers and distributors (e.g., Dole Food Company, Del Monte), and food retail chains (e.g., Super Valu, Giant Eagle, Kroger) participate as members of the Board of Directors and in 5 A Day program activities. All industry partners are required to adhere to strict licensing standards developed by the Foundation and the NCI. These standards cover the use of the 5 A Day logo and taglines, and carefully lay out what claims advertising and promotions can make about increasing consumption of fruits and vegetables. Any materials developed by a partner independently of the Foundation or NCI are voluntarily submitted for review to assure that the messages are in compliance with standards set by the Food and Drug Administration. (We should also note that 43 state health agencies have similar licensing agreements with the NCI that govern their use of the 5 A Day logo and materials—Havas et al., 1994.)

Currently, there are more than 150 industry partners. One of the communication challenges facing the 5 A Day effort is to coordinate both the private and public sector efforts. The use of joint meetings has been one mechanism to provide a forum in which each partner can keep the other apprised of their activities and also plan cosponsored events—such as the launch press conference and 5 A Day Week. However, the sheer number of industry participants who all wish to put programs out to their customers provides numerous challenges for program coordinators—not unlike attempting to herd cats. Rather than choosing to force a highly centralized planning and control structure on 5 A Day efforts, the NCI and the PBHF have shared strategic direction and objectives with industry representatives. These objectives and strategies are based on the data provided earlier in this chapter. Through presentations at meetings such as The Produce Conference and the Produce Marketing Association annual conference, opportunities have been available to present, and discuss, the core target audience of the program and possible tactics that might be implemented by the industry to reach this group of consumers with relevant messages.

## Assessing Message Reach and Impact

### MEDIA TRACKING

Determining how many people—and who—a media campaign reaches is always difficult. Americans are bombarded with a vast array of media-channeled information. Those reached with a message do not necessarily remember being reached, especially if it is their first exposure to the message.

Conversely, people who are reached multiple times with the same message may not remember all the sources of the message. Therefore, asking consumers if they have seen or heard a particular message tends to underrepresent the true number of people who in fact saw or heard it.

In addition, as program planners we not only want to know who was exposed to our message, but how that message was delivered. What channels were used? Was it changed in any way? Because we are not advertisers, and therefore usually not buying time and space, we frequently do not control the form in which the message reaches our target audience. So, in addition to tracking changes in awareness, knowledge, and behavior among our target audience, we also find it useful to examine both the quantity and the content of our program's media coverage. Although measuring media coverage will not tell us who was exposed to our message, it will tell us how many exposures were possible and what the content of those exposures was likely to be.

An analysis of media coverage of 5 A Day during July 1992, the month the national program was launched, focused on coverage quantity, not content. It revealed that media response to the press conference and the campaign was extensive. During July 1992, the campaign generated more than 1,800 media placements in print, television, and radio, accounting for approximately 122 million gross media impressions. The bulk of these placements were editorial print—48%, or nearly 900 stories—and retail advertising—43%. 5 A Day received coverage in all the major national newspapers, such as *The Washington Post, USA Today,* and *The New York Times,* as well as many other publications in large and small cities across the nation. On television, *CNN Headline News* and three national morning shows—*Good Morning America, CBS This Morning,* and *FOX Morning News*—broke the story before the press conference. *ABC World News Tonight* and *ABC World News This Morning* also carried the story, and local stations in 68 markets across the country featured the NCI video news release. In addition, all three major radio networks—ABC, CBS, and NBC—broadcast 5 A Day stories.

Preliminary analyses of the impact of the 1993 5 A Day Week found more than 225 newspaper stories that highlighted the week—reaching more than 27.2 million readers. A 1-hour National Public Radio program sponsored by the PBHF was aired through 160 radio stations in all 50 states. Proclamations of support for 5 A Day efforts were signed by every governor, and more than 1 million brochures were distributed through supermarkets and the NCI's Cancer Information Service (1-800-4-CANCER). Currently, the 5 A Day team is analyzing the message content of the 7,142 editorial print placements generated by 5 A Day between July 1992 and September 1993. To date, this editorial coverage alone has generated 371,127,141 gross impressions.

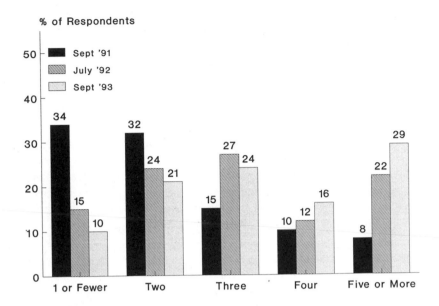

**Figure 12.3.** Results of the Omnibus Survey of U.S. Adults for Self-Reported Daily Fruit and Vegetable Consumption

## CONSUMER TRACKING DATA

The baseline survey conducted in 1991 provided benchmark measures for public perceptions about the benefits of consuming fruits and vegetables. In order to track the impact of the 5 A Day campaign, these same measures are collected on an annual basis using a cost-effective omnibus survey. Several commercial suppliers, including The Gallup Organization, Market Facts, the ICR Survey Research Group, and Opinion Research Corporation, offer national omnibus surveys.

For the 5 A Day project, several questions were added to EXCEL, the telephone omnibus survey by the ICR Survey Research Group. The 5 A Day questions were asked in 1992 and again in 1993 among a nationally representative sample of more than 1,000 American adults. According to the tracking data, both the campaign and its principal messages have had substantial penetration during the first 2 years.

As shown in Figure 12.3, prior to program launch in 1991, only 8% of Americans reported that five or more was the number of servings of fruits

% of Respondents

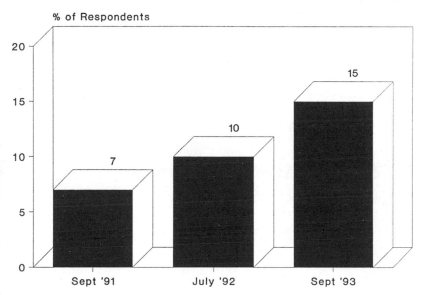

Figure 12.4. Results of the Omnibus Survey of U.S. Adults for Awareness of the 5 A Day Program

and vegetables to eat each day for good health. In 1992, that number witnessed a sharp increase to 22%. By 1993, the number rose further still to 29%. There were corresponding declines in Americans who felt that one or fewer servings (34% to 15% to 10%, respectively) or two servings (32% to 24% to 21%, respectively) were the appropriate number of fruits and vegetables to eat daily.

Awareness of the 5 A Day program has increased steadily. Beginning with a baseline of 7% in 1991, the percentage of Americans who had heard of the 5 A Day program rose to 10% in 1992 and to 15% in 1993 (see Figure 12.4). Finally, the percentage of people who believed that eating fruits and vegetables would be "quite likely" to help prevent cancer, an idea central to the 5 A Day campaign, stood at 48% in 1993. This represents a significant increase over the 41% from the baseline and is comparable to the 1992 measure (45%). Also shown in Figure 12.5 is the enhanced perception that fruit and vegetable consumption can help with weight loss and maintenance, from 52% in 1991 to 64% during the second year of the 5 A Day program.

Despite 5 A Day's positive impact on awareness and perceptions, the tracking data revealed there was still much room for improvement in behavior. There remained a sizable discrepancy between knowledge and actual behavior.

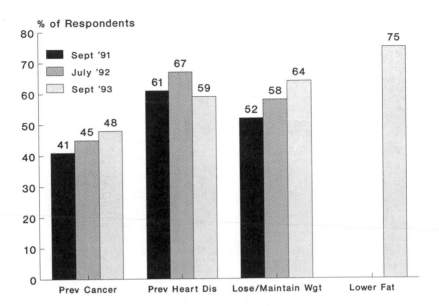

**Figure 12.5.** Percentage of Respondents Believing It "Quite Likely" That Eating More Fruits and Vegetables Has Specific Health Effects

Even though 29% of Americans in 1993 believed that eating five or more servings a day was healthful, only 13% claimed actually to consume five or more servings each day. And total daily consumption was reported at an average of 3.1 servings a day, still substantially below the goal for an adult daily average of 5 or more expected by the year 2000.

Omnibus tracking also affords an opportunity to monitor the impact of highly specific messages and to hone and refine strategy accordingly. The ease-and-convenience messages initiated for the 5 A Day campaign in 1993, for example, had achieved little penetration when the 1993 survey was conducted in September. In fact, the opposite seemed to be occurring, because 13% (up from 8% in 1992) reported it would be "very hard" to eat five servings of fruits and vegetables a day. Considering the CHC model, one possible conclusion was that the "aperture" and communication tools were inappropriate for the target audience. The reliance on free placements for radio PSAs during 5 A Day Week, for example, may have limited exposure to the busy, harried target group.

# Conclusions

In designing messages for specific target audiences, many program planners are usually challenged by the relatively few resources available with which to conduct consumer research. This oftentimes results in little to no empirical support for the development of communication strategies and tactics. The CHC model clearly points to the necessity of specific information on selected target audiences.

What we have presented in this chapter may appear to be a series of formative studies that required a great amount of time, personnel, and money resources to complete. In planning the 5 A Day program, however, once the target was clearly identified, all of the consumer research came from secondary sources—marketing databases—that were analyzed with the specific intent of answering the CHC's strategic questions. The costs for such searches is a fraction of what it would have taken to develop, implement, and analyze our own surveys. As these databases continue to expand, and consequently decrease in cost, they will be much more accessible to health communicators. Vendors such as Donnelley Marketing Information Services, INFORUM, and Equifax/National Decision Systems already have databases available that employ geographic mapping capabilities (based on annual updating of the 1990 Census) along with audience segmentation systems (ClusterPlus, PRIZM, and MicroVision, respectively) that can then be linked with myriad smaller databases to answer almost any question about a consumer group one wishes to ask. The impact that this information technology can have on the effectiveness of messages developed for health promotion is waiting to be explored.

# Note

1. Market Research Corporation of America, Chicago.

# References

Block, G., Patterson, B., & Subar, A. (1992). Fruits, vegetables, and cancer prevention: A review of the epidemiological evidence. *Nutrition and Cancer, 18,* 1-29.
Bunton, R., & Macdonald, G. (1992). *Health promotion: Disciplines and diversity.* London: Routledge.
Cafferata, P., & Tybout, A. (1989). *Cognitive and affective responses to advertising.* Lexington, MA: Lexington Books.

Green, L., & Kreuter, M. (1991). *Health promotion planning: An educational and environmental approach.* Mountain View, CA: Mayfield.

Havas, S., Heimendinger, J., Reynolds, K., Baranowski, T., Nicklas, T., Bishop, D., Buller, D., Sorensen, G., Beresford, S.A.A., Cowan, A., & Damron, D. (1994). 5 A Day for Better Health: A new research initiative. *Journal of the American Dietetic Association, 94,* 32-36.

McGuire, W. J. (1989). Theoretical foundations of campaigns. In R. E. Rice & C. K. Atkin (Eds.), *Public communication campaigns* (2nd ed.) (pp. 43-65). Newbury Park, CA: Sage.

National Research Council. (1989). *Diet and health: Implications for reducing chronic disease risk.* Washington, DC: National Academy Press.

Prochaska, J., & DiClemente, C. (1983). Stages and process of self-change in smoking: Towards an integrated model of change. *Journal of Consulting and Clinical Psychology, 51,* 390-395.

Sutton, S. M., Balch, G. A., & Lefebvre, R. C. (1994). *Strategic questions for consumer-based health communications.* Manuscript under review.

Steinmetz, K. A., & Potter, J. D. (1991). Vegetables, fruits and cancer: I. Epidemiology. *Cancer Causes and Control, 2,* 825-857.

U.S. Department of Agriculture and U.S. Department of Health and Human Services. (1985). *Dietary guidelines for Americans.* Washington, DC: Government Printing Office.

U.S. Department of Health and Human Services. (1988). *The Surgeon General's report on nutrition and disease.* Washington, DC: Government Printing Office.

U.S. Department of Health and Human Services. (1990). *Healthy people 2000.* Washington, DC: Government Printing Office.

Wells, W. W. (1989). *Planning for R.O.I.: Effective advertising strategy.* Englewood Cliffs, NJ: Prentice Hall.

Ziegler, R. G. (1991). Vegetables, fruits, and carotenoids and the risk of cancer. *American Journal of Clinical Nutrition, 53*(Suppl.), 251S-259S.

# PART III

# Combining Theory and Practice: Additional Considerations

Health information comes from myriad sources, many of which are informal (e.g., conversations with co-workers), incidental (e.g., "information" gleaned from entertainment media), and possibly inaccurate (e.g., tabloid accounts of health risks or remedies). When surveyed, people typically cite their physician(s), their family members and friends, and the media as the most common sources of health information in their lives. Our point is that health message design does not occur in a vacuum. Health communication campaigns, of any form, at best supplement people's existing health information and sources of influence.

The admission that planned efforts at health communication are only a supplement to people's existing sources of health information and influence carries with it an obligation. The obligation is to understand and respond to those other sources of health information and influence relevant to a target audience. The audience-centered message design strategies presented in Part II are, in part, an effort to do so. In planning this book, however, we felt that readers could benefit from a more direct examination of the notion of message design as a process of supplementation. Sharon Lee Hammond brought to our attention the fine job of supplementation currently being done by the Food and Drug Administration and certain pharmaceutical manufacturers. Her suggestion provided a venue for exploring the topic of supplementation.

Failed compliance with prescribed pharmaceutical regimens is both common and costly in terms of negative health outcomes and subsequent health care expenditures. In Chapter 13, Hammond discusses factors that contribute to poor compliance and describes how these factors are being addressed with both interpersonal and mediated supplemental information. Patient package inserts and related programs of information provide a unique opportunity to blend all that is known about effective interpersonal and mediated communication. Moreover, they provide an opportunity to supplement the communication of most people's preferred source of health information, their physician, and that of another highly credible source of health information, the pharmacist. Hammond's chapter nicely illustrates another important message design consideration: the need to use multiple methods and means to convey a message to an audience.

The final topic examined in this Part concerns an even more fundamental consideration: What conditions must be in place before we should consider designing messages intended to motivate individual health behavior changes? The flip side of this question is: Who should our messages target? Health promotion activities in America typically focus on the individual, apparently because of our long-standing societal preference for individual autonomy and freedom from government regulation. The ethics of the individual approach dictates that the people, once properly informed, must be allowed to decide their own best health interests and act accordingly. The hazard in this approach is that neutralization of many health threats is beyond the means of most individuals. The locus of many health problems resides in public policies at the local, state, and national levels.

In the closing chapter of this volume, Parrott, Kahl, and Maibach provide a framework for considering the issues and limitations that may constrain individual behavior, and therefore should constrain individual-focused approaches to health communication. The chapter presents strategic questions to consider before proceeding with health promotion activities. Answering these questions will help identify who may need to become involved in the process of enabling health—other than those persons whose health is threatened. The answers to these questions may necessitate strategies more akin to political communication and social advocacy than to traditional concepts of health communication.

# 13 Supplementing Health Campaign Messages

## RECENT DEVELOPMENTS IN INFORMING PATIENTS ABOUT THEIR PRESCRIPTION DRUGS

SHARON LEE HAMMOND

A pproximately 1.5 billion prescriptions are filled each year, all of which have been prescribed to treat and alleviate a multitude of diseases and conditions. These medications cannot be effective unless they are used properly, however. Evidence suggests that inadequate communication about medications is one of the principal reasons why as many as 55% of patients deviate from their medication regimens, seriously compromising their care and often resulting in dangerous health consequences (Office of Inspector General, 1990). Yet a recent review of empirical studies found that the proportion of patients receiving no verbal consultation for new prescriptions ranged between 17% and 30% for physicians and between 30% and 87% for pharmacy practitioners (Weiderholt, Clarridge, & Svarstad, 1992). In addition, a 1987 federal government survey found that only 26% of participants received any written information at the pharmacy with their last prescription (Morris, Grossman, Barkdoll, & Gordon, 1987). This is clearly an area of concern for health message designers. The importance is at least twofold. First, failure to use medications correctly may lead to undesirable health outcomes and resistance to future health promotion efforts that encourage consumers to seek care from providers. Second, the failure leads to added expense for the entire health care system. For these reasons, health campaigners and message designers should carefully consider the design of medication messages that are likely to supplement information provided in campaigns when individuals seek screening and treatment, and receive medical prescriptions.

## Overview of the Problem

There are many reasons why patients deviate from their therapeutic regimen. According to Johnston, Clarke, Mundy, Cromarty, and Ridout (1986), "patients may fail to comply with medical recommendations either because they choose an alternative response (intentional noncompliance), or because they do not understand and/or remember what they were asked to do (unintentional noncompliance)" (p. 304). Having adequate and understandable information about medications is a critical factor influencing both intentional and unintentional patient noncompliance. This is particularly important for the elderly, in that "forgetting" is frequently cited as a reason for inconsistent use of medications—suggesting the need for patients to have written material to review periodically at home (Green, Mullen, & Stainbrook, 1986).

The purpose of this chapter is to examine a portion of the voluminous compliance literature, focusing specifically on the influence of written information on patients' knowledge of and compliance with medication regimens. This review will be followed by a description of several of the current patient information initiatives of the Food and Drug Administration (FDA), as well as a description of several programs created by pharmaceutical manufacturers to inform patients about products, using both written and interpersonal strategies. Because many of these programs are relatively recent, outcome evaluation data to support or refute their use is not available. Nonetheless, they illustrate the innovative efforts being taken to design effective messages about medications to supplement more global campaign efforts and messages designed to promote health.

## Medication Information and Compliance

Determining why patients do not comply with their therapeutic regimens has been the subject of a great deal of research. A 1987 overview of the compliance area identified more than 200 variables related to noncompliance (Meichenbaum & Turk, 1987). A subsequent Inspector General synopsis of the Meichenbaum and Turk article divided the identified variables into several categories, including physiological (e.g., impaired vision or hearing deficits), behavioral, treatment related, and those resulting from the provider/patient relationship (Office of Inspector General, 1990). The behavioral and treatment-related variables influencing noncompliance are of particular interest to those designing health messages. For instance, in the category of behavioral variables, the Inspector General report presents some patient misconceptions regarding the use of medications that are astonishing: "You need to give your body some rest from medicine once in a while or else your body becomes dependent on it or immune to it"; and, "If one dose is good, two must be better." It is not difficult to see how misconceptions like these might contribute to noncompliance with medication regimens, especially those for long-term, asymptomatic diseases such as hypertension or high blood cholesterol.

In relation to treatment variables, drug therapy discontinuation is often related to patient apprehension about the safety and potential side effects of the medication (see also Janz & Becker, 1984). Patients often misunderstand the purpose of the therapy, and they lack confidence that the prescribed therapy will produce a beneficial outcome. Medication noncompliance is particularly prevalent in the elderly population, in that many people over 65 confront the "three Ms"—multiple diseases, multiple medications, and multiple physicians. Those 60 years and over, who constitute 17% of the population, use 39% of all prescription drugs, and two thirds of the elderly also use nonprescription medications on a regular basis (Ascione, James, Austin, & Shimp, 1980; Lamy, 1990). Lamy (1990) reported that one study found that the elderly were associated with one third of all hospitalization reports due to adverse drug effects and with 50% of all reports of fatalities due to inappropriate use of prescription medications.

Much of the research on patient compliance has focused on the influence of written and oral communication about medications on patient knowledge, compliance, and satisfaction with the medication regimen specifically and medical care in general. Among the factors contributing to decreased knowledge about and compliance with medications are lack of individualized medication counseling and lack of written instructions to reinforce verbal instructions (O'Connell & Johnson, 1992). Several studies have shown that when given a choice of whether they would like to receive verbal counseling, written information, or both, the majority of patients choose both (Culbertson, Arthur, Rhodes, & Rhodes, 1988; Harvey & Plumridge, 1991).

Although patients may want as much information as possible about their drugs, some practitioners have argued that giving patients more information about their drugs, particularly about the possible side effects of their medication, may make patients more susceptible to experiencing these side effects—a type of "placebo effect" (Shapiro & Morris, 1978). Research on the influence of written communication on the reporting of adverse side effects is mixed. For example, a 1984 experimental study of patients given information about their depression medication found that those patients who received verbal and written information about the beneficial effects of treatment without mention of adverse effects reported fewer experiences of side effects than those patients who were given information about the side effects (Myers & Calvert, 1984). Other researchers, however, have found the opposite. George, Waters, and Nicholas (1983) found that patients who had received a leaflet with their prescription for a pain medication were no more likely to experience or report adverse effects from the medication than those who did not receive the leaflet. In addition, Van Haecht, Vander Stichele, and Bogaert (1990) found similar results in Belgium, where the government mandates that informational leaflets be provided with all prescription medications. Further, a 1990 review article on providing written information to patients found that the majority of studies have shown that forewarning patients about potential side effects does not result in less adherence and can actually enhance compliance (Weinman, 1990).

The research about the effects of giving patients more information about their drugs is ambiguous with regard to the symptoms patients report. Research is not ambiguous, however, about the influence of written information on patient knowledge of and satisfaction with their medication regimen. Many studies have shown that providing written information improves patients' knowledge about their medications and decreases utilization errors (see Brown, Wright, & Christensen, 1987; Dodds, 1986; Morris & Schulz, 1992; Robinson, Gilbertson, & Litwack, 1986). In addition, patients who receive information (both oral and written) report more satisfaction with their medical care than those who do not receive information (Gibbs, Waters, & George, 1989; Isaacman, Purvis, Gyuro, Anderson, & Smith, 1992; Opdycke, Ascione, Shimp, & Rosen, 1992).

Even though communication may be the key to improved knowledge and satisfaction, a critical finding from this research for designers of health messages is that the provision of written or oral information alone is insufficient for improving compliance with long-term medication regimens (Gibbs, 1992; Schwartz-Lookinland, McKeever, & Saputo, 1989). The authors of a 10-year review of research on compliance interventions found that: "to date, there has been no study that has satisfactorily shown that a single intervention of any sort is sufficient to improve long-term compliance. . . . Thus, at present, long-term compliance enhancement requires combinations of interventions" (Haynes, Wang, & Da Mota Gomes, 1987, p. 160). Morris and Schulz (1992) further stipulated that the most effective intervention should incorporate a combination of educational and behavioral strategies.

Increased knowledge or satisfaction does not necessarily alter behavior or compliance; the patient must be motivated to use his or her knowledge to obtain optimum therapeutic benefit. Educational strategies, like written materials, are needed to increase knowledge and satisfaction, and must be combined with behavioral strategies, like telephone reminders and pharmacist counseling, to improve compliance. Recognition of the effectiveness of these combined strategies has resulted in the dissemination of medication information, fast becoming a growth industry. Health care providers, including physicians, pharmacists, and nurses, have long recognized the importance of communicating to their patients information about their therapeutic regimens. There are now a host of other organizations in the medication information arena, too. These include voluntary organizations such as the American Association of Retired Persons; voluntary disease-specific organizations such as the Arthritis Foundation; collaborative associations like the National Council on Patient Information and Education; mail-order pharmacy associations like Medco; and others. Two of the most active players in this arena are the federal government, through the Food and Drug Administration, and the pharmaceutical industry itself.

## Food and Drug Administration Initiatives

One of the principal responsibilities of the Food and Drug Administration (FDA) is the review and approval of all drugs and drug products produced, marketed, distributed, and/or sold in the United States. Other than requiring certain information on the label of prescription and over-the-counter drugs, however, the FDA historically has not dictated that drug manufacturers provide additional information to patients about all of their products. Nevertheless, the FDA believes that providing complete and readily understandable information about drugs to patients can help achieve maximum benefits from use of the drugs and reduce their potential for causing harm. To this end, the FDA has a number of ongoing programs and initiatives to encourage and/or require the dissemination of medication information in "patient language."

The FDA initiatives partially address the responsibility given to this agency in relation to *Healthy People 2000,* "a national strategy for significantly improving the health of the Nation over the coming decade. It addresses the prevention of major chronic illnesses, injuries, and infectious diseases" (U.S. Department of Health and Human Services, 1990, p. i). Specifically, the FDA was given express responsibility for achieving Objective 12.6, which encourages an increase to: "at least 75 percent the proportion of primary care providers who routinely review with their patients aged 65 and older all prescribed and over-the-counter medicines taken by their patients each time a new medication is prescribed" (p. 343). Before any evaluation of the progress made toward improving routine counseling could be conducted, however, research was necessary to determine the baseline level of counseling currently being performed. In 1992 the FDA began the process of conducting a survey to determine the answer. After careful examination of this baseline data, the FDA will plan appropriate strategies to increase and improve the nature and extent of routine counseling about medications in the primary-care setting. In the meantime, the FDA commissioner is moving ahead to promote communicating about medications to patients (Kessler, 1991).

## COMMISSIONER INITIATIVE

Patient information and education about drugs is a subject high on the FDA's agenda. In 1992, the Agency launched a campaign to persuade primary health care providers to intensify their communication with patients. In a 1991 *New England Journal of Medicine* Sounding Board article (Kessler, 1991), FDA's commissioner challenged pharmacists to expand and enhance their medication counseling to patients both verbally and by providing computer-generated printouts on how to take the drug, along with information on possible side effects. He called on physicians to examine whether the timing and techniques of their drug counseling should be adjusted so that patients would leave the doctor's office armed with the information they need. The Agency has also directed a similar appeal to registered nurses.

## PATIENT PACKAGE INSERTS

The FDA is particularly supportive of providing written information to patients about every drug they take. In the 1980s, the FDA proposed a regulation requiring written patient package inserts (PPIs) for 10 classes of drugs. These leaflets would have included information related to the drugs' benefits and risks and directions for use, and were to have been distributed by pharmacists to patients with new prescriptions for these drugs. After much public debate, however, the Agency withdrew the proposed regulation. The essence of the opponents' arguments against the proposal was that the private sector would be a better conduit for encouraging health care providers to inform their patients about medications. To this end, the

National Council on Patient Information and Education (NCPIE) was born out of a grant from a major pharmaceutical firm. NCPIE materials describe its members as "national, state, and local organizations interested in improving communication about prescription medicines between patients and health care professionals." It currently has 352 member organizations and is growing.

Even though PPIs may not currently be mandatory for all drugs, the FDA has historically approved, as part of the official labeling at the time of a new drug application, PPIs for drug products that potentially have very serious risks and/or have alternative therapies—situations that would then involve some level of patient consent to take the drug. Having a PPI approved as part of a drug's official labeling means that it is illegal to distribute the drug to a patient without including the PPI. For example, a PPI for the drug Accutane (also discussed in the next section) is part of its official labeling. Accutane is prescribed for patients who have severe recalcitrant acne and, in and of itself, is not dangerous to the patient. Taking Accutane while pregnant, however, would cause serious harm to the fetus. Accutane would not have been approved for marketing in the United States if its maker had not agreed to provide a PPI that includes an informed consent document for the patient to initial and sign. On the other hand, the product Rogaine (also discussed in the next section), which is used to stimulate hair growth, also has an officially approved PPI. Although the drug has very few risks, its use provides patients with only minimal cosmetic benefits and no therapeutic benefits (i.e., it takes a long time to see any new hair growth, and what progress there is may be very limited). FDA determined that Rogaine users needed to be informed in writing that this product is not a panacea for baldness.

As of the end of 1993, the FDA had approved a PPI as part of the official labeling for 25 individual drug products. These products are indicated for a variety of health problems, including glaucoma, smoking cessation, endometriosis, angina, psoriasis, benign prostatic hyperplasia, stroke, migraine, and hypertension. In addition, the FDA requires a PPI for four classes of drugs: oral contraceptives, intrauterine devices (which incorporate a drug to aid contraception), progestins, and estrogens. Every drug that falls into any of these four classes must have a PPI distributed with it. These PPIs are often very detailed, describing most of the many risks and benefits of these classes of pharmaceuticals. Only a very small number of approved drugs are required by FDA to have written information disseminated along with the drug package.

When a decision has been made that a PPI is necessary for a product, the FDA has traditionally worked closely with the manufacturer to develop the language for the insert. At the core of this development process is the commit-ment on the part of both the industry and the Agency to provide information to the patient that he or she is able to understand and utilize. One example of this commitment is the PPI that was developed for Proscar, a drug for benign prostatic hyperplasia (also discussed in next section). The makers of Proscar, in consultation with the Agency, used readability testing procedures on the draft PPI and conducted copy testing with consumers, using a targeted research approach. The resulting PPI uses a simple and easy-to-understand format, yet provides important information about the risks, benefits, and directions for use of the product. The Proscar PPI is shown in Figure 13.1.

## Industry Programs

Along with the FDA, pharmaceutical firms are taking an active role in providing information to patients about their products. In many ways, it is in the industry's best interest to communicate carefully the risks and benefits of their products to consumers. First, a patient's failure to continue and/or complete a course of drug therapy directly affects the profits of the maker of the drug products. Statistics show that 7% of prescriptions are never brought to the pharmacy for dispensing and, of those that are, 4% are never picked up (Coccia, 1992). Even more to the point, drug-related malpractice law suits account for 10% of all malpractice suits brought in this country. A substantial number of these cases are due to a failure to warn patients of foreseeable side effects (Quaid, Faden, Vining, & Freeman, 1990).

Many companies have begun their own efforts at patient education, some using what has been called "complete compliance packaging." Compliance packaging itself is defined as a prepackaged unit of a drug that provides one treatment cycle of medication for the patient, usually in the form of blister packs. These separate dosage units for separate days help to remind the patient to take the medication or remember that the medication has already been taken. A "complete compliance package" is the newest innovation in com-pliance packaging. According to Smith (1989), the complete compliance package serves to expand the pharmaceutical companies' definition of their "product" beyond that of just the medication itself: "The complete package consists of the medication plus the complete set of compliance packaging and the educational materials necessary to help the patient obtain the desired therapeutic outcome" (p. 44).

The FDA is responsible for reviewing all compliance packaging and patient support materials produced by the pharmaceutical firms for intended distribution to patients to assure that the information contained in them is accurate (i.e., consistent with approved labeling) and balanced as to the risks as well as benefits of the product. The variety of materials submitted to the Agency is diverse, using communication channels such as videotapes, audio-tapes, pamphlets, diaries, 1-800 numbers, flip charts, newsletters, and a host of others. These materials and programs are often designed with multiple goals and purposes in mind. Some programs are designed to support physicians in their efforts to communicate important information about the drug to the patient; others are directly aimed at helping patients comply with the medication regimen. Some programs are purely promotional in nature, designed solely to improve brand name recognition or increase brand loyalty. Some programs are available only to patients taking the brand name product; others provide disease-specific information to anyone suffering from the disease or symptom. Some are given to the patient by the physician; some are available directly from the manufacturer by enrollment; some are provided by the pharmacist. Several of these pharmaceutical programs are described below in order to further illustrate the outcomes of the FDA's and the drug industry's efforts in this area. Each program provides examples of goals associated with summative evaluation in message design (see Chapter 9 in this volume).

## Examples of Pharmaceutical Compliance Programs

USING COUMADIN
SAFELY AND EFFECTIVELY

Coumadin is an anticoagulant used to prevent abnormal clotting and is prescribed to prevent harmful blood clots from forming or moving. Often-times, patients are prescribed Coumadin while in the hospital and, therefore, must be educated as to how to use the drug at home. Patients on Coumadin must have regularly scheduled prothrombin time tests, which compare the length of time it takes the patients's blood to clot to the time it takes for normal blood to clot.

The Coumadin patient education kit includes: (a) an 11-minute videotape, (b) an 11-minute audiotape, (c) a "Patient's Guide to Using Coumadin at Home," (d) a series of tabletop size flip charts for use in one-on-one educational sessions between the health care provider and the patient (entitled "Using Coumadin at Home: Questions You May Have About Coumadin Therapy), and (e) a dosage calendar and drug identification card for emergencies. These

# Patient Information about
## PROSCAR® (Prahs-car)
Generic name: finasteride
(fin-AS-tur-eyed)

7763700
78583/100892

**PROSCAR is for use by men only.**

Please read this leaflet before you start taking PROSCAR. Also, read it each time you renew your prescription, just in case anything has changed. Remember, this leaflet does not take the place of careful discussions with your doctor. You and your doctor should discuss PROSCAR when you start taking your medication and at regular checkups.

**Why your doctor has prescribed PROSCAR**

Your doctor has prescribed PROSCAR because you have a medical condition called benign prostatic hyperplasia or BPH. This occurs only in men.

**What is BPH?**

BPH is an enlargement of the prostate gland. After age 50, most men develop enlarged prostates. The prostate is located below the bladder. As the prostate enlarges, it may slowly restrict the flow of urine. This can lead to symptoms such as:

- a weak or interrupted urinary stream
- a feeling that you cannot empty your bladder completely
- a feeling of delay or hesitation when you start to urinate
- a need to urinate often, especially at night
- a feeling that you must urinate right away.

**Treatment options for BPH**

There are three main treatment options for BPH:

- **Program of monitoring or "Watchful Waiting".** If a man has an enlarged prostate gland and no symptoms or if his symptoms do not bother him, he and his doctor may decide on a program of monitoring which would include regular checkups, instead of medication or surgery.

- **Medication.** Your doctor may prescribe PROSCAR for BPH. See **"What PROSCAR does"** below.

- **Surgery.** Some patients may need surgery. Your doctor can describe several different surgical procedures for BPH. Which procedure is best depends on your symptoms and medical condition.

**What PROSCAR does**

PROSCAR lowers levels of a key hormone called DHT (dihydrotestosterone), which is a major cause of prostate growth. Lowering DHT leads to shrinkage of the enlarged prostate gland in most men. This can lead to gradual improvement in urine flow and symptoms over the next several months. However, since each case of BPH is different, you should know that:

- Even though the prostate shrinks, you may NOT see an improvement in urine flow or symptoms.

- You may need to take PROSCAR for six (6) months or more to see whether it helps you.

- Even though you take PROSCAR and it may help you, it is not known whether PROSCAR reduces the need for surgery.

**What you need to know while taking PROSCAR**

- **You must see your doctor regularly.** While taking PROSCAR, you must have regular checkups. Follow your doctor's advice about when to have these checkups.

- **About side effects.** Like all prescription drugs, PROSCAR may cause side effects. Side effects due to PROSCAR may include impotence (or inability to have an erection) and less desire for sex. Each of these side effects occurred in less than 4% of patients in clinical studies. In some cases side effects went away while the patient continued to take PROSCAR.

**Figure 13.1.** Example of a Patient Package Insert

258

Some men taking PROSCAR may have a decrease in the amount of semen released during sex. This decrease does not appear to interfere with normal sexual function.

You should discuss side effects with your doctor before taking PROSCAR and anytime you think you are having a side effect.

- **Checking for prostate cancer.** Your doctor has prescribed PROSCAR for symptomatic BPH and not for cancer — but a man can have BPH and prostate cancer at the same time. Doctors usually recommend that men be checked for prostate cancer once a year when they turn 50 (or 40 if a family member has had prostate cancer). These checks should continue while you take PROSCAR. PROSCAR is not a treatment for prostate cancer.
- **About Prostate Specific Antigen (PSA).** Your doctor may have done a blood test called PSA. PROSCAR can alter PSA values. For more information, talk to your doctor.
- **A warning about PROSCAR and pregnancy.**

PROSCAR is for use by MEN only.

PROSCAR is generally well tolerated in men. However, women who are pregnant, or women who could become pregnant, should avoid the active ingredient in PROSCAR.

If the active ingredient is absorbed by a woman who is pregnant with a male baby, it may cause the male baby to be born with abnormalities of the sex organs. Therefore, any woman who is pregnant or who could become pregnant must not come into direct contact with the active ingredient in PROSCAR.

Two of the ways in which a woman might absorb the active ingredient in PROSCAR are:

*Sexual Contact.* Your semen may contain a small amount of the active ingredient of the drug. If your partner is pregnant, or if you and your partner decide to have a baby, you must stop taking PROSCAR and talk to your doctor. If your partner could become pregnant, proper use of a condom can reduce the risk of exposing her to your semen (discuss this further with your doctor).

*Handling broken tablets.* Women who are pregnant or who could become pregnant must <u>not handle broken</u> tablets of PROSCAR. PROSCAR tablets are coated to prevent contact with the active ingredient during normal handling. If this coating is broken, the tablets should not be handled by women who are pregnant or who could become pregnant.

If a woman who is pregnant comes into contact with the active ingredient in PROSCAR, a doctor should be consulted.

Remember, these warnings apply only if the woman exposed to PROSCAR is pregnant or could become pregnant.

**How to take PROSCAR**

Follow your doctor's advice about how to take PROSCAR. You must take it every day. You may take it with or between meals. To avoid forgetting to take PROSCAR, it may be helpful to take it the same time every day.

Do not share PROSCAR with anyone else; it was prescribed only for you.

Keep PROSCAR and all medicines out of the reach of children.

FOR MORE INFORMATION ABOUT PROSCAR AND BPH, TALK WITH YOUR DOCTOR. IN ADDITION, TALK TO YOUR PHARMACIST OR OTHER HEALTH CARE PROVIDER.

MERCK & CO., INC.
West Point, PA 19486

materials have been produced in both English and Spanish and, except for the flip charts, are intended to be given to the patient by the health care provider.

## PROSCAR PATIENT
## SUPPORT PROGRAM

Proscar is a relatively new drug indicated for the treatment of symptomatic benign prostatic hyperplasia (BPH)—or enlarged prostate. Compliance with Proscar is a particular problem because a minimum of 6 months of treatment may be necessary to determine whether an individual will respond to the drug (i.e., symptoms will decrease). It is often difficult for patients to continue to take a drug in the face of persistent uncomfortable or painful symptoms.

The Proscar Patient Support Program has a physician-initiated component as well as a pharmacist component. When a patient is started on Proscar, his physician will give him a patient starter kit that contains disease awareness information and a patient starter certificate for a 30-day complementary supply of Proscar. In order to enroll in the program, the patient must redeem his certificate at the pharmacy. At the pharmacy, the patient is given a free supply of Proscar; the pharmacist is then reimbursed by the pharmaceutical company for a $4.00 handling charge and is sent a replacement bottle of 30 tablets. When the pharmacy submits the completed certificate to the company for reimbursement, the patient is automatically enrolled in the program and will begin receiving the support program mailings. Patients receive six mailings the first year they are taking Proscar. The first mailing includes: (a) a patient information sheet explaining the materials in the package, (b) a wellness newsletter of interest to men over 50, and (c) punch-out calendar cards to help the patient remember that he has taken his pill for the day. The materials from this mailing are also included in all subsequent packages, with the addition of: (d) a compliance education brochure, (e) another certificate for a complementary 30-day supply of Proscar, (f) a 7-day pillbox, and (g) a brochure entitled *7 Tips to Help You Remember to Take Your Medicine*. The pharmaceutical company also maintains toll-free telephone and fax numbers for patient support.

## INSOMNIA: PATIENT
## EDUCATION MATERIALS

The drug Halcion is often prescribed by physicians for their patients who have difficulty sleeping. It is one of several benzodiazepine sleeping pills that have several important risks and limitations, including diminishing effectiveness with continued use and possible development of dependence and mental changes when the drug is used for more than a few days. In fact, in the past few years the news media has reported on several criminals who have used Halcion as an excuse for their illegal actions; hence, the "Halcion defense."

Patient education materials are provided to physicians for distribution to their patients who have questions about insomnia and sleep disorders. The folder-type packet includes: (a) a 17-minute PBS educational video titled "Journey Into Sleep," (b) a 12-page booklet on "What You Should Know About Insomnia," (c) a packet of tear-off sheets listing "Tips for a Good Night's Sleep . . ." and "If Your Doctor Has Prescribed a Sleep Medication . . .", and (d) a packet of tear-off sheets listing bulleted suggestions for promoting better sleep. All of these materials are educational in nature, not a promotion of Halcion.

## ROGAINE: CLINICAL EXPERIENCE PROGRAM

Rogaine was recently approved as a topical solution for stimulation of hair growth. The chemical in Rogaine, minoxidil, has been used in tablet form since 1980 to lower severe high blood pressure. The product therefore poses a particular risk to patients who have underlying coronary artery disease.

Rogaine requires that patients apply the solution twice a day for at least 4 months before any hair regrowth may be observed. The application procedure is somewhat complicated and the pharmaceutical company has assembled a box of materials to be given to patients by their physician when prescribed Rogaine. The 13" × 10" box and its inserts are produced in two colors: mauve for female patients and gray for male patients. The box contains: (a) a 10-minute videotape featuring three patients who have had personal experience with Rogaine (female patients in the video for women, male patients in the video for men), (b) a 27-page booklet containing a coupon for patients to send in to receive a $10 certificate and money-saving rebate coupons, (c) a 7-inch comb to use during application, and (d) an illustrated guide for applying the product. The box also contains a package with three applicators for demonstration purposes only; no minoxidil is included in the package. The pharmaceutical company also maintains a 1-800 number for patient support.

PREGNANCY PREVENTION
PROGRAM FOR WOMEN ON ACCUTANE

Accutane is prescribed for patients with severe recalcitrant acne who are unresponsive to conventional therapy. However, severe birth defects are known to occur in babies of women taking Accutane in any amount, even for short periods of time, during pregnancy. As a result, female patients must be counseled to avoid pregnancy while undergoing treatment with Accutane and should undergo a serum pregnancy test before starting therapy.

The makers of Accutane have assembled a comprehensive package to help health care providers conduct this counseling. The package is set up as a narrow file box with eight tabular sections. The sections include: (a) a tear-off package of patient qualification checklists for the physician to use to determine suitability for Accutane treatment, (b) an 11-page informational brochure titled *Important Information Concerning Your Treatment With Accutane,* (c) a packet of tear-off sheets with a toll-free number to call to hear important information about Accutane in 13 languages, (d) an informational booklet on birth control, (e) a packet of tear-off reimbursement information sheets for the initial visit to a consulting physician [if the patient has been referred for expert counseling on contraception and serum pregnancy testing, the makers of Accutane pay for the consultation and pregnancy test], (f) a health care provider's guide to qualifying and counseling candidates for Accutane therapy, (g) copies of a true/false test for patients to take after speaking with their physician and reading the informational brochures, and (h) a packet of tear-off informed consent sheets to be signed by the patient or her guardian and the physician [also contains an enrollment form for a follow-up survey conducted by the School of Public Health at Boston University to gather information on how Accutane is used by women of child-bearing potential].

ALTACE ALLIANCE PROGRAM
AGAINST HYPERTENSION

Altace is prescribed for patients with hypertension and is one of several "ACE inhibitor" drugs (ACE stands for angiotensin-converting enzyme). As with any drug for what is basically a "symptomless" disease, noncompliance with the medication regimen is a widespread problem. In fact, noncompliance with the entire long-term therapeutic regimen for hypertension, which may include diet, exercise, and sodium components, is a severe problem.

The makers of Altace have assembled a professional sample kit intended to aid patients in complying with their regimen. The kit is to be given by the physician to patients beginning a regimen of Altace. It includes: (a) a free 1-week supply of Altace capsules; (b) an emergency identification card; (c) an informational booklet titled *Hypertension: What It Is, and What YOU Can Do About It* [discusses how Altace and other nondrug regimens, such as diet and exercise, contribute to hypertension control]; and (d) a pocket-sized patient recordbook to help patients keep track of their medication-taking, diet, and exercise program. The kit also contains Volume 1, Number 1 of a newsletter produced by the makers of Altace titled *Lowering Your Blood Pressure—It's Up to You*. A postage-paid card is included for patients to enroll in the Altace Alliance Program in order to receive future issues of the newsletter.

## TENORMIN WELLSPRING SERVICE

Tenormin, like Altace, is indicated for the management of hypertension and, again, compliance with the therapeutic regimen is troublesome. The Wellspring Service for Tenormin patients is a long-term support service purporting to enhance the physician/patient relationship by reinforcing the physician's advice about cardiovascular disease, its treatment, exercise, diet, and a healthier lifestyle in general.

The Wellspring Service particularly appeals to pharmacists who are concerned about low refill rates of antihypertensive drugs. In fact, promotional materials for the Service directed at pharmacists point out research that has found that the majority of patients delay renewing antihypertensive medication an average of 15 days (Jackson & Huffman, 1990). Enrollment in the program includes monthly mailings consisting of newsletters, money-saving coupons, and samples of health products such as "no salt" marinades. Most important, a customer representative of the Wellspring Service telephones patients once a month for the first few months to remind them to refill their prescription. In this way, the makers of Tenormin claim an increase in refill compliance as a result of enrollment in the Service. Additional benefits of the Service include a $3.00 store credit when a proof-of-purchase card for a Tenormin refill is sent to the company and a 1-800 patient support number.

## HANDS-ON-HEALTH

The makers of another antihypertensive medication, Verelan, have also developed a patient support program for their product. The Hands-on-Health program begins when a physician gives the patient a sample pack of

Verelan that contains a mail-in registration card. Once the enrollment card has been received and processed, the patient receives the introductory package, which includes a videotape and newsletter developed in cooperation with the Philadelphia Heart Institute and an important enrollment card. The unique feature of this patient support program is that once the patient fills out and mails the enrollment card and it is received and validated by the firm, he or she receives by mail a free digital home blood-pressure monitor and diary. The manufacturer claims that the monitor and diary motivate patients to chart their own progress and points to published research that shows that a home blood pressure monitor improves medication compliance and is helpful in evaluating the effectiveness of the therapy. After 3 months the patient receives a second newsletter. Promotional materials for the Hands-on-Health program state that as of 1993, more than 30,000 Verelan patients have enrolled in the program.

## THE PRAVACHOL
## PARTNERS PROGRAM

Pravachol, like Lopid, is a cholesterol-regulating agent. The Pravachol Partners Program was designed "with the help of over 250 physicians across the country who routinely prescribe lipid-lowering therapy" to support physicians' efforts to communicate to their patients the necessity of a long-term commitment to treating their cholesterol problem. The makers of Pravachol cite the results of an internal, nonpublic study of 300 patients receiving lipid-lowering drug therapy that showed that more than 45% could not remember any of the information shared at the time they were given their prescription. The makers have therefore developed a program that includes an informational videotape, hosted by Regis Philbin and Kathie Lee Gifford, with an accompanying brochure to help patients keep track of their cholesterol levels. Patients also receive three subsequent newsletters designed to "remind them of their commitment to cholesterol management." The newsletters include articles to keep patients up to date about issues in cholesterol management, advice for developing a low-fat, low-cholesterol nutrition plan, and special discount offers on healthy products. The program is available free of charge to Pravachol patients, with an enrollment form and a pharmacy receipt for their first Pravachol prescription.

## HEALTHQUEST PATIENT SUPPORT PROGRAM

The makers of Questran, another cholesterol-lowering drug, have also developed a patient support program to help patients comply with their therapeutic regimen. Unlike Lopid and Pravachol, one factor influencing compliance with Questran is that the drug comes only in powder form and must be mixed with water, juice, soup, or pulpy fruits with a high moisture content—like applesauce or crushed pineapple—and taken twice a day. This procedure requires considerably more time and effort on the part of the patient, thereby possibly affecting compliance with the regimen.

To combat this problem, the HealthQuest patient support program is designed to reinforce physicians' instructions to patients about lowering their cholesterol and to motivate patients to continue their prescribed therapy. Physicians are asked to encourage their Questran patients to call a 1-800 number to enroll in the program. Many innovative reminder devices are provided to physicians to help them remember about the availability of the HealthQuest program, such as silver adhesive stickers with the 1-800 number imprinted on them for placing on phones, clipboards, patient folders, and more; a plastic stethoscope identification tag with the 1-800 number; a phone index card; and a tabletop tent card advertising the program with tear-off 3" × 5" sheets with the 1-800 number. Patients calling the toll-free number hear a computerized script that briefly discusses cholesterol, its management, and the HealthQuest program. They are then asked to press any key on the phone keypad and another computerized voice asks them to state clearly their name, address, and telephone number. Enrollees are then sent a series of four newsletters "designed to support, entertain, and inform people taking Questran." The newsletters contain articles on cholesterol and what it does, suggest changes in diet and lifestyle, offer stories and tips from people who use Questran, and include low-fat, low-cholesterol recipes. If they have not already received one, patients are also sent the Start Smart Patient Information Kits for users of Questran. The kit includes an informational booklet entitled *Cholesterol, Questran and You,* a mixing guide for Questran with tips and recipe ideas, an audiotape titled *A Patient's Guide to Questran,* a recipe card for mixing a one-quart quantity of Questran, and a folder titled "Short Cuts to Success" containing three helpful guides to using Questran.

## Conclusion

If the goal of medication communication is to provide information the patient is able to understand and utilize, no one communication strategy is likely to be effective when used alone. The research suggests that a combination of interventions, both educational and behavioral, are necessary to improve compliance with therapies. Organizations that engage in communicating about medication with patients have taken this advice and developed multiple strategies to help patients comply with their regimens. In many instances, these programs are a direct application of traditional communication theory. In fact, an April 1993 article in an industry trade press bulletin cited a 1985 article by Marshall Becker that recommended several goals for pharmaceutical companies' patient support programs, including:

- increasing patients' specific knowledge of the disease and the restoration of health
- influencing patients' health beliefs
- helping patients adopt lifestyle changes if necessary
- increasing provider-patient communication
- extending care beyond the doctor's office and pharmacy, using reminder strategies and techniques
- showing the importance of family and social support as a means for enhancing adherence to therapies. ("Drug Companies' Patient Support," 1993)

At this time, only two published studies specifically evaluate any of the industry programs described in this chapter to determine their success vis-à-vis their stated goals, both of which are evaluations of the Tenormin Wellspring Service. One, a 1-year, company-funded study of 985 members of HMOs in seven states, found that hypertensive patients who received the Wellspring service refilled their prescriptions 16% more often than those on the drug who were not enrolled in the program. In addition, during the study period, Wellspring enrollees spent an average of $127 less in physician fees and hospital bills than did those not in the program (Podolsky & Newman, 1993). The second, an experimental study of 453 outpatient HMO enrollees in three states, found that existing hypertensive patients who received the Wellspring kit and reminder telephone calls ordered an average of 27 days more medication than the control group; and new hypertensive patients ordered 40 days more medication than the control group (Sclar et al., 1991). It must be noted that refill rates are at best an indirect measure of actual daily compliance with a medication regimen.

In sum, this chapter illustrates that written patient information may be used to help patients understand and use their medications appropriately, although no single information strategy is effective for all patients under all circumstances. Designers of medication messages should take into account the objectives to be achieved by the drug information, the characteristics of the patient population, the nature of the message to be communicated, and the circumstances under which the strategy is to be used (Mullen & Green, 1984). Formative and process evaluations of programs' effectiveness should be undertaken to guide ongoing and future efforts to communicate about medications. In this way, individuals who respond to campaign messages to seek screening and treatment, and receive (as is so often the case) prescriptions for medications, will be provided with messages that facilitate rather than inhibit societal health promotion efforts.

# References

Ascione, F., James, M., Austin, S., & Shimp, L. (1980). Seniors & pharmacists: Improving the dialogue. *American Pharmacy, 5,* 30-32.

Becker, M. (1985). Patient adherence to prescribed therapies. *Medical Care, 23*(5), 539-555.

Brown, C. S., Wright, R. G., & Christensen, D. B. (1987). Association between type of medication instruction and patients' knowledge, side effects, and compliance. *Hospital and Community Psychiatry, 37,* 55-60.

Coccia, B. (1992, June). Creative marketers help physicians communicate with a diverse U.S. patient population. *Product Management Today,* pp. 10-13.

Culbertson, V. L., Arthur, T. G., Rhodes, P. J., & Rhodes, R. S. (1988). Consumer preferences for verbal and written medication information. *Drug Intelligence and Clinical Pharmacy, 22,* 390-396.

Dodds, L. J. (1986). Effects of information leaflets on compliance with antibiotic therapy. *The Pharmaceutical Journal, 11,* 48-51.

Drug companies' patient support programs on the rise. (1993, April). *FDA Advertising and Promotion Manual Monthly Bulletin, 1,* pp. 1-7.

George, C. F., Waters, W. E., & Nicholas, J. A. (1983). Prescription information leaflets: A pilot study in general practice. *British Medical Journal, 287,* 1193-1196.

Gibbs, S. (1992). Prescription information leaflets for patients. *European Respiratory Journal, 5,* 140-143.

Gibbs, S., Waters, W. E., & George, C. F. (1989). The benefits of prescription information leaflets (1). *British Journal of Clinical Pharmacology, 27,* 723-739.

Green, L. W., Mullen, P. D., & Stainbrook, G. L. (1986). Programs to reduce drug errors in the elderly: Direct and indirect evidence from patient education. *Journal of Geriatric Drug Therapy, 1,* 59-70.

Harvey, J. L., & Plumridge, R. J. (1991). Comparative attitudes of verbal and written medication information among hospital outpatients. *DICP, The Annals of Pharmacology, 25,* 925-928.

Isaacman, D. J., Purvis, K., Gyuro, J., Anderson, Y., & Smith, D. (1992). Standardized instructions: Do they improve communication of discharge information from the emergency department? *Pediatrics, 89,* 1204-1208.

Haynes, R. B., Wang, E., & Da Mota Gomes, M. (1987). A critical review of interventions to improve compliance with prescribed medications. *Patient Education and Counseling, 10,* 155-166.

Jackson, R. A., & Huffman, D. C. (1990, July). Patient compliance: The financial impact on your practice. *NARD Journal,* pp. 67-71.

Janz, N., & Becker, M. (1984). The health belief model: A decade later. *Health Education Quarterly, 11,* 1-47.

Johnston, M., Clarke, A., Mundy, K., Cromarty E., & Ridout, K. (1986). Facilitating comprehension of discharge medication in elderly patients. *Age and Aging, 15,* 304-306.

Kessler, D. A. (1991). Communicating with patients about their medications. *The New England Journal of Medicine, 325,* 1650-1652.

Lamy, P. P. (1990). Adverse drug effects. *Clinical Pharmacology, 6,* 293-307.

Meichenbaum, D., & Turk, D. C. (1987). *Facilitating treatment adherence: A practitioner's guidebook.* New York: Plenum.

Morris, L. A., Grossman, K., Barkdoll, G., & Gordon, E. (1987). A segmentational analysis of prescription drug information seeking. *Medical Care, 25,* 953-964.

Morris, L. S., & Schulz, R. M. (1992). Patient compliance—An overview. *Journal of Clinical Pharmacy and Therapeutics, 17,* 283-295.

Mullen, P. D., & Green, L. W. (1984). *Measuring patient drug information transfer: An assessment of the literature.* Houston: University of Texas Health Science Center, Center for Health Promotion Research and Development.

Myers, E. D., & Calvert, E. J. (1984). Information, compliance and side-effects: A study of patients on antidepressant medication. *British Journal of Clinical Pharmacology, 17,* 21-25.

O'Connell, M. B., & Johnson, J. F. (1992). Evaluation of medication knowledge in elderly patients. *The Annals of Pharmacotherapy, 26,* 919-921.

Office of Inspector General. (1990). *Medication regimens: Causes of noncompliance* (DHHS Publication No. OEI-04-89-89121). Washington, DC: Government Printing Office.

Opdycke, R.A.C., Ascione, F. J., Shimp, L. A., & Rosen, R. I. (1992). A systematic approach to educating elderly patients about their medications. *Patient Education and Counseling, 19,* 43-60.

Podolsky, D., & Newman, R. J. (1993, March 29). Prescription prizes: Drug makers hope giveaways and discounts will snag customers. *U.S. News & World Report,* pp. 56-60.

Quaid, K. A., Faden, R. R., Vining, E. P., & Freeman, J. M. (1990). Informed consent for a prescription drug: Impact of disclosed information on patient understanding and medical outcomes. *Patient Education and Counseling, 15,* 249-259.

Robinson, G. L., Gilbertson, A. D., & Litwack, L. (1986). The effects of a psychiatric patient education to medication program on post-discharge compliance. *Psychiatric Quarterly, 58,* 113-118.

Schwartz-Lookinland, S., McKeever, L. C., & Saputo, M. (1989). Compliance with antibiotic regimens in Hispanic mothers. *Patient Education and Counseling, 13,* 171-182.

Sclar, D., Chin, A., Skaer, T., Okamoto, M., Nakahiro, R., & Gill, M. (1991). Effect of health education in promoting prescription refill compliance among patients with hypertension. *Clinical Therapeutics, 13,* 489-495.

Shapiro, A. K., & Morris, L. A. (1978). Placebo effects in medical and psychological therapies. In A. E. Bergin & S. L. Garfield (Eds.), *Handbook of psychotherapy and behavior change: Empirical analysis* (pp. 213-222). New York: John Wiley.

Smith, D. L. (1989). Compliance packaging: A patient education tool. *American Pharmacy, NS29*(2), 126-134.

U.S. Department of Health and Human Services. (1990). *Healthy people 2000: National health promotion and disease prevention objectives* (Conference ed.). Washington, DC: U.S. Department of Health and Human Services.

Van Haecht, C.H.M., Vander Stichele, R., & Bogaert, M. G. (1990). Package inserts for antihypertensive drugs: Use by the patients and impact on adverse drug reactions. *European Journal of Clinical Pharmacology, 39,* 551-554.

Weiderholt, J., Clarridge, B. R., & Svarstad, B. L. (1992). Verbal consultation regarding prescription drugs. *Medical Care, 30,* 159-173.

Weinman, J. (1990). Providing written information for patients: Psychological considerations. *Journal of the Royal Society of Medicine, 83,* 303-305.

# 14 Enabling Health

## POLICY AND ADMINISTRATIVE
## PRACTICES AT A CROSSROADS

ROXANNE LOUISELLE PARROTT

MARY LOUISE KAHL

EDWARD W. MAIBACH

*Since the ethical laws, which concern the individual duty of each man in himself, are so hard to frame . . . it is no wonder if those that govern so many individuals are more so. (Frame, 1973, pp. 112-113)*
                                        —Montaigne, 16th century philosopher

A substantial knowledge base has accumulated in relation to understanding human behavior and health. When combined with communication theory and public health practice, this knowledge highlights the means and methods to design messages that promote individual responsibility in relation to health. The outcomes associated with such efforts, however, depend upon the environment in which an individual lives, as constructed by state and local, national, and even international health policy and administrative practices. Before constructing health messages aimed at the individual, therefore, one should carefully evaluate the larger social scene, examining the administrative health policies and practices that provide the backdrop for health promotion programs. Such examination fulfills an ethical obligation to understand the external barriers that may inhibit the success of health enablement activities.

## Health Message
## Designers' Ethical Obligations

The first two decades of the 20th century saw the U.S. middle class evolve toward greater social awareness. An urban population increasingly dealt with indigents in a concerned and public manner, adopting consumer protection laws and public regulatory commissions. Individual free choice, and the belief that a human being's material fortune depends on character traits and morality, became unrealistic to the early 20th-century progressive. The new American industrial society's working-class citizens suffered ill health and injury, often through no fault of their own. As a result, middle-class progressives considered social insurance, a means to furnish part of the population with protection that others may need less or afford for themselves, using society's resources to maintain the laborer's traditional self-reliance (Hirshfield, 1970). One specific area that Americans felt warranted government action and social insurance was health and medical care. Supporters structured disconnected ideologies into the beginnings of a political myth, and in 1906, the American Association for Labor Legislation (AALL), an educational pressure group concerned with health reforms in industry, sought compulsory health insurance as a solution to indigent medical care (Hirshfield, 1970).

The AALL, with leaders versed in European social insurance experiments, concentrated initially on a campaign to implement workmen's compensation laws, the first successful social insurance in the United States. With that achievement, the AALL's membership grew to include progressive politicians and university professors, Woodrow Wilson among them. The group's executive secretary, John B. Andrews, worked with other influential AALL members to insert the social insurance plank into the 1912 Progressive Party's platform (Andrews, 1938). The AALL's efforts spanned the decade of 1910 to 1920, a predecessor to modern efforts to reform health policy and the vision that inspires these activities. The AALL's efforts were inhibited by failure to address labor leaders, who felt that the enactment of social insurance would weaken labor unions; employers, who felt they would pay an unfair portion; and commercial insurance companies, who viewed national health insurance as a threat to business (Hirshfield, 1970). These same issues will always challenge health policy makers and administrators, forming the context within which efforts to empower and enable individuals to be healthy must be framed. These issues suggest several broad questions that health campaigners should address during the process of planning, implementing, and evaluating their messages:

1. To what degree are there clear statements of *national standards* applicable to health?
2. To what degree have *domestic laws* been created to observe the national standards?
3. To what degree do *federal administrative goals and institutions* support the domestic laws?
4. To what degree do *state and local rules and actions* exist to facilitate or inhibit the attainment of federal administrative goals and institutions?
5. To what degree do cultural norms *allocate legal responsibility and mobilize support* for health policies and practices?

## NATIONAL HEALTH STANDARDS

The identification of national health standards is a tenuous proposition at best. One problem with forming statements of national health standards is that any individual might consider almost anything to be within the realm of just claims. For example, is clean air a birthright? Does every human being have a just claim to breathe air that is noninjurious to her or his health? If so, does an individual have the right to bring suit against a state that does not guarantee that the air she or he breathes is noninjurious to health?

In the United States, a Bill of Rights guarantees citizens certain inalienable rights, and one individual's rights stop where another individual's begin. The difficulty in establishing national health standards, then, is to determine where to draw that line, particularly if one considers life in terms of mental and physical health, and work-related activities harm one's mental and/or physical health. These are issues that nations have wrested with both internally among states and externally at the level of international law.

The relationship that exists between an individual and the state forms an underlying notion of human rights and provides a way to frame discussion about national health standards. In particular, two United Nations' documents that address human rights illustrate the tension around the topic of national health standards. The Covenant of Civil and Political Rights was designed to acknowledge an individual's freedom of religious expression, peaceful assemblage, and movement, in addition to the inherent right to life (von Glahn, 1981). The Covenant on Economic, Social, and Cultural Rights, on the other hand, directly addresses issues relating to economic and social areas, such as: the right to work, medical care, education, and mental or physical health (von Glahn, 1981).

The United States had reservations about being a signature party to both U.N. covenants, recognizing the potential for conflict between what one citizen does to satisfy the right to work and another citizen's inherent right to life. Underlying this issue, as articulated by the AALL decades earlier, is the struggle to address whether or not an individual may be held responsible for his or her own ill health. In other words, if someone willingly works, and the work harms physical/mental health, is the worker or the employer responsible?

In relation to something such as the air we breathe or the water we drink, national health standards appear to be clearly necessary. Without such standards, one state or an area within a state may adopt policy that undermines the efforts and policy of a neighboring state or region. Few would disagree with the statement that national health standards appear to be of vital importance to safeguard the food supply, too. The use of some forms of pesticides, however, may threaten the quality of the air or water we use, while promoting the quality of the food we consume. Such conflicts must be addressed, and health message designers should start with an analysis of the national health standards within which their efforts are to be framed. Two questions should guide this undertaking, which leads to the ability to examine potential conflicts:

1. *What is the relationship between the health activity being planned and the right to life;* and
2. *What is the relationship between the health activity being planned and the right to work?*

To extend the discussion of pesticide use as an example, message designers who seek to evaluate national health standards relating to pesticides should examine the relationship of use to the right to life and the right to work. In relation to the right to life, health promoters might list the fact that pesticide use is related to respiratory and skin ailments that negatively affect quality of life and may even threaten one's survival. On the other hand, pesticides protect the food supply from spoilage due to insect infestation, and food is necessary to sustain life. An evaluation of the relationship between pesticide use and the right to work might demonstrate that use is related to farmers' ability to make a profit and stay in business. Production of pesticides also creates jobs. Having reached these conclusions, message designers should recognize the clear potential for conflict to occur in the face of attempting to restrict pesticide use. The evidence of conflict or potential for conflict signifies the need to include messages for multiple audiences, with arguments and counterarguments designed to address different sides of the issue.

Evaluation of the national health standards that relate to a particular influence topic is the first step in efforts to examine the societal system that frames the message designer's efforts. The next undertaking in this analysis is an examination of whether domestic laws exist to observe the national health standards.

## DOMESTIC LAWS TO
## OBSERVE THE NATIONAL STANDARDS

To make comparisons about health standards from one nation to another, indicators such as infant mortality rate are used. These provide a gross summative measure of a number of national health standards, including sanitation and nutrition levels, as well as available medical care. The United States has a relatively high infant mortality rate in comparison to other developed nations (Willis & Fullerton, 1991), suggesting that national health standards in support of a lower infant mortality rate have not been clearly articulated, are in conflict, and/or are unsupported by domestic laws.

Legislation to support a national health standard often occurs in reaction to an event that costs lives and/or captures media attention. In relation to air quality, for example, early in this century, Trail Smelter emissions in British Columbia caused damage to the state of Washington and injury to persons and property. Under a 1935 treaty, the dispute was arbitrated in favor of the United States, and the assertion was made that no State had the right to use its territory to the injury of another State's persons or property (von Glahn, 1981). Determining responsibility for fallout and other by-products of nuclear testing also illustrates issues that require domestic law to support national air quality standards.

National health standards are broad guidelines that articulate philosophy and principles to direct health-related activities undertaken within a nation. For every standard, multiple domestic laws are likely to be necessary to evolve the principle toward practice. To assess whether domestic laws exist which observe the national health standards, message designers ask:

1. *What domestic laws exist to support the standards;* and
2. *What domestic laws exist to oppose the standards?*

In relation to the discussion of pesticide use, message designers may determine that domestic laws exist that support use to safeguard the food supply. Laws may also exist that oppose use in areas that have a certain population density. No law may actually exist to support use to protect farmers' profits, but use for the purpose of safeguarding the food supply may at the same time promote farmers' profits. No law may exist to oppose use that endangers farmworkers' health, but use for the purpose of safeguarding the food supply may at the same time endanger farmworkers' health.

As in the case of national health standards, message designers should identify situations in which domestic laws create conflict or potential for conflict, thereby gaining a better understanding of the audiences to be addressed and the appropriate content for messages. American farming is one arena that clearly illustrates the competing demands between domestic laws designed to support the right to life versus the right to work. Farmers often depend upon workers who work for low wages and demand few benefits. The agricultural labor force is "the only sector of the U.S. economy to be given preferential treatment in the Immigration Reform and Control Act (IRCA) of 1986" (Thompson & Martin, 1991, p. 527). Migrant and seasonal farmworkers reside in very poor conditions and often have ill health with no one enforcing labor protection laws on their behalf (Linder, 1990). To enforce laws on behalf of seasonal farmworkers, however, jeopardizes the already small profit margin of farmers. In other words, to protect the health of one group puts at risk the right to work and make a living of another group. Both groups and both goals must be addressed in message designers' plans to enable health.

The major weakness of domestic laws aimed at supporting national health standards is in the area of implementation. Having identified domestic laws that relate to observing particular national health standards, an examination of federal administrative goals and institutions designed to implement these laws is an appropriate next step to fulfill the message designer's ethical obligation.

## FEDERAL ADMINISTRATIVE GOALS AND INSTITUTIONS TO IMPLEMENT DOMESTIC LAWS

The design and passage of domestic laws to support national health standards is a necessary but not sufficient condition to enable health. To implement the laws, the support of federal administrative goals and institutions are frequently required. At any point in time, the current federal administration's goals have a substantial impact on whether or not the necessary institutions exist to support laws created to uphold a national health standard. The basic purpose of national health care policy and reform is to provide leadership and direction for efforts to improve the health and well-being of a nation's citizens. This includes the design and implementation of the means to grant access, both geographically and financially, to health and medical care.

As part of the effort both to create jobs and to protect individual health and safety, statements of policy to reflect federal administrative goals are written and presented to the public. These policy statements comprise what has been termed bureaucratic discourse, which is, "any report produced by an organization for evaluation and other practical purposes that is targeted for individuals, committees, or publics who are unaware of its promotive character and the editing processes used to shape it" (Altheide & Johnson, 1980, p. 5). Federal government agencies and departments employ bureaucratic discourse frequently when they address both internal and external audiences "in the exercise of power" (Combs & Nimmo, 1993, p. 122). The purpose of bureaucratic discourse is to create, mobilize, and continue support for administrative goals, while concomitantly limiting and restricting any opposition to them.

This nation's public statements of administrative goals about health care emanate largely from the Department of Health and Human Services, address multiple audiences, promote the particular viewpoint of the President and advisers, and endorse specific courses of action, often in the face of opposition. The very process of articulating health care priorities, of "setting the agenda," demonstrates significant political powers. Health message designers should assess:

1. *What administrative goals underlie bureaucratic discourse;* and
2. *What institutions exist to create, mobilize, and continue support for these goals?*

Analysis of both these issues is critical to understand the likely success or failure of health enablement activities.

If administrative discourse promotes prenatal care as a practice for all pregnant women, for example, this may be a means to articulate the goal of reducing the infant mortality rate. Such a goal may be the result of efforts to implement the Healthy Birth Act, which was passed as one domestic law in support of a national health standard. Campaign planners assigned the task of promoting prenatal care, however, ought to ask themselves whether there are an adequate number of accessible providers and clinics to give the care. Promoting the desire for prenatal care without assuring access to such care perpetuates and exacerbates the underlying inequities in the health care system (see Parrott & Daniels, in press).

Health problems of the poor and minorities have often been found to be exacerbated by the inadequacies of institutions that provide services. This is particularly true for pregnant women and young children. The report of the National Commission on Children (1990) concluded:

> fragmented, narrowly defined policies and programs often create financial, administrative, and geographical barriers to early and regular care. The result is a disjointed tangle of services that reach some but not all of those who need them.
>
> As in other areas of human services, it is typically those women who need prenatal care most who are least likely to receive it. (p. 124)

In another area of the nation's health policy, naming the prevention and detection of HIV as a priority alerts health planners and campaigners that there will be support for activities in relation to HIV. What varies with different administrations is the specific vision that forms the approach to be taken. The Reagan, Bush, and Clinton administrations have all been criticized for making HIV prevention a priority in name only. Former President Bush's appointment of Earvin "Magic" Johnson to the National Commission on AIDS illustrates action taken to support a health goal. This administrative action captured widespread attention and approval, as the Bush administration heralded Johnson's affiliation with the Commission as proof of its commitment to outreach on the issue of AIDS and evidence of ongoing attempts to publicize measures contributing to prevention of the disease. When Bush refused, however, to adopt the suggestions of this very Commission, notably with regard to the distribution of condoms in public schools, the sometimes inevitable clash that occurs between health care priorities and electoral politics became apparent.

Curbing alcohol and drug use has also long been named as an administrative health care priority in the United States, suggesting yet another sanctioned focus for campaigners' messages. Millions of Americans require treatment for alcohol and drug abuse, but the cost of programs to reduce drug demand is excessively high. Because the federal government's willingness to fund drug treatment has not kept pace with the demand for drug treatment among low-income people, there is a large treatment availability gap. The approval of additional funding for facilities to treat drug abuse is necessary to provide institutional support for an administrative health goal and reflects support for domestic laws that make drug use illegal.

Having evaluated whether or not federal administrative goals and institutions exist to support the implementation of domestic laws, message designers should next consider state and local rules and actions. These may complement, denigrate, or be unrelated to federal policies.

## STATE AND LOCAL RULES AND ACTIONS TO SUPPORT ADMINISTRATIVE GOALS AND INSTITUTIONS

State and local rules and actions to support administrative goals and institutions are frequently necessary to empower individuals to be healthy. If clinics and providers are available for pregnant women to use to receive prenatal care, for example, but eligible women have no mode of transportation to get to the clinics, or have to wait for hours to receive care, the existence of the institutions does little to ensure proper care. An examination of the community environment in which a target audience lives often reveals barriers to the use of institutions designed to provide health services. Moreover, state and local rules and actions are often needed to enforce federal laws passed to promote well-being. An analysis of state and local rules and actions may thus highlight necessary reforms to move promise forward into the realm of performance.

Health message designers should assess:

1. *What state and local rules/ordinances exist to support federal administrative goals and institutions, and domestic laws created to observe national health standards;* and

2. *What state and local actions have been taken to support federal administrative goals and institutions, and the domestic laws created to observe national health standards?*

In recognition of the significant role of state and local ordinances and actions, consider the consumption of alcohol, which has often been limited by state laws that assign age limits to purchasers. If local convenience store workers sell beer to minors, however, the law proves to be an inadequate means to enable health. Similarly, laws have been passed to constrain the sale of tobacco products, but stores and vending machines allow underage consumers to purchase and use tobacco products. These practices, once identified, provide an important avenue for message designers to target efforts to enable health.

Many state and local ordinances illustrate the symbiotic relationship that exists between federal and state laws, as one state may adopt a more liberal policy than another state, so individuals cross state borders to imbibe. In the absence of a federal regulation, these state activities are sanctioned. State and local rules also importantly affect whether or not federal institutional support will be granted to a particular state or locale. A state must sanction and support the reporting of injuries, illness, and/or disease, for example, to provide evidence of a need for federal institutional support. Health message designers increase the likelihood that their messages will succeed by evaluating whether or not a situation lacks institutional support because of an absence of need or an absence of state and/or local action to demonstrate the need. In the event of the latter, message designers may conclude that a precursor to enabling health is to promote recognition at the state and local level that a need exists.

In recognition of the vital role that state and local communities play in health enablement efforts, campaigners have moved toward emphasizing community-based programs. Health planners seek to identify the local opinion-leaders and to work with them toward enabling health. At the same time, the vital need to gain insights about the cultural norms that guide health behavior becomes apparent.

## CULTURAL NORMS TO ALLOCATE RESPONSIBILITY AND MOBILIZE SUPPORT FOR STATE AND LOCAL RULES AND ACTIONS

The information that individuals have about health depends upon communication with friends, family, physicians, and others, as well as exposure to mediated messages about health. When an individual's family or friends fail to support a health recommendation, the likelihood of following the advice is reduced (e.g., Alcalay & Taplin, 1989). Past investigations demonstrate that social support systems are as likely to lead to negative as to positive health habits (e.g., Pearlin & Aneschensel, 1986). Health message designers must therefore seek to understand cultural norms that affect the interpretation of and behavior associated with state and local rules and actions taken to support administrative goals and institutions, and domestic laws designed to attain national health standards. Health message designers should assess:

1. *What cultural norms exist to allocate responsibility for behaviors affecting health;* and

2. *What cultural norms mobilize support for state and local rules and actions?*

In relation to alcohol and drug abuse, an analysis of the health objectives attained by the end of 1990 as specified by the Surgeon General's Report in 1979, "Healthy People," revealed that 19 goals had been set, and only approximately half were met, with another one-fourth viewed as unlikely to be met (McGinnis, 1991). The objectives that the nation had made progress on included educating the public about the effects of alcohol and drug use, and changing societal attitudes that glorify alcohol use. Among the objectives yet to be attained are those that focus attention on issues that result from drug and alcohol abuse, including the spread of HIV and child and spouse abuse (Stoto, Behrens, & Rosemont, 1990). To attain these goals necessitates that the cultural norms that allocate responsibility in relation to drug use and support for drug use must be examined. In some cultures, norms associated with drug- and alcohol-related child and spouse abuse include "looking the other way" or "blaming the victim," exemplifying the failure of state and local ordinances to be carried out because of cultural norms.

When an individual's cultural group eschews care in an organized setting, the individual is less likely to obtain such care, even when institutions exist to provide the care (e.g., Flay & Burton, 1990). Health message designers may enter campaigns with the assumption that the appropriate starting place for their efforts is to change the norms that fail to support the behavior that campaigners seek to change. Garnering support for desired behavior from the individuals for whom the behavior is requested is an important component of designing health messages. It is by no means the best or the only starting place, however, nor the one that is most likely to enable health, as suggested throughout this discussion of health message designers' ethical obligations. The analysis that has been advocated leads to several conclusions with subsequent implications for fulfilling the message designer's goal to enable health.

## Implications and Conclusion

Incidents that unnecessarily cost human life appear to happen all too frequently and are the bane of the existence of health message designers, who aim to promote individuals' well-being. For example, these events occur in plants where chickens are being processed and fire exits are locked, and on farms where pesticides are used to protect crops but personal safety equipment is deemed to be too expensive to purchase to protect humans during pesticide use. Health message designers ought to weigh such issues during the process of constructing a campaign. These barriers have little to do with whether or not individuals understand particular health messages and far more to do with the activities of those who make and enforce policies. Thus, the issue for the message designer becomes: Who should be the target of messages? For example, if we are concerned about the toxic effect of pesticides, should we be targeting:

- individuals with the message "don't eat pesticide-laden foods"
- farmers with the messages "don't use particular types of pesticides" and "don't use any pesticides without wearing personal protective equipment"
- manufacturers with the messages "don't manufacture toxic substances" and "educate farmers about personal safety when using pesticides and risk of failure to practice personal safety"
- lawmakers with the message "don't license manufacturers who fail to provide safety measures for using pesticides"
- the general public with the message "support the enactment of laws to safeguard personal health and safety"

As a result of recognizing the multiple audiences involved in the effort to enable health, message designers will recognize the need to construct message content aimed at attaining the goal most appropriate for that target.

To assist message designers during the process of planning a campaign and selecting target audiences and goals to be associated with messages, the following questions can be used to guide an ethical analysis:

1. Does the absence of domestic laws to support a national health standard reduce the likelihood that a message will enable health? If yes, an appropriate starting place and audience for health messages is the lawmakers rather than the general public.
2. Is there a conflict among present domestic laws that reduces the likelihood that a health message will enable health? If yes, once more, the appropriate starting place and audience for health messages is the lawmakers rather than the general public.
3. Do federal administrative practices inhibit the design of appropriate messages? If yes, proceed if the health of most audience members could still potentially be improved within the constraints of message design; otherwise, do not proceed.
4. Do institutions exist to provide the services recommended to enable health? If not, the appropriate starting place and audience will be the group(s) responsible for allocating support for the institutions.

5. Do state and local rules and actions support the use of institutions designed to provide services to enable health? If not, an appropriate starting place and audience will be the group(s) responsible for enforcing federal policy.

6. Do cultural norms support the actions advocated by state and local health promotion efforts? If not, revise the practices and aims to acknowledge cultural traditions.

This analysis aims to encompass approaches to mobilize social support to change administrative policy and practices, and may involve media advocacy approaches to change administrative policy and practices. Recognition is given to the fact that when administrative conditions do not warrant an emphasis on individual enablement, health message designers are ethically obligated to cease such promotions.

In sum, an analysis of administrative policies and practices extends the health message designer's formative evaluation into a realm too often forgotten, neglected, or relegated to post hoc explanations for failure. Ultimately, the goal is to garner opportunities for individuals to elect behavior that fosters well-being. Individuals judge political programs and decision making about health in terms of personal access to care and the quality of that care, an elusive and multidimensional phenomenon (Parasuraman, Zeithaml, & Berry, 1985). Such analysis is thus up to message designers, who must exercise an ethical framework, concerning the individual duty of each one unto him- or herself, and everyone they purport to enable to be healthy.

# References

Alcalay, R., & Taplin, S. (1989). Community health campaigns: From theory to action. In R. E. Rice & C. K. Atkin (Eds.), *Public communication campaigns* (pp. 105-130). Newbury Park, CA: Sage.

Altheide, D. L., & Johnson, J. (1980). *Bureaucratic propaganda.* Boston: Allyn & Bacon.

Andrews, J. B. (1938). No time to falter. *American Labor Legislation Review, 29,* 147-148.

Combs, J. E., & Nimmo, D. (1993). *The new propaganda: The dictatorship of palaver in contemporary politics.* New York: Longman.

Flay, B. R., & Burton, D. (1990). Effective mass communication strategies for health campaigns. In C. Atkin & L. Wallack (Eds.), *Mass communication and public health: Complexities and conflicts* (pp. 129-146). Newbury Park, CA: Sage.

Frame, D. M. (1973). *Selections from the messages of Montaigne.* Columbus, OH: Columbus University Press.

Hirshfield, D. S. (1970). *The lost reform.* Cambridge, MA: Harvard University Press.

Linder, M. (1990). Crewleaders and agricultural sweatshops: The lawful and unlawful exploitation of migrant farmworkers. *Creighton Law Review, 23,* 213-233.

McGinnis, J. M. (1991). Health objectives for the nation. *American Psychologist, 46,* 520-524.

National Commission on Children. (1991). *Beyond rhetoric: A new American agenda for children and families.* Washington, DC: Government Printing Office.

Parasuraman, A., Zeithaml, V. A., & Berry, L. L. (1985). A conceptual model of service quality and its implications for future research. *Journal of Marketing, 49,* 41-50.

Parrott, R. L., & Daniels, M. (in press). Promoting prenatal care to women: Promises, pitfalls, and pratfalls. In R. L. Parrott & C. M. Condit (Eds.), *Women's health care campaigns: The rhetoric of reproduction.* Urbana-Champaign: University of Illinois Press.

Pearlin, L. I., & Aneschensel, C. S. (1986). Coping and social supports: Their functions and applications. In L. H. Aiken & D. Mechanic (Eds.), *Applications of social science to clinical medicine and health policy* (pp. 417-437). New Brunswick, NJ: Rutgers University Press.

Stoto, M. A., Behrens, R., & Rosemont, C. (1990). *Healthy people 2000.* Washington, DC: National Academy Press.

Thompson, G. D., & Martin, P. L. (1991). Immigration reform and the agricultural labor force. *Labor Law Journal, 42,* 528-536.

von Glahn, G. (1981). *Law among nations: An introduction to public international law.* New York: Macmillan.

Willis, W. O., & Fullerton, J. T. (1991). Prevention of infant mortality: An agenda for nurse-midwifery. *Journal of Nurse-Midwifery, 36,* 343-354.

# Index

# About the Contributors

**Erica Weintraub Austin,** Ph.D., is Assistant Professor of Communication and Head of the Public Relations sequence at Washington State University in Pullman. Her research focuses on the development of decision-making skills through uses of mass media and interpersonal sources, particularly in the realms of substance abuse and public affairs. She is also interested in how parents can affect their children's interpretations of media messages, thereby affecting the decisions children make about a variety of important issues. Recent work includes publications in *Communication Research, Journal of Broadcasting & Electronic Media, Journalism Quarterly,* and a contribution to *Relational Communication and Health Outcomes* (edited by G. Kreps and Dan O'Hair, in the SCA Applied Communication Series). She recently worked with the state of Washington to develop a statewide alcohol abuse prevention campaign aimed at the parents of 3- to 10-year-olds.

**George I. Balch,** Ph.D., is Visiting Associate Professor in the Department of Marketing at the University of Illinois at Chicago. He is currently conducting social marketing research at the Prevention Research Center of the University of Illinois and consulting with the National Cancer Institute and the U.S. Agency for International Development to develop and monitor the effectiveness of communication interventions. He was formerly Vice President, Associate Director of Strategy and Research at DDB Needham Worldwide, one of the world's largest advertising agencies.

**David Cotton,** Ph.D., M.P.H., is Research Psychologist in the Behavioral and Prevention Research Branch, Division of STD/HIV Prevention at the Centers for Disease Control and Prevention. He received his doctoral degree in Clinical Psychology from the University of Alabama while concurrently pursuing his public health degree at the University of Alabama at Birmingham.

His current research interests are in the development of social science-based interventions modifying STD- and HIV-related risk behaviors in community-level, small group, and one-on-one settings.

**James Price Dillard,** Ph.D., is Associate Professor at the University of Wisconsin in the Department of Communication Arts. His research examines compliance-gaining in interpersonal relationships and has been published in such outlets as *Communication Monographs* and *Human Communication Research.*

**Lynne Doner,** M.A., is Vice President and Director of Research at the Washington, D.C., office of Porter/Novelli. Her research interests include applying commercial market research techniques and data to target audience development in social marketing programs, and developing useful process evaluation methodologies for mass media components of health promotion and disease prevention programs.

**Jerold L. Hale,** Ph.D., is Associate Professor in the Department of Speech Communication at the University of Georgia. His research interests include social influence and relational communication. His research examines persuasion and influence in interpersonal relationships. His work has been published in *Communication Monographs* and *Human Communication Research,* as well as other national and regional outlets.

**Sharon Lee Hammond,** Ph.D., is Adjunct Assistant Professor at the University of Maryland's Graduate School of Management and Technology, where she teaches the graduate-level quantitative research methods and marketing research methods courses. She received her Ph.D. from the University of Maryland's Health Communication Program in 1990. She has conducted survey and experimental research in the areas of cancer, AIDS, environmental health risks, and medication communication, resulting in publications in a variety of journals and edited books, including *Science, Technology & Human Values, Communication Research, Health Communication, Health Education Quarterly, Communication Yearbook,* and *Health Education Research.* She is also the editor of a special issue of *Health Communication* on the topic of communicating with patients about their medications.

**David R. Holtgrave,** Ph.D., is the Acting Assistant Director for Behavioral Science, Office of HIV/AIDS, Centers for Disease Control and Prevention, and is an adjunct faculty member in the Emory University School of Public Health, Division of Behavioral Science and Health Education. He received his Ph.D. in Quantitative Psychology from the University of Illinois and did postdoctoral work at the Harvard School of Public Health, Interdisciplinary Programs in Health. His work on decision analysis and the psychology of decision making has been published in such outlets as *Risk Analysis, Medical Decision Making, Journal of Behavioral Decision Making, Journal of Family Practice,* and *Archives of Internal Medicine.* His research interests include behavioral decision making, risk communication, and the evaluation of prevention programs.

**Cecile Johnston,** Ph.D., is the Director of Communications Research at Prospect Associates. In this capacity, she is responsible for the design, implementation, and analysis of research projects devoted to the promotion of social programs, particularly those involving health communications. As project director, she designs and oversees implementation of formative, process, outcome, and impact studies of health programs for the Office of Cancer Communications, National Cancer Institute.

**Mary Louise Kahl,** Ph.D., is Assistant Professor in the Department of Communication at the State University of New York in New Paltz. Her research interests include the rhetoric of women's health care.

**Linda S. Kay,** M.P.H., is a Public Health Analyst in the Behavioral Studies Section, Behavioral and Prevention Research Branch, division of STD/HIV Prevention, National Center for Prevention Services, Centers for Disease Control and Prevention. Her current research interests emphasize health communication and behavioral science, especially as it relates to HIV prevention in adolescents and in the workplace.

**R. Craig Lefebvre,** Ph.D., is Chief Technical Officer and Vice President, Health Communications at Prospect Associates, a health communications firm located in Rockville, MD. He has authored more than 50 publications in the areas of social marketing, health promotion, and community-based programs. His current work includes planning, developing, implementing, and evaluating cancer communications programs; social marketing and media advocacy approaches to tobacco control; international communications efforts directed toward HIV prevention; and applications of social marketing to health reform.

Kay Loughrey, M.P.H., R.D., is a Public Affairs Specialist in the Office of Cancer Communications of the National Cancer Institute. She directs the 5 A Day for Better Health's media campaign and coordinates nutrition education programming for NCI.

Edward W. Maibach, M.P.H., Ph.D., is Assistant Professor in the Division of Behavioral Sciences and Health Education and Director of the Center for Health and Risk Communication at the Emory School of Public Health. He is a communication scientist with research interests in the use of mass and interpersonal communication campaigns to promote health enhancement. He is actively involved in social marketing research, and is currently conducting both experimental and evaluation research studies on effective communication strategies for the prevention of cancer, AIDS, STDs, and adolescent pregnancy. He has written a number of articles and book chapters on these topics, including several examinations of the implications of Bandura's social cognitive theory for HIV prevention campaigns.

John McGrath is the Chief of the Communications and Marketing Section at the National Heart, Lung, and Blood Institute, part of the National Institutes of Health in Bethesda, MD. N.H.L.B.I. coordinates national health education campaigns on blood pressure, cholesterol, asthma, and warning signs for heart attacks that make extensive use of mass media. He is a doctoral candidate at the University of Maryland.

Jennifer L. Monahan, Ph.D., is Assistant Professor in the Department of Speech Communication at the University of Georgia. Her research focuses on emotion and affect in communication. She has published her work in such outlets as *Communication Monographs* and the *Journal of Communication.*

Glen J. Nowak, Ph.D., is Assistant Professor in the Department of Advertising at the University of Georgia. He is also a Visiting Communication Scientist at the National AIDS Information and Education Program at the U.S. Centers for Disease Control.

Roxanne Louiselle Parrott, Ph.D., is Assistant Professor in the Department of Speech Communication and a Fellow in the Institute of Behavioral Research at the University of Georgia. She also has an adjunct appointment in the Department of Medicine at the Medical College of Georgia. She is coauthor (with Michael Pfau) of *Persuasive Communication Campaigns* and primary author of *Women's Health Care Campaigns: The Rhetoric of Reproduction.* Her research interests include an examination of how mediated and interpersonal communication interface, affecting individuals' involvement with message content.

**Michael Pfau,** Ph.D., is Professor in the School of Journalism and Mass Communication at the University of Wisconsin-Madison. He has authored more than 40 articles, many dealing with influence strategies in health campaigns, appearing in such journals as *Communication Monographs, Human Communication Research,* and others. He has coauthored four books, the most recent, *Persuasive Communication Campaigns* (1993) with Roxanne Parrott. He is a past recipient of the Speech Communication Association's Golden Anniversary Monograph Award.

**Michael J. Siska,** M.S., is Health Communication Research Specialist in the National AIDS Information and Education Program of the Centers for Disease Control and Prevention.

**Michael D. Slater,** Ph.D., M.P.A., is Associate Professor in the Department of Technical Journalism at Colorado State University in Fort Collins. He received his doctoral degree in Communication at Stanford University in 1988, and was a predoctoral fellow with the Stanford Center for Research in Disease Prevention; prior to that, he was a public relations executive in New York City specializing in technology, health, and education. He is currently principal investigator of a study funded by the National Institute on Alcohol Abuse and Alcoholism on adolescent responses to alcohol advertising, and recently conducted or consulted on audience research and message/channel evaluation studies for AMC-Cancer Research Center and the U.S. Department of Agriculture (on minimizing exposure to pesticides). His research on message effects, attitude influence processes, and audience segmentation has appeared in journals including *Communication Research, Health Education Quarterly, Journal of Communication, Journal of Public Relations Research,* and *Journalism Quarterly.*

**Sharyn M. Sutton,** Ph.D., is currently the Director, Nutrition Marketing and Education in Food and Nutrition Services at the U.S. Department of Agriculture where she is directing the national nutrition education efforts of F.N.S. Prior to joining USDA, she was Chief of the Information Projects Branch, Office of Cancer Communications at the National Cancer Institute where she directed NCI's health communications and communications research activities. She teaches, speaks, and publishes on social marketing issues, consumer research, and human information processing.

**Barbara J. Tinsley**, Ph.D., is Associate Professor in the Department of Psychology at the University of California at Riverside and Clinical Associate Professor in the Department of Gynecology and Obstetrics at Loma Linda University Medical Center. She received her M.S. and Ph.D. degrees in Human Development, Educational Psychology at the University of Illinois at Urbana. Her research interests include family health risk management, interactions in health contexts, child health socialization, and predictors of maternal and child health services utilization.

**Kim Witte**, Ph.D., is Assistant Professor in the Department of Communication at Michigan State University. Her research focuses on the role of fear in public health campaigns. Recently, she has begun to examine how members of diverse cultures respond to fear appeals. Her work has appeared in *International Quarterly of Community Health Education, Social Science and Medicine, Communication Monographs,* and elsewhere.